The
End
Doesn't
Happen
All At
Once

The End Doesn't Happen All At Once

a pandemic memoir

Chi Rainer Bornfree
Ragini Tharoor Srinivasan

ALEPH

ALEPH

ALEPH BOOK COMPANY
An independent publishing firm
promoted by *Rupa Publications India*

First published in India in 2025
by Aleph Book Company
7/16 Ansari Road, Daryaganj
New Delhi 110 002

ISBN: 978-93-6523-664-4

1 3 5 7 9 10 8 6 4 2

Printed in India.

For sale in the Indian subcontinent only.

For our children

'I saw what I saw very clearly.
But I did not know what I was looking at.'
—V. S. Naipaul

'Everything comes to an end but what I'm writing to you goes
on. Which is good, very good. The best is not yet written. The
best is between the lines.'
—Clarice Lispector

'There are things that can only be understood retrospectively,
when many years have passed and the story has ended. In the
meantime, while the story continues, the only thing to do is tell it
over and over again...'
—Valeria Luiselli

CONTENTS

Prologue   xv

BOOK 1: THE CAVE

FIRST SPRING: THE SHOCK   3
March 23, 2020 | *Day 19*   3
March 26, 2020 | *Of course I'll write*   4
April 2, 2020 | *The end doesn't happen all at once*   5
April 9, 2020 | *We're not dead yet*   8
April 16, 2020 | *On privilege*   12
April 23, 2020 | *Knowing differently*   15
April 27, 2020 | *An unforgivable idea*   17
May 8, 2020 | *God is mad*   20
May 15, 2020 | *Corona vs. consumers*   23
May 21, 2020 | *Patchwork pandemic*   25
May 29, 2020 | *The future habit*   27
June 4, 2020 | *Keep moving*   29

FIRST SUMMER: THE FIRE   32
June 17, 2020 | *Dr Sayed*   32
June 20, 2020 | *The hills are burning*   34
June 27, 2020 | *The zombie stage*   36
July 4, 2020 | *Learning our class position*   38
July 11, 2020 | *Dissent becomes consent*   41
July 18, 2020 | *'Families choose'*   45
July 22, 2020 | *What the fuck have I been doing?*   47
July 31, 2020 | *Erring*   49
August 8, 2020 | *Conflict causes growth*   52
August 15, 2020 | *There are no cookies*   56
August 29, 2020 | *For the listener*   59

FIRST FALL: THE NUMBERS 65
September 6, 2020 | *Reid Park Zoo* 65
September 17, 2020 | *Never play defense* 68
September 27, 2020 | *We're still swimming* 73
October 2, 2020 | *How to be a good human in a civil war?* 76
October 10, 2020 | *Slippery slope* 79
October 17, 2020 | *A madhouse inside this skull* 82
October 23, 2020 | *Back to school* 86
October 29, 2020 | *Horror show* 88
November 6, 2020 | *On Sunday she died again* 89
November 14, 2020 | *Rewarmed Chinese* 92
November 21, 2020 | *Indian summer* 94

FIRST WINTER: THE DARK 99
December 18, 2020 | *What if?* 99
December 21, 2020 | *The ninth month of March* 101
January 3, 2021 | *Winter cocoon* 103
January 9, 2021 | *Driving distance* 106
January 14, 2021 | *Happy button* 108
January 17, 2021 | *We choose our own lives* 110
January 23, 2021 | *Political pageantry* 113
January 30, 2021 | *For the yearbook* 116
February 7, 2021 | *As if no one's watching* 119
February 16, 2021 | *News from Johannesburg* 121
February 20, 2021 | *Impossible choice* 124
March 1, 2021 | *It's March again* 126
March 6, 2021 | *Dark chasms* 129

BOOK 2: THE PORTAL

SECOND SPRING: THE RETURN 138
March 17, 2021 | *The world keeps ending* 138
March 30, 2021 | *Change is possible* 140
April 4, 2021 | *Easter Sunday* 143

April 13, 2021 | *What to wear to a vaccine appointment?* 146
April 19, 2021 | *The Lodhi cluster* 148
April 25, 2021 | *A hug in a letter* 152
May 2, 2021 | *Hope for what?* 154
May 8, 2021 | *What they call freedom* 158
May 15, 2021 | *Fuck the CDC* 160
May 22, 2021 | *Social calendar explosion* 163
June 1, 2021 | *Rehearsing return* 165
June 8, 2021 | *Cave syndrome* 169

SECOND SUMMER: FOREVER 175
June 13, 2021 | *I booked my ticket* 175
June 19, 2021 | *Why take that risk?* 179
June 25, 2021 | *Is this the truck?* 181
July 2, 2021 | *Reunion without union* 185
July 9, 2021 | *Cruel optimism* 188
July 16, 2021 | *Vacation is exhausting* 191
July 23, 2021 | *The Dean at midnight* 194
July 28, 2021 | *Covid forever* 198
August 5, 2021 | *Be careful what you wish for* 200
August 11, 2021 | *The flooding of Atlantis* 203
August 19, 2021 | *Where's the lie?* 206

SECOND FALL: THE BOTTOM LINE 213
August 26, 2021 | *A damn good disguise* 213
September 2, 2021 | *The opposite of relief* 215
September 8, 2021 | *A new friend* 218
September 16, 2021 | *The pleasure-pain dialectic* 220
September 22, 2021 | *Happiness depends on being free* 224
September 30, 2021 | *Owning it* 227
October 8, 2021 | *Willing to find out* 231
October 13, 2021 | *Breaking the fourth wall* 235
October 19, 2021 | *Permission to be* 239
October 28, 2021 | *The egg and the chicken* 243
November 5, 2021 | *Product reviews* 247

November 12, 2021 | *Walk through lightly* 250
November 18, 2021 | *Subtraction* 254

SECOND WINTER: THE END OF THE BEGINNING 259
December 25, 2021 | *Omicron (once more with feeling)* 259

THIRD SPRING: TURN THE PAGE 264
February 24, 2022 | *Happy birthday, pandemic* 264
March 26, 2022 | *Goodbye to all that* 267

BOOK 3: THE WOODS

THIRD SUMMER: THE AFTERLIFE 274
June 28, 2022 | *Houston, we have a problem* 274
July 6, 2022 | *Timing* 279
August 3, 2022 | *Did you pray?* 283
August 24, 2022 | *Touch of a hand* 286
September 20, 2022 | *Afterlives* 288

THIRD FALL: THE STRENGTH 294
October 12, 2022 | *The strength to be different* 294
October 23, 2022 | *The view from normal* 298
November 12, 2022 | *What is most important?* 303
November 24, 2022 | *Germ warfare* 306
December 10, 2022 | *Choice of errors* 311

THIRD WINTER: FIDELITY 315
December 20, 2022 | *The view from Delhi airport* 315
December 27, 2022 | *(Un)happy holidays* 321
January 8, 2023 | *When the object comes back to itself* 324
January 21, 2023 | *What is a safe distance?* 329
January 31, 2023 | *The gift of multiple stories* 333
February 9, 2023 | *Fidelity to the event* 336
March 4, 2023 | *The view from the banks of the Rhine* 341

FOURTH SPRING: TWO ROADS   349
March 22, 2023 | *Life returns*   349
March 29, 2023 | *Doubt*   352

EPILOGUE: FIFTH SPRING   361
C | May 2024 | *Rearranging the world*   363
R | May 2024 | *Looking directly at the sun*   367

List of Illustrations   376
Notes   378

PROLOGUE

Surreal. Distorted. Distant, yet too close. Perhaps that is how the Covid pandemic seems to you now.

Because of the letters you are about to read, we remember it differently: crisp and ever present. Because of these letters, we lived it differently: as a challenge to witness it fully, to change ourselves. Because of these letters, we loved each other differently.

We also remember what are now the before-times. We remember the end of the before.

For C, the end started with watching videos taken on cell phones in China, of deserted streets and boarded up doors. Supplies started accumulating in the basement, masks we didn't yet know how to use. In mid-February, C and the children got very sick. They got better, and then fell sick again. In bed, weakened, C was stricken with fear: the void of tastes and smells seemed to foreshadow the grave. The lost senses returned, but the fear stayed. C tried to tell friends who didn't know yet. C told them, I think many people will die.

For R, the end came on Monday, March 9, the first day of the university's spring break. That morning, she walked through the empty halls of the English department with hands and fingers balled in her sleeves, to avoid touching doorknobs, handles, faucet, and wall. She had spoken that morning to her mother, who was in Delhi, and warned her that the world she was scheduled to fly back to on Friday, March 13, was going to be another world entirely.

We were texting frequently.

Almost exactly eleven years prior, at a different university, we had met as newly admitted graduate students on either side of a cheese platter. Late afternoon sun slanted through the big windows of the department library, buzzing with gossip. At the welcome meeting, earlier, C had launched their ideas with panache and the name of a certain German philosopher, R recalls. Her own performance was self-effacing, full of disclaimers, and carefully calibrated. C had noted R's poise. It made C reach over the hors d'oeuvres and social preliminaries to the real question of the day. 'So, are you coming too?' A half-shrug, a warm smile. 'It's sort of overdetermined for me.' C didn't know exactly what that meant, but they wanted to find out.

We remember eleven years of dinners and initiation rituals, of rifts and reconciliation. We remember two bikes leaned up against the yellow siding of a small apartment under the Berkeley sequoias. We remember what we used to order at the bar-and-pizza patio joint near campus, because it was always the same: spinach artichoke dip and two glasses of the house red.

We remember the night in 2011 that we marched on the ports of Oakland, some weeks after C's husband Micah floated the original call to Occupy. C was hounded at an assembly by a local reporter with questions about their backstory, their family connections to the US government.

We remember the birth of R's daughter, Mrinalini, in 2013, and a couple years later, of C's son, Zia.

We remember saying goodbye together to the campus where we met. The ceremony was tedious; the professor at the podium mispronounced R's name. We hugged and took giddy pictures on the steps by the side entrance of the department, where C had always locked their bike.

We remember a dream, an intimation slipped into a birthday wish.

It was 2017, and C's birthday. R remembers writing to C from a window seat on a crowded airplane, with clouds in her peripheral vision. She wrote of gratitude and gifts, but also of the unmistakable violence of the Sonoran desert where she and Brandon, her mathematician husband, had just begun junior faculty jobs. She paused before writing what she most wanted to say:

> If I were to suddenly die (I know, I know), would you be willing, one day long in the future and in no hurry, to do something with my unpublished work? I have these half written projects that would need curating, editing. It's a bit like asking you to be the godmother of my writing. It's maybe too much. But every time I get on a plane I wonder what would happen to those files and then I think, if I'm lucky enough, maybe C will find them and make them live.

At the window of an urban fourth-floor walk up, C understood the request as a sacred gift. The brief reply held infinite feeling.

> Yes, I will care for your writing with all the tenderness I would bring to raising your child, and, instead of praying that you won't die for many years to come, why don't we make a different kind of wish—to write something together while we are still alive.

More life would come first. R's son Shai was born in May 2018, and five months later, C's daughter Areté. We remember the carefully constructed routines of sleep, feeding, and care, routines that would have been outgrown and forgotten—if not for the rupture of 2020, if not for the division of our lives into after and before.

That Monday in March 2020, R signed on to her office computer to find an email from C. The subject: 'Info.'

> Hi darling, wonderful to hear your voice today. Don't panic but please do act fast to prepare materially and mentally for a major shift in routine. Talk to the kids. It's when, not if, and you protect yourselves and others by bowing out early. Take heed of Italy where the death rate

is 7 x South Korea because they did not take it seriously. Prisoners escaping there; social unrest will follow. We'll get through this but it is historic, I think.

Just repeating myself because I love you so much! Showed Zia and Areté old pics of playing with Mrinalini in Ann Arbor over dinner.

Shopping list below; more soon.

Lots of love,
C

The list included foodstuffs and treats for the children, hand sanitizer and Lysol wipes, Mucinex and Zinc. The stores were already out of most of this stuff before the newspapers caught on, before 'cancel everything'. There was no Lysol in Target that week, no hand sanitizer, no detergent. Only ravaged shelves with displays of glitter pens and commuter mugs, travel pillows, and obsolete tech.

We knew. A lot of us knew. Some of us knew quickly and some of us knew slowly and some of us knew all at once in the toilet paper aisle. Many of us knew for a very long while before we would admit it. Others of us knew right away that we knew, but we did not foresee how we would have to hold that knowing against a tremendous, calculated machinery of forgetting.

That Monday afternoon in March 2020, we spoke by phone. C sat in the small study of their Hudson Valley home, at the desk by the window where so many of the following letters were written. R stood beside her car in the graveled carport shaded from Tucson's desert sun, and bargained for time.

Can't I go later, R asked, can't I do the shopping in a couple of days?

A pause. Go today, C said.

∾

Remember?

BOOK 1

THE CAVE

FIRST SPRING: THE SHOCK

MARCH 23, 2020 | *DAY 19*

Hi darling,

I hope you're feeling a little better, but it's okay if you're not. It's snowing today in Kingston. I don't know what to make of this simple, ordinary shift in the weather. I don't know what to make of anything, really.

Here is snow.

Here is my street on lockdown.

My neighbor on the left works for the utility company, so he's still going into the office as an 'essential worker'. (Philosophy and literature are essential too, but we can do it from home.) Last time I checked, my neighbors on the right were still commuting to the city once or twice a week. Maybe that's changed by now.

I read, before my attention dissolved, someone describing coronavirus as a 'noetic shock': a mental blow that entirely disrupts your sense of self and worldview.

Which is a roundabout way of asking: will you do an art project with me for the duration of this virus? Will you write letters back and forth with me once a week?

I could use the sense of weaving, building something.

How are the children? For the first week, we kept packing their lunchboxes as usual for them to use at lunchtime, but now they're just stacked on top of the fridge.

It's day nineteen of (very disciplined) self isolation.

Love always,
C

MARCH 26, 2020 | *OF COURSE I'LL WRITE*

Hello love,

You're on 'week three' so you will remember the difficulties of 'week two'. It's been harder for us than the first. It's been challenging to keep to the schedule we designed so that Brandon and I can each take a break from the kids and do 'work' or work-like things. Somehow, we are settling into a rhythm, the four of us. We are slowly getting used to inhabiting this space together, to eating all our meals together, to dancing, playing, and digging around in the backyard together.

I am conscious of a kind of gratitude for this time, and then also guilt about that gratitude, since it is a sign—or more accurately a symptom—of our considerable privilege. But then: we've always had that privilege. We've just been more significantly inoculated from the burden of thinking about it.

Of course I'll write letters with you.

I said 'week two' but we are not as isolated as you four are being. We are still taking walks, though abiding by your and Micah's 14-foot rule as much as possible, and not the conventional 6-foot. I went grocery shopping this morning, with gloves and mask and wipes, and was appalled at the lack of caution displayed by workers and customers. Weird things were out (no tofu). Weird things were in (chicken galore). We ordered delivery through Instacart once but generally don't feel comfortable with having someone else do our shopping, absorbing our risks, taking fewer or lesser precautions than we might, and using all that awful plastic.

Saying this in the spirit of conversation. We have to draw some lines, and we're all trying, in different ways. This is another way of saying that we will make our bed and lie in it, even if it kills us.

It was my mother's sixtieth birthday yesterday. She got back from Delhi less than two weeks ago; yesterday Modi announced a three-week national lockdown in India, on four hours notice. Deadly chaos. My mum's in a daze. I organized a series of 'surprise' Zoom calls for her with friends and family. I had made her a book of messages and tribute poems in early March, and finished it just in time to get it to her by mail. Pleased with myself for not having procrastinated on that!

And I wrote her a poem yesterday morning, instead of preparing for my undergraduate students. It's called 'On Having a Terrible Birthday'. Here's how it opens: *First the flights went, and / the children who would visit / to celebrate you with / a marzipan cream cake, / impossible now, / to go anywhere*...

There's an ironic middle: *'Today, you could fly for $50 to Beijing, / $75 roundtrip to Rome. / You could drive to San Francisco / in half an hour / and leave as late as you want to / for the airport'*...

And an overdramatic close: *'It's the knowing, now / and for always, / that far more terrible / than a terrible birthday / is the thing we can't speak: / the alternative.'*

I cooked baingan bharta at 10 p.m. for the same reason I wrote the poem: as an homage. As I mashed the eggplant, I listened to Mrinalini's playlist. The Australian pop song 'Youngblood' by 5 Seconds of Summer, on repeat. Felt oddly exhilarated.

Sending you all my love. Is this my first letter?

R

APRIL 2, 2020 | *THE END DOESN'T HAPPEN ALL AT ONCE*

Hi dearest,

Welcome to April. I'll skip the attendant foolery and cruel clichés. I'm not in the mood for jokes or readymade sentiments. I will say, this letter writing may be harder than I initially thought. I have thought of writing you every day since yours arrived, without putting fingers to keyboard. But that it's hard sometimes means it is a good thing to do.

Hard to write because of time. Not enough of it—the one thing that's the same as always! But more because the numbers, the mood, the moment, are happening all the time in different places, different ways. Time isn't flowing, it's jolting. For example: I wrote all this yesterday, April 1. Wanted to add more—so much more to say—but just sending as is today, April 2, before I head downstairs to help with the kids.

Turns out the end of the world doesn't happen all at once.

And it's hard to write because times are hard. Midway through loading the washer today, I began to believe the very worst: civilizational collapse, à la the Mayans, à la the dinosaurs (who continue as birds, scientists say). Which would mean doing laundry by hand! Which would mean, for me, wearing dirty clothes.

To stave off the spiraling, I started an online Latin class. It seemed like a constructive thing to do although I don't really have time for it (see above). I like it, something to focus on that is not the news. The structure of the language, of the class, are a familiar room. And online, I feel a certain liberation from the gendered expectations that attach themselves to my body in real life—a physical invulnerability that enables intellectual boldness.

Of course I immediately began worrying that this is my way of 'staying busy' and stopping myself from writing and therefore 'bad'. I did also start a blog. Nothing as beautiful as your poem to your mother, which captures so much about being alive in this time. I honor you for your work making her day special. I failed at that with Micah's lockdown birthday last month, Micah who is himself so attentive. I suspect we will all have other chances.

Parents: my mom is doing well. We talk every night for the first time in my life and I am committed to keeping her alive by doing this. She is strong. My father: angry shrug. I have to wonder what is keeping him in Cairo, presiding over a university that is on hold. Poor health care, high risk, why does he stay when the whole point of 'non-pharmaceutical interventions' (new jargon I have recently learned) is to work remotely? He's putting himself and others, especially his Egyptian staff—the cook, the maids, the butler—who are still commuting two hours each way on crowded public transit, at unconscionable, unnecessary risk. So why?

Sparrow outside my window with a little broom of grass. It is their fault our gutters are clogged but I welcome the visitor with his flag of spring.

As for practicalities, and privilege: dear one, I want to be aware of the way we are prone to use old analytical categories. Beware of the way we are all prone to downplay risk, talk ourselves into doing things we know we should not. Yes, New York is different than Arizona. But the media is not telling the whole truth, and the data is just not there.

Ultimately, as Instacart workers strike and online vendors are sold out with untold delays, you may not have a choice about going to the store. I have never liked the rhetoric of privilege—a conversation for another time. Though it's obvious that we're all in different boats in this flood, you have to row as hard as you can with whatever you've got. Don't underestimate this virus.

Tell me about you, how your family rhythm is evolving. Hungry for news outside this small space.

Love, so much love,
C

APRIL 9, 2020 | *WE'RE NOT DEAD YET*

Dearest C,

I am daily full of self-recrimination about not being the writer I thought I wanted to be, the writer I thought I might have been, the writer I hoped I might be by now. I try to remind myself, as you have told me in the past, that just because I haven't done what I say I want to do doesn't mean I won't ever do it. I am chastened by the fact that all the major outlets are publishing their Covid diaries, and I haven't positioned myself as the kind of writer whose diary anyone has asked to publish.

But then, *you* have asked me to write. And you are worth more than all of them.

And so, I will write.

And I will read. I keep returning to these words from your letter: 'I have never liked the rhetoric of privilege—a conversation for another time.'

I think that time is now. I think that is the conversation to be had *now*. I don't want to put words in your mouth, so tell me. What I don't like about the rhetoric of privilege is the way it is used as a bludgeon against the so-called privileged, without nuance or context. I've been on the receiving end of the 'too privileged' accusation more than once, because I write about South Asian literature and criticism written in English, often by globe-trotting cosmopolitans and diasporic expatriate writers, many of whom are prizewinners who have been celebrated by the international publishing market.

The politics of English in India is fraught (understatement!). English is a colonial bequest and the language of the elites; it's also a tool of advancement and opportunity, especially for those historically excluded from English-language education (but we'll leave that aside for now). There's this pernicious idea in the field that 'real Indians' write in the vernaculars, and that English has limited purchase on Indian lives, that it's time to stop listening to those who are more-British-than-the-Brits. Of course, I agree, we can't just go on reading Salman Rushdie and heirs. And yet: the postcolonial Anglophone tradition must be read and taught. It's no less real. And no less Indian. And those are the writers like me, like us. Am I not also responsible to them? Should I not own up to who I am, to the accident of birth that put me in this particular position of reading?

So, I am more interested in what privilege affords and what it does *not* afford than in self-flagellating over privilege.

That said, our privilege is undeniable in this extended and yet also compressed moment of pandemic time. Is it not?

I read on your blog the story of Areté and the worm, but it broke my heart a little reading the phrase '18 months' and knowing I haven't even met your daughter yet! You were there for Shai's naming ceremony; I was so deeply touched that you came all that way, for a day. I wonder if or when I will ever meet your baby girl.

Our family's Covid count is ticking up. My cousin in London had it; he's recovered now after two weeks. He had a bad time of it, but no hospitalization. His girlfriend took care of him and was totally exposed, but apparently she didn't get it, or had no symptoms anyway.

Brandon's brother and his girlfriend had it. They got it in New York but went to Maine before they knew they had it, and they are holed up now at my in-laws' lakeside compound. They are two weeks in. She told us it felt like someone was sitting on her chest. They are going to be ok, I think. Though who knows who my brother-in-law infected when they first landed from the city, and he went out to stock the house.

My cousin's wife and her family have the body count: four grandparents in assisted living contracted Covid, two in New York and two in New Orleans. Both grandfathers died this week, within two days of each other. One of her grandmothers is very ill now. It's devastating.

And yet, the mundane business of living goes on. I haven't been to the regular grocery this week, but I did go to the Indian store for parathas and that was uncanny. Leaving the house, I expected to see a world on fire and yet it all looked and sounded just the same. So many cars on the road and people on the streets holding hands! I went into the store masked and gloved. There were a few furtive others, similarly dressed. There were largely empty shelves and 'take one only' signs everywhere. Some masks were more like attempts at mummification. I grabbed one of everything and ran.

Having already ventured out once, I gave in and lost an hour filling an online shopping cart for a Safeway delivery. After the delivery, it was an hour-long operation of bag transfers, hand washing, container sanitization, more washing.

I want to leave a gift for the mailman, but I'm worried I mis-remember his name.

Your mother, your sister, your father, your husband, your children, your in-laws, everyone, how are they?

Against your better judgment, we let the kids go to my in-laws for visits this week and have agreed to a seder for Passover on Saturday. They are being about as careful as we have been, which is more careful than most, but less careful than you tell me to be. Brandon asked me if we were going to keep the kids away from his parents despite their professed vigilance, and if we did it for months and then they got Covid and died, wouldn't we feel terrible to have kept them away? It was a bit of melodrama and he's not prone to that, even-keeled and calm as he is, so it caught my attention.

He said something striking about my going running in the neighborhood, too. I have done so a few times, and apart from one horrifically stressful run when the entire Tucson Fire Department was on my route, I can generally avoid everyone I see by a dozen feet or more. Brandon said: well, if you're going to get Covid while going for a run, we're all getting it, and we're all going to die.

We may be dying but we're not dead yet.

And I'm cooking up a storm, more and better than I've ever cooked before. And the children are healthy and Mrinalini has gained three pounds since the worst of her sickness.

Feels like another world, but actually it's only been a few months since that horrendous time—since Mrinalini's first, bizarre vomiting episode at the end of September. Remember? All fall we were in daily and nightly agony, wondering how to make this six-year-old child stop spiraling into anxiety about the idea of food. She had to stop vomiting. Then, she had to stop panicking about vomiting. I had never seen her depressed before. I had never seen her panicked before. I had never seen her eyes so vacant. How many doctor's visits we made, how many tests we did, how many times I had to pick her up from school almost immediately after dropping her, because she couldn't make it through the morning!

Well, we don't have to worry about school anymore.

The house is not as clean as if our cleaner was here (I've paid her through May not to come, will keep paying her not to come), but certain things are better organized. That horrible drawer in the kitchen full of dead pens and rubber bands, for one. I let Brandon throw away all the used ziplocs with cashew butter residue that I was saving for the next sandwich. And the liquor cabinet is stocked.

Tell me, love, why you chafe against the rhetoric of privilege.

Love and more of it,

R

APRIL 16, 2020 | *ON PRIVILEGE*

Hi dearest,

I wanted to write you back immediately—was restless that night thinking of it—and I should have, because instead I am just narrowly skating in under the deadline, and as I type I can almost hear Micah's angry thoughts about how I am not making enough time for our relationship. In fact I do hear his angry vacuuming downstairs.

Nevertheless, I will write and take the consequences later.

On privilege—what I do not like about it as a term of analysis (as distinct from what I do not like about it in-the-world) is that it doesn't accomplish anything, except the bludgeoning that you mention. Empty moralism, a form of censorship, not to mention, sloppy on purpose. The basic problem is not that particular slices of people have privilege, it is that the majority live without adequate resources and without power. That's the thing that needs to be understood/changed, and though I can hear someone saying that those are two sides of the same coin, the way it lands matters. Are you pulling down the privileged or powering up plurality?

Once again, the underlying intuition behind this somewhat vitriolic, very partial, and surely 'wrong' response is my impatience at seeing a new situation resurface old narratives. If what Covid-19 teaches us is only what we already knew (America is deeply racist), then we are not really learning. And I think the first lesson of Covid-19 is that we desperately need to learn from this. We must let change be our teacher. We must let it teach us how to change.

But fine, let the articles and data come. Everyone should write and think what they need to write and think. I will keep trying to make it all part of what I am trying to learn, which is how to think about change at all (Western philosophy is historically bad at this, as inheritors of Plato's forms), and about this change in particular.

The thing I'm most afraid of (besides the fear of losing you, which I do not allow myself to consider) *is* that the entrenched forces will succeed in re-establishing normal, as the Arundhati Roy article you sent me said so well:

> Historically, pandemics have forced humans to break with the past and imagine their world anew. This one is no different. It is a portal, a gateway between one world and the next...
>
> Nothing could be worse than a return to normality.

Is it a privileged fear to worry that the normal systems of injustice will prevail despite this shock?

As for daily life: we watch from the window the evidence of Governor Cuomo's decrees taking hold. Across the street, our elderly neighbors fly their flag half-mast, wear masks when they go out to their medical appointments. The white man next door comes and goes freely and gets awfully close to other neighbors, even leaning down into the old man's car window. (He doesn't come near us—must be our anti-social vibes.) On the other side of us, the black and Brazilian lesbians, refugees from NYC, seem to be on our wavelength. We talk over the fence about planting, food delivery, and their friends still in the city who are sick.

Even this distant contact with the neighbors makes Micah anxious. I don't think he would be able to re-enter 'normal' very easily. Each of us becomes more of what we are in a crisis, I read somewhere, and so he shows himself to be anxious, deeply self-insulated, tending towards extremes; but also steady and resolved, very creative, extremely intelligent and supportive. Mostly I feel very lucky, though I couldn't live with only him—I sometimes sorrow, as you know, over his lack of connection with others.

We worry about what will become of his career, now

that the speaking events are all free on Zoom. Already from Davos he was texting me videos of the Chinese lockdowns. By the time he left the Extinction Rebellion founders in the UK, he knew it was probably his last flight for a long time. In truth, I think he will welcome the reprieve from the stresses of the speaking circuit, a performance we jokingly call the 'ideological zoo'.

But what *is* the long arc for radicals? Micah tells me stories: about Jerry Rubin, 1960s counter-culture icon who became a successful businessman in the 1980s. About Gene Sharp, whose influential ideas on non-violent protest have aided in the CIA's efforts at regime change. Some activists lapse or ascend into traditional politics, as when we dreamed of moving Occupiers out to our small Oregon town and getting the crew elected to city council. And then there are those whose arcs are not long at all, whose lives are cut short by suicide or assassination (King, X), or madness (Jason Russell, organizer of Kony 2012). On a podcast we recently did together with the director of the Hannah Arendt Center about the pandemic, Micah was more convinced than ever that protest is over. And yet social rebellion is at the core of who I know him to be. So who will he become?

A month into lockdown, and still the plague is only touching me at the periphery of my circles.

The world I can see is shrinking but something else—what?— is growing to compensate.

All love,
C

APRIL 23, 2020 | *KNOWING DIFFERENTLY*

Dearest C,

It is Brandon's turn to play with the children, so I am writing to you from the little desk inside my closet. There are roses, so many, pink and red and white, outside my window.

I agree with you about the use of the rhetoric of privilege (as bludgeon): that it (the rhetoric) does not address actual structural inequalities and imbalances of power. It serves as an alibi, and it assuages guilt. It gives some of 'us' (using the term advisedly) a language for reckoning with our relative security that is mildly but not substantively censorious. Yes. Pulling down, or lifting up, you ask. A million times yes.

And yet: how do we grapple with the fact that this pandemic has given more to some of us than it has taken? That, for instance, I always wanted the mornings, and now that I am not packing school lunches or going into my department office, I have them.

I wanted to cook more and feed my children mustard greens and toor dal and make beautiful, round, crisp dosas that make them squeal and now I do, regularly.

I wanted to sit out in the garden (I felt badly about all the wasted outdoor space that we barely inhabited) and now I do; we do. We fly paper airplanes and dig for shells that we have buried in the sand. We found a bird's nest with eggs and two watchful birds tucked into a desert palm in our yard, and delighted in it. Later we cried for the birds when the wind blew the nest onto the concrete, killing the baby and smashing an egg. And Shai constructed a whole narrative about it: *uh oh baby bird tree fell down uh oh baby bird trash can.*

(I know, we should have buried it.)

Privilege might be a failed language, it undoubtedly is, but how then to reckon with being afforded a new position of thinking and writing? Maybe, as you might say, the answer is to quit with the self-flagellating 'reckoning' and just do the thinking and writing.

You wrote this: 'If what Covid-19 teaches us is only what we already knew...then we are not really learning.' Yes. And there's a lot of that not-really-learning going on: about racism, about health disparities, about the nightmare that was the American dream, about the sham of American exceptionalism, and about the failures that were trafficked as successes.

But I would add that there is value in learning again what we already know. That in fact this is how we come into knowledge in the first place, not from spaces and places of non-knowledge or not knowing, but through new awareness and understanding of what we have already known but are now positioned to know differently.

I haven't seen my neighbors recently. They are all much older, in their 70s and 80s, and staying indoors. Brandon's parents continue to see us and help take care of the children a couple times a week. It is good for the four of them, but not so much of a break for us, since we only send one child to their house at a time. We've had two or three lovely dinners together. We are continuing to deal with all of our PTSD from Mrinalini's sickness, so this feels like healing. We had dinner in our backyard the other night, and Mrinalini was not only eating but recounting with pleasure misadventures from our last India trip in summer 2019, when Shai was just fifteen months old and met both of my grandmothers for the first time. It was cool in the night air; she was hugging her knees to her chest and grinning away. Joy.

If, as you say, we are becoming more ourselves, maybe we are also learning to better live with ourselves and in our lives. I feel moved to try to understand and appreciate the decisions I've made over the years, the things I've done, what (and who) I have held close and let go, over and above what I didn't do, or haven't done. I am striving toward greater intentionality in every breath. That is what I hope for. The growth I seek in what you rightly describe as a shrinking world.

I should acknowledge also the mundane worries: how will we sustain this for months yet? How to anticipate the next Covid waves? And what about the children? You say that Micah will not easily re-enter normal. Will we ever want to send the little ones back to school? I wonder about this with Shai especially. He is thriving and beautiful, and I don't wish to send him back to that den of snotty noses and divided attentions.

Privilege.

There's more. On April 12, eleven days ago, Brandon unceremoniously took over Shai's bedtime routine, and so, with that, he's weaned. I'm maybe not weaned yet, in that I haven't returned to the scene of his bedtime. I'm afraid he will ask to nurse and only then, belatedly, realize what he has given up. So I stay away, and he doesn't ask for me, and I have turned instead to Mrinalini's bedtime, and she's grateful for it.

And so, in this new world of closeness and always togetherness, my baby enacts his own tentative and brilliant form of separation.

All my love,
R

APRIL 27, 2020 | *AN UNFORGIVABLE IDEA*

Dear heart,

I'm so glad I have you to write with during this time. That I can trust someone so sensitive (here, as a synonym for intelligent) and articulate with my feelings and wrongness and blunderings-about-looking-for-light-switches. You nail the point about learning as learning anew, my dear.

More than that. Your letter gives me hope. And courage, too, to speak my lunatic feeling. It's this: what if this virus is here to help humanity?

We say we are 'at war' with the virus. But what if the coronavirus is trying, navigating its own limited affordances along with its considerable powers, to help us...evolve?

This suggestion might be an unforgivable idea. It does nothing for those who are suffering and dying. Worse, it could be seen to sanction the criminal actions/inactions of our federal government. And perhaps the notion is also a foolish one, in the ways that faith is always foolish. But to ask whether we might manage a symbiosis with corona that is superior to what we were managing before is not more foolish than putting one's faith in a vaccine, I genuinely think. And so I need to find a creative form I can infuse with this feeling, so that it can be seen 360 and not taken halfway. I'm thinking of Octavia Butler's *Xenogenesis* series, in which an extraterrestrial species of 'gene traders' arrives to cure cancer, save the planet, and save humanity—but only by making humanity into something else.

Which is to say, indirectly, yes, absolutely: it's not privilege but what you do with it. This is what John Zerzan, that gentle aged doyen of Green Anarchism, said to me once, when I was impossibly young. In my memory, he was passing on this wisdom from an indigenous activist fed up with those using their privilege mainly for self-flagellation.

But even this comeback to the conversation about privilege should be forgotten. I held my baby girl in my lap as she scribbled, and noted how her fierce pleasure lies simply in the completion of the steps it takes to make her marks: choosing and uncapping and grasping and stabbing and moving the arm. Whereas my creative time is all scarred with the fall of whips like 'privilege' and 'women's writing' and 'not good enough' and 'your career' and a thousand others.

Writing is not a privilege, it's just what some of us were put here to do. None of us escapes suffering. None of us knows how much suffering is 'too much'. And besides, to riff on Solon:

a person might be as privileged as Jeff Bezos, but call no one happy until they are dead.

That doesn't address the structural issues, of course. The problem of unequal power and resources, nor the personal choices, what to do with the assortment you've been handed. What to do with my privilege? Some questions just have to be lived.

That's all inside—what about the outside? To me it seems like something small has shifted. Do you feel it where you are too? Like the beginning has ended. It's starting to sink in, I think, the timescale of this event. Not two weeks or two months but two years, the talking heads are starting to say more openly, and that means privately they are perhaps thinking twelve or twenty or always. That's why the reopen-now idiots are so terrifying. They haven't got it yet, or they have, and they're going to try to make this time a dying hell.

One of the parts of my dissertation (is there any more embarrassing word as long as one has not written a book?) that I never really understood to my own satisfaction was why the reciprocal analogy between war and disease crops up so much in the Greek canon. Now I am starting to learn firsthand. The deaths and suffering, the terrifying upended timescale, the way no one really knows how it will end but we make our peace with that. The way it is either the foreground or the background but never not the ground. And historically, disease and war do arrive together sometimes. I fear this may be one of them.

As for the minutiae, as Micah and I call it:

Latin class ends tomorrow. I hadn't been planning on taking the next installment—not enough time to write—though I already drew up a more leisurely self-study schedule. But all of a sudden I feel scared. What am I afraid of when I fear the end of Latin class? Is it what I would have to write? Is it not having that external structure and focus and regular casual facetime? I need to think carefully about this question because

I am addicted to the pleasures of being a 'good student' and so I am very close to convincing myself to go on with it.

Other bits and bobs: Areté is beginning to use the potty. She had started resisting diaper changes, so this simply became the easier option. So many things are easier with the second child! Zia and I are deep in an imagination game involving four animal finger puppets. We build forts and race up and down the driveway and I don't worry about teaching him to read but I do slip in little games about secret codes. I give them as much love as I can and enjoy doing it.

Tell me more about the beautiful flowers and the beautiful children and the small deaths that don't stand in for bigger ones. About what you think about the choices you've made. About the end of this semester for you. I am glad you can have the grandparents as part of your quaranteam, just as I'm glad your brother will be with your parents. Stay safe.

Love always,
C

MAY 8, 2020 | *GOD IS MAD*

Dearest C,

I read you many times this week, and I realize, reading you this morning, how many of my thoughts this week were preceded by yours. As if I spent all week slowly coming to understand and see what you had already prised open.

Last night, my in-laws came for dinner. 'Indian food.' My version, anyway, which daily and weekly improves. I am becoming the cook I always wanted to be, but never bothered to become, a pale shadow of my mother, but a shadow now, with definition. In the course of our lamenting those you rightly call 'the reopen idiots' and wondering over our respective blessings and privileges, my father-in-law and I had an exchange about

God. Referring to Trump and his maniac followers, and the kinds of people who have power and are using it to run the death machine, I said to him, *clearly, there is no God.*

My father-in-law looked at me and said, *isn't there though? There's clearly a God, and God is mad.*

Something about your positing—slyly, tentatively, and even quickly taking it back—the idea that corona might be here to help us, makes me pause over this exchange. Is there a God? Is God mad?

The powers that are (though they are not the powers that should be) have plainly decided that the deaths in the making are tolerable. The white supremacist state has taken off its hood, and it's every man for himself as it always has been, but minus the pleasantries. The American dream is dead; the American nightmare is nigh.

Tellingly, my immigrant parents' anguished mourning of that dream is far more acute and earnest than my own grief for this nation will ever be. My parents came to the United States from India in the late 1970s and early 1980s—my mother for a BA in 1979, my father for a PhD a year later—because they thought America was the future. Now they have a front row seat for the horror show that is the decline of the West. Horror show not because the West is declining, mind you, but because it is determined to take the world down with it. I feel for my parents more than I feel for my cursed American children, born without their choice on this sinking ship.

And yes, there has been a shift, something is shifting, the beginning is ending, but I'm having a hard time disentangling it from the premature reopening. A friend in the Bay Area marked the end of the beginning with the return of her nanny, two weeks ago. Others have returned to the neighborhood playground and restaurant. The masks are already loosening, and we'd barely learned to put them on. Brandon and I feel new resentments brewing as we try to think in terms of years and months, now that we know we can manage the days and weeks. Two of Mrinalini's four summer camps have written with plans to proceed; two have canceled. Of course, she cannot go to summer camp. Can she go to summer camp?

At the university, our president is playing chicken with the faculty and students. He's hired a PR team of high end frat brothers who most recently consulted for Mitch McConnell and Bibi Netanyahu and he is on TV touting our plan to 'reopen' in the fall. It's a shameless ploy for tuition dollars, and we faculty have not been advised of the plans. On a townhall Zoom this week, the president dared the faculty to oppose him. *It's a gamble,* he essentially said; *we'll set up infirmaries across campus and see if we can make it. Otherwise, the layoffs start now.*

I'm on leave from teaching in the fall (junior research leave, what a joke!) and Brandon is going to request online teaching, and we anticipate that the kids will be home, with Mrinalini in some hybrid form of second grade. So this is our life. Will this be our life? Is this the life we always wanted, I wonder? If I could read and write for another two or three hours a day (three feels greedy but I'll say it), maybe this is actually what we would want. Maybe this is what Marx said about being a poet in the morning, a hunter in the afternoon, and a cook in the evening. Our movements and actions are far more purposeful and directed now than they ever were before. Feeding, caring, watering. So much less idling. We are closer to the lizards and rabbits and woodpeckers and bees that live with us than we've ever been.

I love that you are taking Latin and reveling in the pleasure of being a good student. Shai, inspired by Areté, though he does not know it, has had a few successful pottying episodes this week. Mrinalini teeters occasionally toward a relapse of we-still-don't-quite-know-what issues (GI, anxiety...the only thing she was definitively diagnosed with after those many months of starving was Small Intestinal Bacterial Overgrowth, but what the hell caused *that?*). Overall, she is coming into her own as an epic daydreamer and reader.

Meanwhile, Brandon and I are deep into articles about the inflammatory component of Covid. You can understand why this is particularly concerning to us given his issues (and Mrinalini's history). If in fact part of what Covid does is exploit overactive immune systems, I wonder if his being immune-suppressed by biologics will actually prove to be a good thing? He takes biweekly Humira shots for what is technically called 'ankylosing spondylitis' (aka arthritis in his back, with bizarre-o dinosaur name!), though I think the shots have mostly had the effect of treating his ulcerative colitis (an inflammatory bowel disease, also probably auto-immune).

And it's hot now: 41°C in the day. We managed to keep the windows open until just a couple days ago, when we finally had to turn on the AC at night. I miss the voices of the birds in the morning, coming in through the mesh.

Tell me about the voices you're hearing.

From the desert with love,
R

MAY 15, 2020 | *CORONA VS. CONSUMERS*

Dear R,

You and your words are a pillar of my sanity (I knew you would be) as the country slips into collective delusions. When I see the struggle as one between coronavirus and consumerism, I find myself rooting for the virus. Let it change us! May it block the return of the endless consumption economy, in which I, too, am complicit. For your father-in-law is right that the gods are mad—crazy-angry—and the gods are right to be mad.

Micah likens the reopening to watching everyone go out and have unsafe sex. Consumer libido spilling out again. In the early days, they didn't understand the Spanish flu; they thought AIDS was a cancer, he reminds me. We still don't know what this thing is—and the most dangerous thing is thinking we do. No theory of the virus accounts for this mysterious Kawasaki-like development in children, a syndrome I would not have known to fear if it were not for your Mrinalini.

Everything we thought we knew so far about this entity has turned out to be false. But we are supposed to believe that we now know it is safe enough to open up?

I feel it too, of course, the urge to loosen up, let go. My mom, sad after Mother's Day, talked about flying to Jordan, about coming here this summer. Pretending she can control her risk. Pretending she'll endure a two week quarantine in a vacation rental after the trip. I indulged her fantasy, but the very thought sends Micah into an honest panic. In the CDC guidelines that Trump trashed, one important recommendation has been left out: no traveling between 'zones'.

For Mother's Day here, Micah helped me fix up my side of the study: installing shelves and speakers and, most importantly, a bulletin vision board above the desk. I hung up an Egyptian hand of Fatima and two wooden masks, from Rwanda and Indonesia, and a beautiful tapestry that I bought in Palestinian Jerusalem. I overpaid out of heartbreak, and later found from the tag it was made in Delhi. Assembling pieces of my past around me, it begins to feel like something could get brewed in here.

Anyway, Covid. It's normal now. The government buffoonery is normal. It's fine, we'll go out, some of us will get infected, some of us will die, what are you gonna do, it's normal. Do we always have to balance safety and freedom in a zero-sum equation?

I am still looking for the framework for replacing the talk of privilege. Because it does seem as though the world will be split into two. Not just before and after, not just virtual and physical, but differentials of speed, access, online code-switching.... To teach in the Fall, to keep living in this world, I'm going to need to learn to see a kind of class striation and bottlenecking that the glitzy internet is so good at distracting us from.

I am learning, though. Latin and other things. Re-learning, as you say. Learning how to love. How to be there for Micah in his panics. To listen to Zia's endless, impassioned sobs over a vacuumed-up lego piece. To hear the quiet questions that bubble up in myself. To be patient when Areté insists on eating only in the lap of a parent (usually yours truly) and not her formerly-beloved chair. She's normally so easy-going that her occasional fits unseat me more than they should.

Got my rehiring paperwork today, which was a relief.

To be continued...

With love from my room,

C

MAY 21, 2020 | *PATCHWORK PANDEMIC*

Hello dearest C,

You talk about 'the world split'. Ed Yong—who has been writing the best of the mainstream Covid essays for *The Atlantic*—called it 'the patchwork'. You're both right.

These days I am experiencing more cognitive dissonance than in the last many weeks, as we feel the increasing fraying of connections, and search out our bit of the patchwork, a place we might feel safe, while everything else opens up and goes haywire.

We are newly committed to staying home with the kids. Daycare sent out a note asking if we want to send Shai back for the summer—of course not! Mrinalini's last day of virtual first grade is tomorrow. She won the award for best 'Drama' student in her class, which strikes me as right. She's never been great on stage, but she's terrific on camera. This week, I took both kids for their well-visits and Shai's two-year vaccines, and the pediatrician's office was in violation of its own stated procedures. We have to keep the kids home, because I don't trust anyone.

The institutions are broken. The world is broken. The US is approaching 100,000 Covid deaths. I have stopped attending Zoom meetings with indignant faculty trying to get through to the malignant, incompetent administrative C-suite here at the university. 'It's normal now,' you said. I'm so tired. You're of course right.

A friend in Tucson admits her daughter has regular playdates with the neighbor's kid. My in-laws are plotting their return to Maine, even though they know we need them. Now, my mom is talking about going to India this fall. Oh, how I already miss the early days of the lockdown in mid-March! Days when it felt like enough of the world (ok, our world) was in it together. Mrinalini asked a couple days ago what we're doing this summer and was less than pleased to hear 'more of the same'.

In all this, reading you is the bright spot. I love picturing you in your room, made beautiful not just by the vision board but by your vision. My room is a corner of a closet, but I'm glad for it, and the cool mornings out back while the kids are still sleeping or troubling Brandon.

Sometimes, C, I think about the future when we'll talk about this time, this year, this lockdown, and it will be past, and that future feels impossible, and I struggle to imagine myself into it. But maybe the point is not that we can't imagine ourselves out of this time into the future. Maybe this endless present is where we were headed all along, and the real crazy thing is the fact that most of us (but not you) didn't see it coming.

All the love,
R

MAY 29, 2020 | *THE FUTURE HABIT*

Dear R,

It's bad today. Race riots in Minnesota and elsewhere, possibly cop-instigated. The broken government and world and hearts you wrote of, on full and flaming display. So many ways to break and be broken. No one seems to know any way to heal and repair. Eight minutes the white police officer kept his knee on George Floyd's neck. Four days of uprising, so far, in dozens of cities.

My Bard colleagues are finding ways to go to the local marches. Bringing toddlers in cars with windows up, in masks. I feel the pull too, of course. Remember how beautiful everyone was, that afternoon at the port occupation in Oakland? This too is one of those generation-defining moments. Were you there or were you not there? Micah reminds me that however beautiful, however heartfelt…it will not work. Protest is broken.

Instead of marching or scrolling or tweeting, I listen. I rededicate myself to an old writing project. I resurfaced today from scrapping with it ('Adventures of Nobody'), and wondered if it matters to anyone in a crumbling world, if it could matter in whatever world eventually emerges from the ashes. No way to know. And it doesn't even seem like the right question. To be more creative, I am supposed to exercise. To sleep more. To meditate. If I do all these things, will there actually be any time left for all that creativity to happen? Rhetorical question, we both know the answer.

Our house's version of 'reopening': we are talking about whether it is safe to get Chinese food delivered tonight. Wear gloves, toss the packaging, reheat everything? Need a fucking break. Drew up a new budget. Amazing how much money there is when you're not paying for childcare. We are, of course, paying in time. The Princeton paperwork arrived yesterday. We'll be appointed as lecturers for a class titled 'Rupturing Tradition', co-taught with a couple of Classics superstars. Although there is no way we can say no at this point, I also cannot see any way to do a good job at this class, with both the kids at home. We are pretty sure it'll be completely online. If not, I don't think we would do it.

I read about people forming quarantine pods or double-bubbles. This seems fine but I know it is not an option for us; there is no one we trust that much. We are still so much at the beginning of this undoing of the world. Even my mom, who errs on the side of optimism (my dad is always coming home 'next month', the vaccine research 'looks promising'), wrote that it's unethical to do human challenge trials for Covid vaccines because the subjects can't know what they're consenting to: we still understand this thing too little.

You must survive this plague, R. I find myself thanking god for Brandon's various ailments, for Mrinalini's past experience with Kawasaki's and even her recent illness, because I think these things will help keep you safer now. I read something called 'When we're twenty we think we are invincible', and don't you also still feel twenty, sometimes? Despite my fatigue, the two kids, the ghosts, the repetitions of the past...I do. Sometimes.

The real thing I want to say is that you're right about the difficulty of imagining the new world and our place in it. Have you seen the images of reopened South Korean schools, the video of a young student in China being sprayed with disinfectant and temp-checked before entering? Imagination is the crux of the problem now. Imagination, as much as critical thinking, is what's really suffered.

One thing I know is, I'm not assigning regular academic essays next term. I don't want to write them, I don't want to read them, I don't want to teach that form. But I don't know yet what will replace it.

If that future arrives! Still must always remind myself not to count on it. This habit of believing in a picture of the future, no matter how uncertain, is very hard to break. But I believe you will write back. I believe this exchange of letters will be longer than I imagined when we started it. I believe that we will witness something unfolding that we couldn't have imagined. And that's something to stick around for.

Reading Clarice Lispector's *Água Viva*, which, if it's about anything, is about living deeply in the now. It's comforting, also, because it is surely a book that, before it existed, was impossible, not to mention unmarketable. Feel a deep kinship with it.

Love and more love,
C

JUNE 4, 2020 | *KEEP MOVING*

Ah, my friend. My friend. I am so grateful to have you.

The loneliness is starting to hit—not the salutary solitary, but the lonely, the alienated, the separate, the alone. I have felt the pull of the protests as well, and have stayed home nevertheless. You know I've never been good at marching and slogans. But I feel the moment in my heart, my bones.

Maybe that's why I've been very tired this week, experiencing tension headaches (do I feel twenty sometimes, you ask? Lately I feel much much older). It doesn't help that it is a zillion degrees in Tucson and that what's true most everywhere else in the country (time to go outside!) is not true here. We are indoors more than ever, which as far as Covid goes does not bode well.

What more to say about this place? You have moved a lot, too, which means you know the struggle of trying to build community. From the beginning of our time here, it was clear we didn't belong. We felt disconnected; we had such a hard time making friends; we wondered why we had come. I've been thinking this lately: that if, at the beginning of the lockdown, I felt that I was starting to like Tucson more (because Tucson reduced to my safe-house and swimming pool was in many ways a Tucson enlarged and enriched) I now realize that the overall effect has been that I have withdrawn from this place even more thoroughly.

When it is all over, if it ever ends, we will have to leave this place, because it is now the scene of a slow death, the scene of a crime. I am not traumatized by the lockdown, indeed I take solace in it, but I feel ever more detached from all the reasons we came here and all the people we've found, and there is no longer any part of me that is willing to keep trying to cathect.

Where to go? Is another life possible? How to live in this life?

I started writing this letter with a profession of loneliness, but of course it's also the case that I am never really alone these days. Whether it's the children and their demands or the onslaught of news, opinions, images. I want some quiet, to close my eyes. You meditate. I'm getting some of what I need from the pool. The time I'm spending there is vital and restorative, even joyous. I descend and I picture the body of beautiful Ayman Safiah, who I read about this week in the news, 29-year-old Palestinian ballet dancer who drowned in the Mediterranean, may he rest in peace. I hear his last words, 'keep moving,' and I swim.

I won't apologize for it either, even though I am aware when I sink into the coolly prismed blue that elsewhere the world is on fire.

C, I do want to survive. I want to imagine a new world and it seems clearer now than ever that it has to start with the reimagining of the minutes.

As for the work, for the academic essay which you are writing away from, I agree with you that it's time to write and read whatever the hell we want. If not now, when?

All my love,
R

FIRST SUMMER: THE FIRE

Dear R,

I'm writing you with tears in my throat and on my desk. My dad sent the latest report on the dire pandemic situation in Egypt, ahead of his board meeting, his last obligation before he (supposedly, hopefully) gets on a flight home Sunday. The last paragraph of the article relates the death of a doctor from Covid, one of many. The doctor, concerned about his pregnant colleague, had taken over the care of her coronavirus patient and (because of the lack of PPE) contracted the virus and died. The article quoted a Facebook post by his pregnant colleague's husband: 'May God have mercy on you, Dr Sayed, who died almost an hour ago. I owe you the life of my wife and daughter.'

All of a sudden it became real to me, and I cried.

'It'—the story, the death, the suffering, something peculiarly, generously Egyptian, something deeply human, something about my childhood in Cairo and my wide-smiled swim coach Sayed, something about all the world's mothers. No, I don't really know why this article, out of all of them, should have sliced through all the newsy noise, and through this sound-proofed self-isolation, through the routine-muffled day.

I suppose some part of me is worrying about my dad's exposure on the flight, and whether he will quarantine himself properly from my mom when he arrives. Some part of me is worrying about my cousin, who missed our weekly cousin's morning virtual workout today, complaining of intense fatigue. It's her twenty-fifth birthday Friday (remember twenty-five?).

32

With Dr Sayed I suddenly feel the immense loss of each particular, peculiar, complicated human heart and skill and experience. It glares against the juxtaposed backdrop of New York's apparent 'winning'.

And it's our thirteenth wedding anniversary today. We found an old joint question and answer journal we used to keep in Oregon. Last night's question was: what contest would you easily win together? I wrote: a stay-at-home-the-longest contest. Micah made blueberry pancakes for breakfast. I have a silly idea of seeing if I fit into my wedding dress and wearing it for dinner. We'll see. For Father's Day, I've promised to take on various disagreeable male-coded tasks: mowing the lawn, clearing the sink drain, installing a shelf.

Micah shared another headline: a young woman who had been doing everything right for months. Went out for one night, socially distanced; now she and sixteen of her friends are sick. He found a way to look at the movement data for different zip codes—Pima, where you are, is down 1.5 per cent from last week and 13 per cent since February. Whatever that means. (For Micah it always means the same thing: keep staying home.)

You wrote in your last letter of your loneliness, of headaches, of unwillingness to try to connect and root. Of conversations that go unspoken, of silent dreams and nightmares of the future. I hear you. This letter seems like another letter about nothing. I begin to wonder if Nothingness is not the signature, somehow, of this time. If all of this—loneliness, triviality, death, silences—is the shadow of the Nothing—the way we register the being of what is not—the way what is not constitutes us. If what the virus has to teach us is also, or mainly, this: we come from nothing, we return to nothing, in between, we are also, mostly, nothing.

I love you and am grateful for you, my soul-friend, for your life-light, for your words. Keep going.

Love as always,
C

JUNE 20, 2020 | *THE HILLS ARE BURNING*

C,

I didn't give your letter a week to sit and lift me, as it did, as they always do, before replying. I am writing back almost immediately out of a deep need to reach you through the page.

I read the words to Dr Sayed in your letter and I felt tears in my eyes, too. May God have mercy on all these souls. You are right: the routine, the silences, the solitude, and the relentlessness muffle much of this noise, this pain, the bigness and hugeness and world-historical-ness of all that we are living through. So when it returns, when it punctuates the mood, it takes your breath away.

I am sitting outside sweating. I can feel the drops underneath my shirt as it sticks to my sides. The outside outlet is dead, like our car (for the third time recently: it is an old car, but also we have been allowing Shai to 'drive' and press buttons, which has not helped). The fan does not work. It is already in the high-20s and climbing at 6 a.m. Before mid-day it will reach 42°C. The earth is burning. Last night, we could see from our house in midtown a real fire in the hills.

Shai left his room this morning upon waking, for the first time, instead of waiting for one of us to come and get him. He has been defiant and demanding recently, two things he rarely is; he's coming into his independence in new ways each day. He's tall for two and can open all the doors. He knows where everything is. He's bargaining now. More tears.

For her part, Mrinalini enjoyed her virtual theatre and dance camp. On Friday, they had a showcase for families in the form of a Zoom webinar. They acted out a play (Mrinalini was a doctor, wearing her now languishing Tae Kwon Do uniform inside-out, as scrubs), each child by herself, performing alone in her bedroom. And then they danced, terribly and sweetly, also in their bedrooms. The screen was full of boxes of little awkward bodies swaying and twirling in front of their beds.

I had sent the grandparents the webinar link, and so they tuned in, and this little virtual camp showcase compelled my mother for the first time to write to me in an email: 'Missing the old days which are unlikely to return in the same way again.'

We went through all the feelings this week and arrived anew at the realization of what we already know: that this is it, that this will be it, that nobody is coming to save us, that only we can save us, that this is in fact how it has always been for most people in most of the world.

Brandon is coping by doubling down on work. He's trying to finish some mathematics papers that take him out of this world. Selfishly, I feel like they're getting in the way of various conversations I want to have with him once the kids go to bed. It seems clear to me that not having a strong community here in Tucson, not having friends we want to see, Mrinalini not having a best friend: all of this has been useful, vital preparation for what we are living now. But it can't go on like this, and I want to talk about the future. I want to think together about whether there *is* a future, and if there is, what we want from it, can get from it, can give to it. And how do we reach it? I keep seeing warning lights ahead, off ramps, escape hatches, roadblocks, and I want to talk about them. Brandon is much more focused on the present.

Still, it feels like we are moving into a new stage. Maybe because of this we took a liberty this week. We went to Reid Park, a huge park that takes up a number of blocks and includes the zoo and a lake and many playgrounds (of course we didn't go to any of those places). I've wanted to go for a while, but had been avoiding it. I thought Shai would demand to go on the swings and slides, and I didn't want to have to say no. But we went today, with Shai riding piggyback in the Ergo carrier, and we walked around the lake and fed the ducks (who we are not supposed to feed). Shai was so thrilled that he didn't even see the playground. Mrinalini was thrilled, too, her mood lifted like we haven't seen in months. Then the four of us went to a large and empty field and played tag and ran races. My thighs are still aching from the sprints. They were giggling and gurgling with delight. They slept a little longer that night. The hour after dinner dragged a whole lot less.

Two thoughts are on my mind, now that we've ventured out. One is Micah's comment at the start of it all that we are all 'experimenting'. Yes. This week we desperately needed something and somewhere new, and we experimented and found it. Second, I heard from one of my grad school mates that his and his wife's main goal every day is 'tiring out' their three kids. Huh. Now there's an idea.

Brandon and Shai just came and fixed the outside outlet, so there's a beautiful fanned breeze now on my face, and I'm drinking coffee and writing to you. I hear birdsong and chirps at three or four different octaves. I am tired but feel good. I close my eyes and rest them back on the couch and think that if I can just sit here in this moment for the duration.... A dog barks. I am learning to breathe.

Happy anniversary, darlings. And happy Father's Day.

All my love,
R

JUNE 27, 2020 | *THE ZOMBIE STAGE*

Dear R,

What to say? You know already the scary and infuriating, dismal and utterly predictable national spike in cases, especially where you are. You know what we're trying to think about (with an accent), how that work reaches back to our past selves.

Here, I tried and failed to be heard by my parents about the boundaries we have set. We reached the 'zombie stage' of the pandemic when a disordered elderly lady wandered up our driveway into our backyard. As in a film, our responses felt pre-scripted—we shepherded the kids inside, tried to communicate with her, to ward her off, and failed. We called the police, because there is no one else to call. All this was horrifying to me. We attempted to establish new scripts for next time.

And the end of one script looms, for all of us, with the end of the mobility-power of a blue US passport. Will immigrants still even *want* to come here, this time next year? Smart, hard-working people like your parents, my grandparents? Why would they?

Routines are now well established. Is that why time is going faster? A while back, weren't we complaining that the disease was moving too slowly? That it takes too long to appear and to kill people, so that it takes humans too long to learn the lesson? In any case, time doesn't feel slow any more. The disintegration is moving faster. I think it will keep picking up speed.

On May 11, I posted a sheet of blank boxes to the wall on the right of my desk and began ticking off a box for every day that I write. This is what I look at when I'm trying to comprehend time passing (not the list of future deadlines, which is posted in front of me). I went forty-one days (quarantine originally comes from forty, of course) without missing a box. In the blur of routine, I notice with admiration the family 'firsts' you mark in your letter: Mrinalini's zoom performance, Shai's new defiance, some loss starting to sink in for your mom. Happy-sad. The starry joy that the dark sky reveals. I seem to forget almost everything as soon as it happens, and pay almost as little attention to the uncertain future.

It's funny you mention your car battery dying. Same, exactly, with ours: dirty old hybrid Honda Accord—my parents bought it for us for less than $4000 when we moved up here, me unemployed and broke—that we let Areté play around in. The first time it died, we worried and ordered a jumpstarter from Amazon and fixed it. The second time, we just let it sit for a few weeks. Finally we restarted it again so we could roll up the windows; there's a chipmunk living in the garage and she could certainly find cheerio crumbs in the car if she is diligent. Today it looks like rain, so we might move it out of the garage: I have dreams of constructing a cardboard maze or castle with all our empty cardboard boxes in there. Have I mentioned it has become hard to throw anything away?

Separately I'll send you the virus essay that's been taking up so much of my energy these past couple weeks. It's time, too, to put some thought into my fall classes, so that books can be ordered. In both the Princeton seminar and the Bard course, I'm planning on experimenting with co-creating the syllabus with the students. It feels right to build in empty space to accommodate the unexpected.

I miss you. Send me photos of you, too, and not just your gorgeous children. We've mostly stopped taking them, because they would be the same as pictures I've already taken (playing in the sandbox, painting in the bathtub). To me there's something obscene about my sister in Jordan resuming posting pics of their 'socially-distanced' adventures on the regular. But I don't feel that way about your photos, so, do send.

I miss you. I know I already said that. But I really do.

So much love,
C

JULY 4, 2020 | *LEARNING OUR CLASS POSITION*

Good morning dear C, from virus-ravaged Arizona where, the *Times* reports, 'the rodeo goes on'....

Oh, I don't know what I'm thinking in this moment, but it feels bad! (It's all viral ambiguity, to use your words.) I'm so resentful of those who are buying and paying their way out of the pandemic (everyone's nanny is back). At the same time, that resentment is coupled with feelings of superiority: we will tough it out longer and harder (not longer or harder than *you*! But longer and harder than most everyone else).

Some worries are creeping in about Brandon's parents leaving Tucson for Maine. We've had them as back-up for three months—April, May, June—and anticipate them leaving for August, September, October. Will we manage? Well, yes, we have no choice but to manage, but, but, but...

Ugh. Maybe the bad feeling of the morning stems from my reading too many personal essays by American expatriates pitying the rest of us from their perches in Paris or Reykjavik. Maybe it's being jealous of my mother's cousin who smartly moved to New Zealand two decades ago when everyone else was coming to the United States, or hearing my grad school buddy plotting his move to Taiwan. We have nowhere like that to go. My only other home is India and it's not home. I still haven't processed the lockdown that was imposed on India's poor on March 24—the largest forced movement, they say, since the 1947 Partition.

Or maybe the bad feeling comes from the perversity of my own doomscrolling: my expectation that the Covid-19 numbers will rise, and the grotesque satisfaction I get when I see the little tickers ticking up, the percentages inching toward 100.

Do I want normalcy, or do I want the end of the world?

A too-bald question, perhaps, but I am quite sure you know what I mean.

I saw on Twitter (I know, I shouldn't) some discussion of that article in the *Times* from a couple days ago—the one that said 'you can have a child or a job in the pandemic, not both.' It went around online with many folks commenting that it was a primal scream for a generation of parents. Some Black feminists observed, and these are the words I have been turning around in my mind, that 'some people are learning their class position for the first time.'

Of course, the impossibility of working without childcare, support, or an infrastructure is only new (and news) to a certain class of people. Those who are primal-screaming now have previously been all-too-happy to prop up their lives with the low-paid labor of poor Black and brown women. Writing this, I feel stupidly glad that Shai's nanny was a blonde Mormon, and that Mrinalini's longest serving nannies were underemployed white and Asian wives/fiancées of graduate students and postdocs.

What am I trying to say? Or, in Salman Rushdie's words: 'Oh, spell it out, spell it out.' We started this exchange with a discussion of the insufficient, vacuous language of privilege. Is 'learning your class position for the first time' its inverse?

There is another depressing article in the *Times* this morning about how 'lower and middle class' children are stuck in their bedrooms attending virtual summer camps while 'upper middle class and wealthy' children are off at summer homes in pods with private camp counselors. I felt three things at once, reading this: middle-class solidarity and depression, plus sadness for my daughter; resentment of the wealthy; and real skepticism that an 'upper middle class' exists.

As a demographic (we academics; we, the over-educated) that has status, not wealth, and status, not power, how should we think about our class position?

This morning, the question is mixed up for me with confused thoughts about whether or not I want my job (I don't, and yet...); whether I want to move out of Arizona (I do, god, I do); whether I want to write (I do, but maybe not the things I thought I wanted to write just a few months ago?); whether we should be more focused on making money (which reminds me, we still need to do our taxes); whether our shameful, unspoken plan—and the reason why we have long neglected financial planning!—is to hope we inherit enough money from our parents (will it be enough? also: enough for what?).

Meanwhile, the university continues its reopening charge. Last month, the administration announced plans for 50 per cent of all classes (and 70 per cent of the core curriculum) to be either live or 'flex'. Yeah, right. I haven't talked to a single colleague who is willing to go back to campus. The administration has stopped short of saying that faculty *have* to come back; right now the language is of 'self-assessing' one's own 'vulnerability'. They are also coming for our graduate programs, which to be honest shouldn't ethically exist in the first place (none of these students will get faculty positions). I don't think they'll come for *our* positions, not yet. I admit—though it, too, shames me—that I'm generally keeping my head down and planning to do whatever I need to do to keep my job.

Making this with you—a dispatch from the end of the old world, a record of communion, an exchange—sustains me in the face of all this. May we never stop writing.

What kind of wish is that?

Closing now, with deep, deep gratitude.

Insert here all the questions about you and yours,

R

JULY 11, 2020 | *DISSENT BECOMES CONSENT*

Dearest, dearest R,

Writing you is the most important thing I have to do today.

I've been sleeping poorly, I'm not sure why, which always makes me quick to anger and slow to empathize. Is it because I tuned back into my professor WhatsApp chat, just in time for the arrival of the Open Letter on Justice and Open Debate? The letter, pretty anodyne in itself, is signed by the director of the Hannah Arendt Center here that hosts me, by Bard professor and ousted NYRB editor Ian Buruma, by my acquaintance Thomas Chatterton Williams, by J. K. Rowling, Salman Rushdie, Fareed

Zakaria, and many other unlikely bedfellows designed to inflame our controversy antenna. (PS: now find that TCW is the main organizer behind the letter.)

Have you seen it? If so, you will have smarter/more nuanced thoughts about it than me. The letter positions itself as a broad-based critique of cancel culture, though that goes unnamed as such. It's not very well written, it didn't really speak to me about these times, in short, I don't think it is worth much attention, and yet—it has me thinking more than I wanted to about 'cancel culture'.

I've yet to see a positive case made for cancel culture—or really, even a good definition of it. But reading between the lines of the sometimes histrionic responses to the open letter, I think a sympathetic definition would be something like this: 'cancel culture' is the expression of power of marginalized voices to establish new social norms through material and institutional facts.

I find myself a little conflicted. Like I said, I'm no particular fan of the more progressive than thou, mob-conformity aspects of cancel culture. It's a weapon that is easily used for causes I dislike as much as those I do. I believe in encouraging dissent—a common opinion, surely, which is why I called the letter anodyne.

Yet I'm wondering: is something like cancel-culture a necessary part of establishing new social norms? Is 'the problem' with it only that it's an incomplete part of the movement for change, that it's only the first step in the process of *aufhebung* (cancelling, preserving, transcending) the old world? But Hegel would probably be canceled, or anyway wouldn't be a bodyguard if cancellers came after me.

Maybe the controversy over the letter really comes down to this: cancellers see themselves as the dissenting view that needs protecting, while the letter-writers see themselves as dissenters protecting those who diverge from the progressive dissensus-consensus. A marginalized minority vs. an elite minority. Both positioning and needing to position themselves as defensive, and as broad-based. Both kind of shoddy versions of their respective ideals.

If I'm honest: there's a personal stake to these musings. Micah experienced the rage of the Twitter mob when he went to Davos—a long seven months ago—to talk at the World Economic Forum about elites and activists combining forces to combat climate change. He was called a grifter and a sham, cruelly mocked, and chance backstage encounters were aired in the service of character assassination. From a personal angle, I have no reason to be generous with cancel culture. Maybe that's why I'm trying to be.

Maybe you can read all this processing also as a response to your question, which circles back to the problem of privilege, and whether 'realizing your class position for the first time' is the inverse (and the antidote?!). I do want to think more about this. But now I've *really* written/thought more about this than I wanted to. Sorry darling. I have a feeling we haven't seen the end of this question, and also a feeling that it is both important and wrongly framed. As long as it is wrongly framed it is a distraction, like the bit of kitchen counter that needs tidying so I can get cooking.

We're in this brief moment when it's clear that the powers-that-be, from the President to upper management, aim to make us choose between infection or unemployment. As more and more people choose the former, the cloak of ideology will fall over their actions. They too will start to say versions of 'life must go on'. 'They' will start to include more and more of the people I want to have in my 'we'. Dissent will become consent. I'll feel more and more alone. When (if?) that happens, will my precarious middle-class privilege be enough to construct a barricade against conformity, pessimism, and power? Will anyone remember how they're finally admitting (too late) that airborne transmission is real?

Another reason I might be sleepless in Kingston is that I'm planning my fall classes in earnest now and this involves educating myself not only about the subject (Ancient Greek Political Thought) and anti-racist teaching of it, but also about online pedagogy. The ideas I have about how I want to structure the class fit well with Bard's 'Engaged Liberal Arts and Sciences' initiative, so I applied for a small grant from them for a Course Fellow. Wrote to my dean, registrar, and department chair on Friday to let them know I'm teaching online in the fall. I was very polite and kind. I did not frame it as a request.

I'm intellectualizing my stress, I think. In my body again— we are fine. I'm meditating regularly, twenty minutes twice a day, often on a group Transcendental Meditation call. This is supposed to counter the effects of what one article called 'Covid Brain', though that's not why I'm doing it. Found some online classes on Outschool.com that I think will be good for Zia (ninja-training, legos, a basic preschool circle time). Areté is trying out tiny sentences (he eat, I broke). She's working her way towards a story: every day she prompts me to tell her about the night she was SO MAD, she THREW her BABA (bottle) on the kitchen floor, and the ring-cap BROKE, and the MILK spilled everywhere, but (thank heavens) the CAP of her old baby bottle FIT....

And we found a baby bird, too, a live one, and Zia is mad we didn't let him pick it up, and....

We are going to try to take a 'vacation' next week, which just means, stay home without trying to work. I miss you, dear friend. Keep keeping safe and strong.

Love always,
C

PS: Obviously, during a pandemic, your in-laws should stay put unless there is an urgent need to travel. They should also, ethically, stay to help you. But really it's the first thing.

JULY 18, 2020 | *'FAMILIES CHOOSE'*

C! Good morning, dearest one.

I am reminded every time I read you that we are surviving by grace of my in-laws being here. I don't know how you and Micah are doing it alone. Of course you need a week off.

Even though it doesn't help us get much more 'work' done, my in-laws give the children days to look forward to and we get weekly breaks. However short, those breaks are vital. Shai knows the routine: Tuesday, he goes to their house; Thursday, Mrinalini goes to their house; on Saturday, they both go. Thursday evening: Brandon's parents come to our place for dinner. Sunday evening: we go to their place for dinner. This is our schedule. It gives each week a shape. For all my complaints about the limits of this schedule, my in-laws do many projects with the kids that we don't have the bandwidth for here—papier-mâché, water balloons, rock painting, composing songs, writing skits, planning costumes, learning magic tricks—and I will always be grateful to them.

A confession regarding your smart thoughts on the 'cancel culture' debate: I have no smart thoughts and largely found the conversation irrelevant to the times. Maybe it's my failure to understand the times. But I do hear you about Micah and Davos, and I remember that cruelty well. Two things that I have always admired in you both: your willingness to buck the crowd; and the confidence with which you change your minds. On that point, I remember so keenly you both announcing that you had decided once and for all not to have children. And then, of course, the clarity and purpose with which you did.

Mrinalini's school made a series of announcements this week that I've been parsing. They will be 100 per cent online from Aug 6–Sept 7, after which 'families choose' whether or not to stay online or come back to school in person. I wrote up a little summary of the situation as I understand it.

Here are some highlights (or lowlights!) of their plans for in-person school:

- daily health forms or temperature checks
- a health office for 'well kids' taking routine meds and a 'Covid' waiting room for kids with Covid-like symptoms
- masks required for kids over five (which sounds good, but this means they will not need to be six feet apart at all times)
- no plans to notify the school or school community of confirmed Covid-19 cases
- will only notify those who have been 'exposed' via maskless contact for ten minutes or more; in case of Covid exposure or incidence, affected student (but not the class) will quarantine for fourteen days

So, hello, virtual second grade! We are starting to think about the rearranging we will need to do to set Mrinalini up in a better home-school situation, like where to place her desk. The online program is going to run on a normal school schedule, starting at 8 a.m. with hourly assignments, videos, lectures, and meetings. It's incredibly depressing, but I think she'll handle it better than most. And her school, a charter known for its high academic standards, is rigorously setting up its online platform. Meanwhile, the local school district has unveiled their dystopian plan for kids who come back to school to sit at computers and be watched over by 'monitors' who are likely going to be Instacart workers on their second shift, while teachers record YouTube videos from home. Ghastly.

I've been thinking about our life before the pandemic: me, going to a department I hated to teach students who weren't doing any of the reading; Shai, going to daycare where he had to eat lunch at 10:45 a.m., Mrinalini, going to school having barely recovered from her GI issues and psychological strain; Brandon, I guess he'd been doing the best of us as far as his work was concerned, but his health was not ok.

Actually Brandon hasn't really been ok since spring 2017, the end of the year Mrinalini and I spent in Reno. He had been finishing his post-doc in Chicago, and that's when he first started with the colitis symptoms. It was the end of my first year at the University of Nevada, and I confess I loved every minute of it, even the solo parenting. I feel badly about that, C: how much I enjoyed that year, and how much I relished my independence, next to how sick it made him, how much weight he lost, how pale he got, and how anxious.

Now we eat well, we exercise, we stay away from assholes at the university. What sort of gift is this?

Covid as pharmakon. You know this story. You're writing it.

All my love,
R

JULY 22, 2020 | *WHAT THE FUCK HAVE I BEEN DOING?*

Dear R,

Well, it's only Thursday, and already the pretense of vacation week has faded. I am giving myself more time to do annoying personal things that need to be done—call the bank, transfer prescriptions, give each other haircuts. I finished my grading and a slew of emails. But the one thing I really took a break on is the thing that actually keeps me sane, the one thing I actually need to keep doing no matter what—the writing.

This is all the more important because, on top of my increasing fear and concern about the twin dangers of plague and civil war in this country, I'm now coping with some of my uglier personal feelings. Sometimes I just hate myself, simply and terribly. Last week Micah sent a book proposal that he'd been working on semi-secretly to his publisher, a snappier follow-up to *The End of Protest,* and this week they wrote back with enthusiasm and scheduled a call. When he told me the good news I did a little dance and led the kids in a round of applause and had actual tears in my eyes as I hugged him hard, because such happy personal tidings are so rare and unexpected, and he deserves it.

But—you know me well enough to know there's a but—in a small part of my soul, something feels absolutely crushed. This time last year, I planned to have a book accepted for publication by the time the Princeton class started. That was what I felt I needed to stand on equal footing with my co-teachers. Now Micah is on his way to a second (killer) book and I have to ask myself, what the fuck have I been doing?

I can't use the mother excuse. He's been taking on his fair share of the parenting and often more. So all I can tell myself is that everything happens in its own right time. I tell myself that I just have to keep trying; that I could be closer than I think. I cultivate appreciation for the small good acts I'm doing in the world: helping a friend apply for a new Bard scholarship for adult learners, starting a Disruptive Reading Group at Bard, having difficult conversations with my mom about race, being a good-enough parent and partner and friend.

But my evil demons are whispering that I'll never do it, that I have nothing to say and am no one. They are awfully persuasive.

So I feel anxious and horrible and ashamed. I don't want these feelings to poison my work, but work is the only antidote to the poison. So today I hauled out the index cards where I've been collating the various fragments of writing, and sorted them again, looking for the patterns and form that might hold them together. I felt marginally less anxious, horrible, and ashamed afterward. I know how much time and effort a book cycle takes—to finish it, proof it, proof it again, publish it, promote it—and so I know I'm going to be coping with these toxic feelings of shame, doubt, not-good-enoughness, for some time to come.

Exploring the idea of 'unschooling' for Zia, wanting to protect his passionate brilliance—these toxic feelings have everything to do with how I was schooled.

Feel a little better writing to you. I don't keep secrets from Micah but haven't wanted to ruin his accomplishment with these villainous, bilious feelings.

This shit is hard and long and you are one of the few people that make it worth living through.

Love you,
C

JULY 31, 2020 | *ERRING*

Hi, dearest C,

When I read your last letter my first thought was to reply immediately. And then I realized that you are maybe not sitting with these feelings but purging them, and that I ought not to respond in a hurry. Writing too quickly would mean giving weight to what you call the villainous, bilious feelings, when you have no doubt already sublimated them. But I hear them. And they need not be sublimated.

'What the fuck have I been doing?' is a question I ask myself, too. Often. I had some momentum earlier in the month with a couple different projects. I put something to bed, was about to pick-up something huge, got overwhelmed, pivoted to something smaller. So here's my new plan for productivity in the pandemic: I am going to bring to fruition as many of the half-articles and half-writings from previous years as I can. I am going to err on the side of finishing pieces I've been working on for the last ten years, as opposed to generating brand-new work. This decision has given me a feeling of purpose and a way to tackle this phase. To let what is already here ripen.

Meanwhile: I detest my department. The rot is deep, and I've felt the sick of it since we got here in August 2017. People don't even believe me when I tell them how bad it is. There are factions here that aren't allowed to communicate by email without cc:ing HR. The senior faculty rotate all the leadership positions between themselves (and their spouses!), while never missing an opportunity to tell us more recent 'partner hires' that they didn't want us. The few faculty of color (a very tiny constituency that we are nevertheless hemorrhaging) are daily harassed. Scene 1: Senior white man repeatedly pops his head into black woman assistant professor's office to ask her about the n-word in Mark Twain. Scene 2: Senior white man plays blackface *Othello* for his students, who bring their shocked grievances to the women of color faculty, since nobody else will listen. Scene 3: I have to report a senior white man for excoriating me and another junior woman colleague in a public forum for daring to propose that the World Literature section of the Masters exam should include some texts in translation. Scene 4: A senior white man (hang on, I'm sensing a pattern here) points (yes, he points!) at a black woman junior colleague in a meeting and says: 'instead of doing these diversity hires, we should have done some real hires.'

These old guys: they dislike each other; they dislike the future; mostly, they dislike themselves.

There are lots of horrible Reply-All threads ongoing as the deans slash budgets and hand down pay cuts and threaten to get rid of our graduate program. I feel trapped because: I don't want to be involved in these conversations; I don't care to invest in this institution; I refuse to bloody my head against the brick wall. But I find other people's incompetence so maddening that sometimes I can't help myself but speak up.

As long as I'm doing this job, I am technically still on the tenure clock, and I hate that, because it doesn't feel like a worthwhile pursuit. At the same time, I cannot deny that my professorial perch, broadly construed, is the major enabling condition of my work.

More to be said about all that. The other big thing is plotting my in-laws' return to Maine. Ironically, I'm the one who has been pushing the point. For a few reasons: 1) My mother-in-law is depressed. She frequently complains that she is tired of Tucson, and she worries that Mrinalini doesn't find going to their house 'special' anymore(!). So I think they should go because psychologically they seem to need it. 2) They feel guilty about leaving us, so I feel like we have to create the conditions for them to leave. 3) We need them to go have their vacation, and take their break, because then we need them to come back and help us for the rest of the academic year.

Lots of issues. For them: travel logistics and safety. For us: the loss of the little help we get, just as Mrinalini starts virtual second grade. But we can't keep them here in Tucson, so it looks like they will drive out to Maine at the end of August and return at the end of October.

The next question is whether we can get my parents out here from the Bay Area while my in-laws are gone, to live in their house, to be of some help, and to see the kids, who they haven't seen in months and desperately want to—especially Mrinalini, who they last saw in December 2019, when she was terribly sick.

Meanwhile, Mississippi, where lots of Brandon's family lives, is a total disaster. His aunt and uncle are letting their bachelor son live with them, while still going out and partying with his girlfriend. Another aunt is about to go on a 'girl's trip' to a resort. A cousin with a newborn and toddler is headed to a big-city wedding. A CEO-uncle has kept his business open this whole time with a steady flow of Covid cases ('they're being really careful; they always wear masks'). So CEO-uncle is ok, but what about the workers? If we've learned anything since

March it's the precarity and inequity of this system—one law for the prisons and factories, another for the service sector, another for those working from home. And yet uncle #2 thinks 'the economy is doing great'.

My mother-in-law weekly reports to me how 'careful' so-and-so is being. I ask one or two questions and it swiftly comes out that whoever she's talking about has a circle of at least ten–twenty strong and growing!

I read this week about the fake Covid-negative test results you can buy when your employer wants you to return to work.

And this is why, this is why, all of this is why this idiotic country is never going to get the virus under control.

It was another week of mid-40s here, weather-wise, and we had an algae scare in the pool which is now over-chlorinated, and when I got out yesterday I could feel my whole face tingling. Sitting outside, I can still smell the chemicals, rising off the water.

Have I told you about my brother's long-distance girlfriend, in South Africa? Next time, I'll start there, with a promise of connection. I am delighted by his having this 'pen pal'. Sometimes when I'm swimming I imagine a big family trip to Johannesburg, where she lives, and Cape Town, which is maybe the most beautiful city I've ever seen. For the span of a couple laps, I feel, foolishly, something like hope.

Love you my friend!
R

AUGUST 8, 2020 | *CONFLICT CAUSES GROWTH*

Hello dearest R,

I'm thinking about shaving my head. I sat down, *finally*, to write you, and had to get right back up again for a headband to scrape it away from my face.

In theory, I could go to the hairdresser. It would certainly be nice to have decent hair for filming the Princeton class (which I am plain scared about, but more about that later). And I love getting my hair cut. I'm particularly fond of this particular hair stylist, who is smart and thoughtful and generous, has a daughter about Zia's age, and who certainly seems to be taking all the possible precautions. My region has been fully reopened for four weeks now; the number of new infections hovers around 3.5 per 100,000, which is not quite the 2 per that the most rigorous experts recommend, but is also not so bad that contact tracing becomes utterly useless (as is the case in most of the country). I say all this because I am nowhere even close to the possibility of going to a hair salon. Imagine if I had to teach in person in two weeks?

Anyway, these musings are a weird way into a weird week. The tl;dr version is: conflict causes growth.

The inciting incident: my parents made a lightning trip from Virginia to Massachusetts, flaunting the spirit if not the letter of the new fourteen-day quarantine rule, to see a handful of family members, including my dad's ninety-nine-year-old father and his sister (the anesthesiologist married to an infectious disease specialist with two doctor sons, at least one of whom is working Covid wards). They wore masks and distanced and didn't use any rest stops, and they were patting themselves on the back for leaving before a passel of other more distant family relatives showed up.

While they were there, they found time to give my aunt, who even Micah loves, an earful about how devastated they are that we are 'not letting' them visit. So I hear it from my aunt—with her I can be very honest, thankfully—and I call my mom, and we go through it all again. How I love them, I miss them, it's not personal, this is just our choice to be extremely cautious, and can they please respect it and stop needling me. Micah chimes in with dark facts and data, which frankly never helps, but he needs to be able to say his piece, he says.

My mom is less upset this time than previous versions of this fight, as we each return to our practiced moves, but she tells me that one of the reasons she's been being so cautious is because she wants to see me so much, but since it's off the table, she might as well stop being so careful. I tell her this is emotional blackmail. She says, no it's not. I tell her there is a good reason to keep being careful, so that we can see each other sometime in the future. She sounds unconvinced that future will ever arrive. I ask her again to return to the list of activities I sent her that might work for grandparent-grandchild zooming. She kinda says she will.

This is hard on people. I mean obviously. My aunt's position is that maybe my parents' trip is essential travel. Mine is that they don't want to connect with me as much as they want to get their way. Otherwise they would actually call once in a while, or find some way to be actually supportive, even from afar.

My position is also that I do want to be marginally more open than Micah does. Like, go for remote walks and drives. And I have come to see, in a crazy yet divinely perfect way, that I have selected the exact partner who will force me to revisit the limiting structures of my childhood, and heal and grow from them. So when I perceive Micah as replicating some of the controlling and authoritarian behaviors of my parents, I don't have to throw up my hands in fear—fear that I'm projecting my craziness, or that I'm caught once again, that I'll either have to leave him or put up with this patriarchal garbage my whole life.

No: I picked this man because he represents this challenge to me, and so leaving him wouldn't solve the problem. I solve the problem not with the either/or (submit or leave), but with the both/and (both stay and struggle). This love relationship is my love relationship because it heals that deep question in me, about whether I have a right to a self with my own opinions, or whether I am only worth as much as the positive regard of the people around me.

Anyway, to connect the dots—this conflict is what led us to decide to take the kids to a field to run. We had some good talks (the meditation is really helping), and we picked a nice rainy day, a place we know there's lots of room to maneuver. We got our rain gear, masks, snacks, and hand sanitizer. We took turns trying to get the car started. When I finally juiced it just right, we saw that all the warning lights were lit up. Drove a few feet out of the garage to a horrible scraping sound. We stopped and googled. The brakes are all rusted out, and we need to get it to the mechanic. We backed up into the garage and unloaded everything.

That whole day afterwards was a long, rainy wash of weird feelings. Disappointment, relief. Anger at our stupidity in not taking the car for regular maintenance drives. Annoyance at each other for a dozen dart-tipped words that weren't really what was bothering either of us. Faintly anxious about the mechanic's bill. Gruffly resolved to do better in some vague way. Wondering, at the end of the long weird day, if our failure was maybe also the gods protecting us, just when our resolve faltered.

The next day, sunny again, we took the kids for a short early morning walk up and down our dead end street, before anyone else was awake. They shrieked with joy. Areté pointed to a fire hydrant and made us understand: 'Robot! Red hat robot!' The walk has been our daily habit since then. It has noticeably lifted my energy levels, too, and my productivity, and lessened the difficult emotions I wrote about last time.

I can name the feeling now. Envy. Poison Envy. Name it to tame it, as the parenting books say.

In hindsight, I do not recommend a week of staycation in lockdown. Our work is our sanity.

But tell me all about your major minor mysterious world. Tell me about your brother's Jo-burg girlfriend. And more about the in-laws, and the department sagas. And Mrinalini is now in virtual second grade, right? Remember when that was just a question, at the beginning of our letters?

All love,
C

AUGUST 15, 2020 | *THERE ARE NO COOKIES*

Dearest C,

Oh, the uncanniness of a shaved head fantasy! My daily fantasy, too. Of course, we are sharing in this fantasy across the time zones. Reading you, my immediate thought is that you will do it, before I do. You will have the gumption, and I will continue to make excuses. But also: neither of us is going to a hairdresser any time soon.

What you say here about your parents' lightning trip to Massachusetts—the cracks exposed, the pressures exerted—is at the heart of it all. What is essential travel? What is connection, now? What was it, in the before-times? In what way could they (can any of us) be supportive from afar?

With the horrors of virtual school fully upon us, I find myself increasingly frustrated that my parents have not done more for the kids, that my brothers-in-law who seem to have been on vacation since March have done nothing for them either. For his part, my brother calls Mrinalini sometimes and they talk at length about the books she likes. She tells him stories and asks him questions that she does not tell or ask us, and I am glad for it. They are friends.

I feel, I felt, every word of the abortive trip to the field and the walks around the neighborhood. Reading you, I felt I was there with you in the car that wouldn't start. (So much of what I feel every day is the feeling of being in a car that won't start! Is that the metaphor of the moment?)

Yes, push each other, push back a little against the radical lockdown that you both have chosen and enacted, for all the reasons you say, but also because you know as well as anyone else what you need to do, how to be safe, how much space to create, and when. You know. I know you know. You know you know.

We are in a related moment. We've had a few trips to the field and walks around the block to look at house numbers and broken lamp posts. Shai sweetly thinks that his daddy is the fixer of all the lamp posts in the neighborhood, so he likes to identify them and give Brandon instructions for their repair. He likes purple-colored houses, brown trucks, and unusual front-yard displays of balls or gnomes. We walk around looking for gnarly cacti, and lizards doing push-ups and, bizarrely, rabbits, running all up and down the blistering streets.

Actually we haven't done much of that lately because it is over 43°C every day, and it hurts to go outside. The records are in: it has been the hottest summer in Arizona in 125 years. From May through August, there were 50 days when the temperature was over 40.5°C. There's a GIF going around, about how living in Arizona is 'that feeling when you open an oven to check on your cookies and it burns your face except there's no cookies and you can't escape'.

There are no cookies. And there is no escape.

Back to the related moment: virtual second grade is so horrible that I wrote a desperate Twitter thread about it. The thread did its job. Some acquaintances, friends, and colleagues with same-age kids reached out to me to commiserate. And so, today, I feel slightly better: if we are drowning, we are not drowning alone.

Why not pull her out of school entirely, a friend in DC asked? She, like you, has made that decision with her would-have-been-kindergartener. The same friend has not yet made that decision with her soon-to-be-second grader, for the same reasons, I think, that we are keeping Mrinalini in school.

I don't want Mrinalini to suffer. She is smart and independent. We let her read books instead of paying attention to class. It's her mood I worry about. And her isolation. I suspect from what we learned when she was sick in the fall that she has a tendency toward anxiety and depression. And so, we are wondering if we need to create opportunities for her to see and interact with other children. It's been five months since she's seen any child other than Shai.

Socially distanced dates for children. Do they work? Swim dates? We aren't acting on any of this for now, because of the need to protect my in-laws' health and because we fear the slippery slope and also because: dates with whom? We don't have people here we want to take risks for. This is the heart of our problem.

But we're researching outdoor classes, like tennis, that might get her in spitting distance (ha!) of some other young people.

Being in online school with kids you can't see? Turns out it's a kind of torture.

Another more selfish realization: we were coping pretty well all these months with the schedule we'd created for ourselves. The school's externally imposed schedule is not working for us. We are struggling. We are getting much less 'work' done. Even if it was just two hours a day it was keeping us going. Now, Mrinalini has to be monitored constantly. Her meals have to be made on the school's timeline, and then there's the horror of the ambient noise of her class, the teacher's frustrated pleas, the children's tinny voices. That might be the thing that finally destroys us.

My in-laws are still planning to leave, with our permission and urging. Part of me thinks if they go, it will force change, and that will help us. Because right now, we're living a less-good, less-workable version of what we'd been living these past few months. Better to let them go, let it fall apart, and rebuild.

Should we buy a swingset? A trampoline? A video game console, maybe Dance Dance Revolution? Some sort of heater for the pool in winter? Karaoke? We are trying to make the house livable in new ways for the coming seasons.

The central AC died for the second time yesterday, and we had to sleep the kids in different rooms with the single-AC units. I do think that Arizona is trying to kill us.

And I haven't even told you about the university's purchase of one of those horrible predatory for-profit online schools that has multiple lawsuits pending against it.

They went ahead with huge paycuts: 10 per cent for me, 15 per cent for B.

And the students have started moving in, thousands of them, with thousands more to come.

I have been trying to convince myself that I am working steadily on something. Then, the other day, a senior academic friend asked me about my tenure book and I failed to say anything of substance, just exposed the mess in my head, and I was embarrassed and ashamed, and so envious of how many books and films he has made, and so annoyed at myself.

But. This is the struggle. Is it a beautiful struggle? Sometimes, when I am writing to you or reading you, I think it could be.

Tell me everything.

All my love,
R

AUGUST 29, 2020 | *FOR THE LISTENER*

Dearest R,

What is the word for when you are stressed but so is everyone you know, so there's little we can do to help one another?

Yesterday, I finally managed to get a draft of my column off my chest (it's terrible!), so today I can turn to preparing for the first Princeton class (I'm not worthy!). Am sleeping poorly, and Micah is burned out on childcare so I am trying to step up there (just when I can least afford to), and none of this will be surprising or unfamiliar to you.

You are now, impossibly, one month into second grade, and perhaps a few days into the absence of the in-laws. I can hardly believe either. I wish them a safe journey and you an easeful transition. I read everything you send, with endless hunger for details about your living, surviving, struggling for and with beauty. The poems and books you sent me are beautifying my inner landscape, now. And here is one from Wallace Stevens that you doubtless know:

'The Snow Man'

One must have a mind of winter
To regard the frost and the boughs
Of the pine-trees crusted with snow;

And have been cold a long time
To behold the junipers shagged with ice,
The spruces rough in the distant glitter

Of the January sun; and not to think
Of any misery in the sound of the wind,
In the sound of a few leaves,

Which is the sound of the land
Full of the same wind
That is blowing in the same bare place

For the listener, who listens in the snow,
And, nothing himself, beholds
Nothing that is not there and the nothing that is.

I thought of this poem this rainy morning as Areté led me into a deep 'lake' at the end of our dead end street. Maybe

I'm not really a writer, but a listener, 'nothing myself', but only through you, darling, and the others who feed me with love and poems and soul-emanations I can't possibly perceive and yet, on some level, do. No frozen mind here, just liquid running hot and cold and probably crowded with bath toys and bubbles and possibly overrunning its container. Probably that is why I cannot sleep.

News: spoke via video to my sister and brother-in-law yesterday in Jordan, part of my birthday treat. Covid uptick there. They're 'one week, maybe two' away from pulling my nephew out of the preschool he *just* started and loves. Conflict with their most likely candidates for a pod, the nearby neighbors whose daughter is close with my nephew. The neighbors want my sister to download the state-sponsored contact tracing app. My sister doesn't trust the app not to surveil them, but is willing to download it to a spare phone. That concession is not enough for the neighbor's husband, who canceled the next day's playdate. Meanwhile, my sister wonders why, if the neighbors are being so careful, they went to the beach town of Aqaba over the weekend.

You know this story already, too. We both know so many people who are starting their kids in school even though they know it can't last. Impossible decisions. My sister's neighbor's husband reminds me of how people probably see Micah: intractable, self-absorbed. I wonder if he is as sweet as Micah when the apartment door is closed, and I am strangely comforted to know that these struggles and squabbles are playing out everywhere.

Also learned from my sister that my father is planning to return to Egypt soon, until Thanksgiving. Three words: white male entitlement. As in, 'Those travel restrictions are for other people. My job is *so* important, I just couldn't possibly.' Three more words: I give up. On him only, not the larger feminist struggle. Maybe I can negotiate with Micah to have my mom come and stay locally while my dad is away. Two week quarantine, have a test, and stay in a restricted pod with us while she is here. I am sure the thought of it will send him into a panic. It is probably true that my dad, who is unlikely to accept or follow any conditions, would then try to come and visit at Thanksgiving, making everything more complicated.

We went to the park yesterday afternoon. It was busier than the usual times we go. I could see Zia yearning to play soccer with two older boys who were playing with sticks and a ball. They had masks on. Their moms were wearing masks and sitting far apart on the bleachers. Cases are low in New York and our county, with three straight weeks of an R-naught under 1. It seemed okay; I couldn't think of any reason it wouldn't be okay. But also, I don't want to find those reasons. Micah can: in some possible reality, one of the kids would suddenly pull off a mask and spit and...

I'm out of time, darling. It's been hard to get these words out, a bit undigested. I must need more soul-fiber.... I'll try to work in some time today, to take care of myself, for you, and for the dear and difficult ones around me who continually challenge me to be both stronger and more compassionate than I was yesterday.

I love you and miss you.
C

FIRST FALL: THE NUMBERS

Dearest C,

I'm so glad to have your words to sit with. I revisit them. They change, somehow, day by day. In some ways everything stays the same, and in others, it all gives way. My in-laws are gone now. As Brandon said as soon as they left, *well, it's back to the beginning now.* Back again to March. The endless return to the early days of the pandemic, which have stretched out into the interminable every day of the pandemic, which just might be every day of the rest of our lives.

I keep thinking about what you said about why you were drawn to Micah, about the ways in which he might ironically be like your father, about the specific challenges of your relationship (in addition, of course, to all the joys, the strengthening), and I think you are absolutely right. Sitting outside of it, I feel tempted to urge you: yes, get your mother out there for a little bit of help, for the change for the children, and also for your mother, for some credit or goodwill toward the future and its needs that we can't anticipate.

Of course I say this because my parents are landing up in a week. And to be honest, I'm quite nervous about it. I am always a bit nastier to them in person than I mean to be. I am less of a good host (never mind daughter) than I want to be. I am impatient with my mother. I am resigned to the fact that my parents will not be of much 'help' and that we will have to take time out of our schedules to be with them, since we haven't seen them in eight months. I am also nervous that they will get sick.

The university cases here are steadily ticking up. Some say we are already in a spike; if not yet, then we are heading for one. The university is the largest employer in town. Hundreds of students have tested positive, and the majority are off campus, in the community, doing who the hell knows what.

The K-12 schools are opening at the end of the month. I re-committed to 'distance learning' yesterday, even though Mrinalini is miserable in virtual school and so are we. I hesitated for a moment, wondering if there was anything to consider that would change the inevitable? Well, no, of course not.

It is so perfectly stupid, that the university cases are spiraling upward just as the elementary schools are planning to reopen because on paper we have 'met the metrics'. The metrics are not good enough! Two weeks from now, just when the elementary schools start to open, the metrics are going to have changed, thanks to the university. What a sad and predictable mess.

It's back to the beginning.

So, we are doing something crazy today. I almost don't want to confess it to you. We are going to the zoo. It just reopened with advance tickets only, limited admission, no indoor exhibits and no participatory activities, no water fountains...and I've bought tickets. My in-laws are gone, and it's a long weekend. I want to do something for and with the children.

All night (I realized upon waking) I was thinking and worrying about it. Now it's morning, and Brandon is making breakfast, and then we're supposed to go. Is it Disney World, or is it just an extension of the regular park? My thought: it's all outdoors. Maintain distance. Keep Shai in the Ergo. Everyone stays masked. Take our own water. Stay for a short time, come home for lunch. Nobody uses the bathroom. It's 24 acres, after all.

Yesterday, we drove about an hour toward Mt Lemmon, where normally there's good hiking. Now, because of Covid and the fires, all the trailheads are closed. There's a two horse and five house town up there called Summer Haven, with some touristy shops. We drove by them (full! scary!) and then parked on the side of the road and went exploring in the woods. A few people passed by, but not many. We put out a blanket and had snacks and watched a little mole in his burrow. He was curious about us, the mole. Picked pine cones. The kids made little mud slides, and we looked up at the canopy of leaves and a dozen hawks overhead that had sighted the mole.

They were delighted, overjoyed (the kids, not the hawks). And it was literally thirty degrees cooler up there, which is why we went (it's been 42/43°C again for the last few days).

I reread 'The Snow Man' a few times, once out loud. Tucson-based writer Brandon Shimoda says *one is not a poet when writing poetry, but a poet when reading poetry.* My colleague Johanna Skibsrud just wrote a book of essays called *The Nothing That Is.* Does Areté have the book *None the Number?* That might be 'The Snow Man' for the toddler set.

I can hear steps coming toward me, so I'm going to stop here. More to be said. I will write a postscript about the zoo.

All the love,
R

PS: The zoo! We only lasted an hour and a half, it was in the 40s again, but it was great. I might have enjoyed it the most out of all of us. I've never been to this particular zoo, and I don't much like zoos, so in every way it exceeded my expectations. Not so many people, and most everyone was masked (though of course some were not, and there were many loose, one ear-ed masks hanging off faces). We didn't buy anything or eat anything or use the bathrooms. So it was just like a walk around a park, but a little more cramped. We saw a rhino having a mud bath! And two giraffes munching leaves, and four maybe five elephants including a BABY playing in the dust, and lions staring ahead imperiously, and little yellow pawed squirrel monkeys, lemurs and meerkats and sleeping otter, and anteaters, and a capybara, and a jaguar, and a gibbon asleep high up in a fenced enclosure, fist hanging on to fence, and, some kind of bird with an intense beak, yellow and jagged, I was so sure it was a statue. And then it blinked.

SEPTEMBER 17, 2020 | *NEVER PLAY DEFENSE*

Dear R,

Today, after most of my week's obligations were done (Thursday is the new Friday, around here), I was lying in bed, exhausted but unable to nap, trying to think of what I could do to restore myself, and I remembered that I could write you. How lucky I am that you are here, or there, or in some inter-where, in any case, reachable, writeable, listening, forgiving.

And how lucky you are to have your parents close. The photos, the smiles and hugs and tangible joy at the re-mixing of worlds, made me both smile and cry. If my own mom did come to visit, it would not be like that. Stiff and frozen gestures, Micah receding behind an iron shield of judgment and resentment, my mom captive to her own rigid politeness and introversion. Me and the kids trying to create the semblance of play and connection in the middle, not understanding why our love is ricocheting off hard surfaces, returning distorted.

I grieve it.

There is nothing to be done about it.

There was an awkward grandparents video call on Zia's birthday. We timed it to coincide with a rest stop for my parents, on their way back from Massachusetts where they attended my dad's dad's ('Pa') ninety-ninth birthday party. There was a Zoom version which I did not attend, because it was not convenient and I did not want to. I also did not call Pa, though I know I ought to. I received second-hand notice, from my mother and also my sister, that Pa is still upset about the incident the last time I saw him, at Cape Cod, when he made some nasty remarks about Micah's book, and Micah asked him if he was negging him right at the dinner table, and whether anyone else in the family had written a book at all. My kind cousin, then dating a Nigerian man, jumped in and said to Micah, 'I hope you know the rest of us don't feel like that.' I tried to talk to Big Pa afterwards, feeling I had to say whatever futile thing I said for Micah's sake.

The whole thing was, is, an awful mess with no resolution. The next day I talked a long time to my aunt about it in her spacious beachy kitchen, the kind with two dishwashers in an 'island' that by itself is definitely bigger than those kitchens we had in our Berkeley apartments. (Remember?) Micah hovered nearby, inserted a few things, but couldn't quite bring himself to talk openly about it, though we tried, I felt, to make space for him in the conversation. My aunt is gregarious and generous, early sixties. She told us something of her long history with the man, his anti-semitism towards her Jewish husband, her anger at him, his patriarchal attitudes towards her mother and herself. But she...takes care of him. She forgives him.

Micah can't. Can I? Should I?

In the awkward video call, my in-laws were kind and gracious and invited conversation about pleasant and easy topics. My mom was stiff and my dad chugged soda in the background, obviously signaling his desire to be back on his way. It didn't help that Zia was not cooperating, since he was super hungry after playing a long time on his tablet and demanded two pieces of birthday pie which he wolfed down on screen, forgetting to say his thank yous and generally just wanting to get back to his game. I soon let my parents off the hook ('You probably want to get back on the road'), and then we talked to Micah's parents for forty-five minutes candidly about the difficult racial dynamics with my parents, each of us feeling supported, because each of us is understood and loved and feelings, even ugly ones, are allowed to be said out loud.

There is no time for Micah and I to talk to each other, really talk. We work, a four hour day shift each, and at nights. In the getting-ready and going-to-bed periods, we hand off the kids so we can each take a short meditation break before facing the rest of the hours before us. Micah wants to talk about his meditation, how certain experiences feel, the ones he prefers, could he get something to measure his brainwaves and then try to induce those experiences more often. I just see it as licensed, protected daydream time. Sometimes, lately, I lie down for it and it's almost as restful as nightdream time.

On Thursdays I let myself feel how disorganized I truly feel. The rest of the week, I hold it all together. Routine, routine, routine, and schedule, schedule, schedule. Parceling minutes out to each thing, almost reveling in the fact that there's too much to hold it all in, that something is going to spill out. Example: I sat on the toilet lid this week, one airpod in, listening to my co-professor's recorded lecture, while Areté took a daytime bath. She likes those foam alphabet letters you gave us when Zia was two, as a result maybe of the Leapfrog television shows that are one of our part-time teachers and babysitters.

To be doing actual work sitting on the actual toilet with my actual soapy child in the tub...these are places and objects that are not supposed to coincide.

But in this reality, they do.

In this reality, I am needing to have, but not really having, almost impossible group conversations about racial stress, about what is owed, about the intersection of the personal and the structural.

This teaching together is insanely hard. It is the third class we have taught together, by far the most ambitious, I cannot tell sometimes whether it is brilliance or madness. Useless distraction at the end of the world? Pure foolish egoism? I am terrified of having put a shape on things. What if the shape doesn't work or is ugly? What if, by giving form, and taking form, I invite counter-formations that I can't withstand? We are seeking out the differences.

Disorganized. I won't tell you about the state of the kitchen floors. But everything is spilling everywhere. Everyone is peering into my interior room. I have been obsessive about keeping kid toys out of my office, the one space in the house that is mine. But now that Areté might have to come to seminar, or to the weekly meetings we hold, I keep a bag of special toys, snacks, and juice boxes at my feet. She has shown up to class every time, sometimes more active than others. It's always been fine so far, though yesterday I showed up barely on time and flustered after just getting her to sleep in the stroller, then having to help Micah find his phone (thereby interrupting my own set up and grounding time). Does it matter? It'll be edited out of the final version. It matters.

The shouts, the door slams. Zia sometimes has these 'days'. I guess I have them, also. Moods. When you can't put your finger on it, but everything is just somehow wrong.

It was sweet of you to come to the Zoom event with Kate Manne. I want to tell you one thing she said on the pre-call that she didn't say publicly. It was when I asked her if she has any rules for Twitter. During the event, she talked about not attacking any individual women. On the phone, she told me the same thing. But her first rule was: never play defense.

I have been struck by the force of those words. Like it was the secret code of power, the watchword of masculinity, getting one's way. I recognized my father's strategy, and the trap I always fell into with him, whether it was Connect 4 or talking politics or trying to buy a house: I was *constantly* playing defense, constantly reacting to his moves. I wondered if Manne played sports. You know I mostly took up individual sports, and viscerally hated basketball, which was the one offense/defense team sport I played, really poorly.

Am really glad I am off Twitter. For the Kate Manne event I checked back in after a long absence and was like, yeah, nope, don't need this stream of fear and distraction.

What even is going on? That guy, Michael Osterholm, said the pandemic is like a wildfire, not waves. Then lo and behold, wildfires. Because apparently we humans need an illustration.

I can't seem to stop. One very last thing. A breath of something. I went to drop off a bag to my friend who has been doing a book exchange with us. I wasn't expecting her or her son to be home, but they were. I put masks on the kids, and so did she, and let them run around the backyard together. Let them see the chickens, play chase, take turns on the janky swing and the toddler slide. They fell right into play. I fell into mom conversation. It was maybe twenty minutes? Her child then went off to in-person kindergarten. I washed the kids' hands with the hand sanitizer I keep in my purse, making sure it dried completely, and we went home.

I texted Micah on the way home. 'Nothing to report.' That's the code we use after outings to instantly assuage any anxiety. And told him briefly that I'd let the kids play together. He said he was okay with it and the safety measures I'd taken, but we had to have a long talk that night about how I violated his trust, and can we just talk about new steps before we take them. He's right. I didn't play defense.

Your story about the zoo... I keep rereading it to experience the old, ordinary, glorious pleasure of variety, the love for the profusion of life, all that just for the looking, seeing our animal selves, wild but caged, consuming nature in an alien environment, condensing the myriad species scattered over the globe into a walkable area (because as humans, we like to make polarities, they are interesting for our brains to look at).

Thankful for these letters, dearest, I am hanging onto my sanity by a vise-like pinky finger. Also, it is suddenly cold.

Love,
C

SEPTEMBER 27, 2020 | *WE'RE STILL SWIMMING*

Oh you! I want to reply to every word of this and I will say at the outset that I will fail to do that, but you should know that I read every word multiple times. I don't think I'd ever heard this much about your Pa before.

What was it like for you and Micah to be with your parents in the before-times? I don't mean to challenge anything you say here, but I don't recall it being all hard surfaces. I wonder if there is more give there than you know. (All the same, in Natalie Diaz's words, 'Trust your anger. It is a demand for love.')

Parents, partners, progeny. That's all it is now, feels like. My father is gone; my mother is still here. I love her being here, but I am not as kind to her as I could be, and I try to be warmer, yet there is something in me that mounts a defense with her, in advance. I guess it's all the years of knowing that she wants much from me and wants even more *for* me, and I can't help but experience that latter wanting as a kind of violence.

Related to this is the feeling that I have expressed to Brandon lately, a feeling of us being very much alone together, not only apart from but in some ways *against* his parents and mine, his brothers and mine, the cousins and uncles and aunts and everyone else who frankly *does not get it.*

We are the only people in the extended family with two young children. We have jobs that half don't understand and the others don't think of as jobs in the first place. We don't want to be where we are, and yet we don't know where we want to go. We are not applying for new jobs and yet we don't want the ones we have. We are playing the long game, and everyone else is asking about Thanksgiving.

On the subject of new jobs: this week I realized there are Asian Americanist positions advertised at Duke and Emory and I thought for a very long minute about applying. Ultimately I decided not to. I have so little time that I think I'd better just stick to the plan I have (my how-to-get-tenure-on-two-hours-of-work-a-day plan) and not get distracted by these shiny things.

This is me giving up on the future, giving up on the fantasy escapes that have sustained me during many dark periods these last few months. No, I will not apply for and so will not get those jobs. Yes, we are stuck here. Yes, we might die here. So, what of it?

This new line of rhetorical self-flagellation appeals to me. And I am emboldened to continue working on enhancing the house (the swings!) even as it is also falling apart (this week: a burst water line and suddenly no water, a broken dishwasher, a broken pool pump, algae in the pool, sprinklers malfunctioning—my Eagle Scout husband, bless him, he deals with all that shit).

I thought at one point that we could get the hell out of here before everything comes crashing down but it's already too late, isn't it? Yes, I'm talking about the house, the university, Arizona, *and* this sorry excuse for a country. It's what the poet Arundhathi Subramaniam calls 'Zoomsday', baby: 'A world / full of windows / but no sign / of a door.'

This was the week Ruth Bader Ginsburg died, Amy Coney Barrett arrived, more on the damn Trump taxes. I read too much about all of it on Twitter, and you're right to stay away, but there are some occasional gems, like this poem 'No' by Vsevolod Nekrasov, which was doing the rounds.

no no

no and no

no and no and no and no
and no and no and no and no
and no
and I   no

You didn't play defense.
Here's to you continuing to channel Kate Manne's mantra.
Don't play defense. By which I also mean: know your worth.
License yourself. Or, in the words of Mindy Kaling, *Why Not
Me?* I haven't read that book, but I can't forget the title. I never
ask that question, in that way. Why not me?

My brother and his long-distance girlfriend. Now there's a
topic I haven't done justice to. Since mid-May they have been
talking for many hours each week. About three months in, he
hit a wall (*do I want this? What am I doing? Is this an arranged
marriage?*). I'm sure she asked herself the same questions. But
they pushed through it, and now they are very much together.

They are telling people they 'met' online, but that's not
exactly true. My mother set up an online matrimonial profile
for my brother, which she deleted as soon as he found out
(he was furious!), but not before receiving a message from a
pretty dentist in South Africa. My mum then saw on Facebook
that we have some family friends in common.... She called the
mutual friend for an introduction to the girl's mother, whose
name is the same as my mother's! The mutual friend's sister's
granddaughter is married to the brother of my brother's new
girlfriend.

So it's fate! This is what we Indians call a 'very very close
relation'. Seriously.

So anyway, the girlfriend, who I already know my brother
will marry, is likely to come visit him in December for Christmas,
his birthday, and New Year's. And then, he will go to see her

in South Africa in February for *her* birthday. As far as Covid is concerned, they both see this as essential travel, and I support that. Independent adults, they should know the risks and do their best to mitigate them and hope, ultimately, that they get lucky. I talked to her on WhatsApp video today and found her warm, friendly, big smile, calm, not over-familiar, not pushy, not nosy, but open, relaxed, sweet, and certainly attached to my brother. So, full marks in my book.

Also: what you describe here about the kids playing with their friend is like a scene from another world. We've had grandparents, but we haven't had friends. Friends: what are those, something from the before-times? I wish we had neighbors with children who were friends. I wish my children had nearby cousins. I wish we lived anywhere else, but also this is where we are and where we are going to be, forever maybe, forever and ever until the end. What then?

The pool is cold now, but we're still swimming. I don't know what we'll do without it.

All the love,
R

OCTOBER 2, 2020 | *HOW TO BE A GOOD HUMAN IN A CIVIL WAR?*

Dearest!

Today it is announced that Trump and Melania tested positive. There is widespread disbelief, and widespread cynicism that it will do anything other than increase enthusiasm for Trump. And a murmur: is this the tipping point? Real or fake, recovery or death or something in between, the news is oil to a nation already literally on fire. Two nights ago, in the first debate-spectacle, Trump called on the Proud Boys militia (terrorist group?) to be on 'standby'. I believe all of us may be on standby, now. I believe, as I've said before, we are headed for civil war.

Directly before the presidential debate that may have been the occasion of Trump's infection, I recorded a Zoom conversation with a group of first-years about the *Aeneid* and selfhood for a course required of the entire class. The event was horrible. In the first minutes, I broke out in anxiety sweats, and then stumbled through the hour, hating myself. I had myself on hide-self view, since this is said to be less distracting and exhausting. I briefly turned it on to see if that would help me stabilize. It did not. I turned my eyes to a list of affirmations I keep above my desk to see if that would help. It kept my nerves just barely in check.

I am aware that my physiological response and emotional interpretation of it afterwards are well out of proportion with the reality, which, though I'm sure it wasn't my best performance, was probably passable, or redeemable. That didn't stop me from feeling horrible for twenty-four hours. Now I realize it doesn't matter, anyway.

I mean, *really* doesn't matter. 'Giving up on the fantasy escapes' x1000. I'm not getting a job in academia! There are no jobs—it's about to be civil war. How do I be a good human in a civil war? Fuck that, what does one do just to survive?

Probably I'm exaggerating, just as I exaggerated the suckiness of my performance. Definitely, our 'what is we' conversation is going to be timely.

And I am glad your brother is finding a 'we' to have and to hold in the times to come. It's a sweet, modern story that, as always, builds in its own ambiguity. The three month wall is only the first of many, as it sounds like he is now ready to find out.

But you, you have your ever loyal Eagle Scout. Micah's a help about such things as well, though I chastise him for not keeping track of his tools. In this house, too, there are signs of decay. A floor lamp with no torchere (I learned the word to google a replacement, but never did get around to ordering one) because it broke during a vigorous pillow fight, the closet door that busted in a vigorous game of hide and seek, the leaky refrigerator, the clogged toilet, the leaky shower, the clogged gutters.

I try to hear you about your mother, the micro-violence of her desire to shape and stretch you. To hear you, I have to reach past the jealousy I feel for what I perceive as the warmth and openness between you and her. When I reach past, I glimpse how the love and the violence lie together, and for a moment, I am wise and know how to love my own children, indeed my own self, with soft spaciousness. Then I forget and am my bitter, rough, and selfish self again.

It was a long week of long days in a long year.

On this drizzly morning, I took the kids in the wagon to the small nearby zoo (peacocks, llamas, rabbits, snakes, iguana, a cow, that sort of thing). There was no one else there except for another white-looking woman with a brown daughter probably a little younger than Areté. Through his mask, Zia tried to tell her about Wild Kratts, a show on *PBS* he likes, and through hers Areté said 'Turtles! Turtles over there!' and pointed. At different intervals—near the turtles, by the ducks and chickens—the other mother and I exchanged mask-muffled chitchat, and sensed through small words and small gestures and small arrangements of our bodies, strollers, and wagons that we were probably of similar carefulness. Her eyes seemed to smile under a mop of Miranda-July curls and a blue woolen hat. I was in a huge random red poncho and I had not even checked my hair before leaving the house.

What I am trying to say is, I am starving for human contact and when I receive even a small dose of affinity, like an encounter with an interracial family in the rain, I am longing to spill over into talk, I am sure this is the finest person who has ever existed and I want to know everything about her and her life in Woodstock, where they 'never leave the property', and I want to shower her child with compliments, and yet I am halting, checked, nibbling rather than taking great gulps, and I feel a touch of sadness when Zia is the one who says, 'Mom, do you want to go home?'

Starving for human contact. It's a real thing. And I will keep on starving myself until I no longer can. I accept that part of myself, accept the renunciation of the old world (the before-times) as the price of a plate in the new world.

I have noticed a mild…distaste for food in myself, as well. It alternates with periods of overeating, so that my weight stays within the usual range. I am not worried, it seems like a normal response to the enormous stress. But sometimes, lately, I just can't quite get much down.

no and no and no and no

At first it seems like a nothing poem. But how many times, how many ways, are there to say no, have we said no, over the last year? The no of anger, the no of disbelief, the no of angry disbelief, the no of despair, no to grief that comes anyway, no to the child who wants something you can't give, no to nonsense, no to an invitation, no to an old dream of the future. Until the *and I no*, until all the self is nothing but no.

I have to go, darling. I have to fill out a W-4 and I hear a mischievous laugh behind me.

Love for all and everything,
C

OCTOBER 10, 2020 | *SLIPPERY SLOPE*

C, how many lifetimes ago was October 2?

I slept well and deeply for a few nights after Trump's diagnosis, thinking that maybe he would finally go away. No such luck.

Today and yesterday and inevitably tomorrow, the news is full of Trump's return and the expected East Coast surge. Here, we are tentatively optimistic that the cooler weather (ha! It's still 37/38°C during the day) and more outdoor gatherings will mean that we avoid the worst of the winter wave that is coming for us all.

But it's been a low week. I am tired. I finished drafting an essay that I started writing eleven years ago in my first semester at Berkeley, when I thought maybe I'd defect from literature for anthropology. The essay is about ethnographic methods in a Kerala gurukul, or arts academy. It was hard to get back into it after all these years, and it's one of those papers that ends where it begins, which means, it's about circularity and repetition, and excavating what Christina Sharpe calls the 'ditto ditto in the archives'. So this paper has become an occasion to say again something that has been said before, because, why not? Why not me, in my words?

I like parts of this paper, and I am pleased with myself for (re)writing it, but I am ten days behind when I wanted it to be done, which means I am ten days behind on the next paper I told myself I would write, and I have no juice to begin again.

Add to that the stress of my brother's arrival. He has been mature on the phone—so excited about his girlfriend and the promise of a new partnership—but from the minute he arrived, he has been fighting with my mother, and she is tearful and bitter and they both keep shouting that they bring out the worst in each other, and I am reminded why I don't like to go home to California, and then I feel badly for feeling that way, and I ignore my brother, who is irritating me, and then I remember he is only here for two days, and I try to lift them all up with pleasant conversation and making new cocktails—Palomas, to go with Mexican take-out—and I am spent.

On top of which my father's mother, my Patti who lives alone in Chennai and is immobile and relies on a retinue of part-time servants, had a bad fall. She couldn't get up; they had to break down the door to her second-story flat, and take her to the hospital. No broken bones, but she was in the Covid ward...she doesn't have Covid, at least not at admission...but damn, she can't go on living alone. My father is very depressed. He knows he should go. He also knows that he shouldn't go. It is only a matter of time.

I send Patti pictures of the kids on WhatsApp daily, but I hardly ever call her. The time difference of twelve-plus hours makes it feel impossible. I am too selfish to give up my mornings, and too tired to call before bed. I feel badly about it, but also resigned.

Please forgive the ugly feelings and unburdening in this letter, C. Thank you for bearing the burdens with me. I want to reach you where you are, where you were, you in your red poncho. I know there are decisions in the offing. We are also in a transitional moment. Brandon's parents return from Maine next weekend, but they are driving through half a dozen states and seeing a dozen people along the way. Should we see them when they reach? It's my mother-in-law's birthday next Sunday, same day as precious Areté.

I know what you mean about appetites and starving for contact. I feel a constant low-grade grief but also a desire to retreat even further. How can this be? I know others feel it, too. My mother, for one, is hurting, and she has suddenly become very emotional. My father is remote. Her survival is friends and travel and outings and the vibrant public life. The pandemic has not been kind to this end. And yet, she is writing and reading more than ever. Indeed, she has written a few new children's books in the past few months, and she wrote a book review that ran in a major Indian outlet, and she's just written a personal essay, too, at the invitation of a well-known editor. I worked with her on revising this essay. It brought her to tears, harnessing the power of the 'I'.

Earlier this week, I organized an outdoor playdate for Mrinalini with a colleague's daughter. The two girls went swinging together on the new swingset. All masked, all outdoors. Mrinalini was beyond thrilled. They had such fun. Of course, after a little while, they started dropping their masks. They wanted to blow bubbles. They went inside the house 'to get things'. This is the slippery slope. Verdict: it was worth it.

I am in talks with a preschool, too, for Shai, at a colleague's recommendation. Five children, outdoor classrooms, 8.30 a.m.–12 p.m. only, no lunch, no naps. It's not open currently. They are waiting to meet certain metrics. To send him or not to send him?

We are losing the pool, which is chilly now. I don't want to have to give up this last part of my routine, this huge component of my daily survival. Today, we sent the kids up to be with my mother and brother for a few hours, and now we must go and meet them. I did a little work and swam and read, but also I just sat and was listless. When you only have a few hours break every few weeks, it is almost impossible not to crash hard. In this, I worry a little for you and Micah. I don't want you to crash out when this is all over. You haven't even had these few hours, cruel though they often are.

You must protect yourself, love, at any cost.

All the love,
R

OCTOBER 17, 2020 | *A MADHOUSE INSIDE THIS SKULL*

Dear one,

I love your letters. The letters have become part of how I love you. The letters have become…a portal, like Arundhati Roy said of the pandemic at the very beginning. They have become a portal to your climate, geographical and emotional, and a portal away from my own small world, and a portal for ushering me, and you too I hope, both into our future selves, able to face them with more courage because the letters allow us to allow older versions to tag along.

A portal to your climate: I remember you telling me, when I visited for Shai's naming ceremony, how surprised you always were at how green Arizona is. Maybe I am making this up, but I remember you saying, it's the shock of it, the excessive aliveness of the green surviving in this fucking barren desert. Maybe we were at the botanical garden when you said this, or maybe we had just exited the glass doors of that poetry library (how I liked that place), from the cool absence of temperature into a band of air so hot it is material. Maybe I remember you saying this, or maybe I'm making it up, because I remember having the same impression of Virginia when I arrived there after living in Cairo: the surprise that such greenery could exist.

The greenery there, staying green as the forest leaves light up here. The greenery there means that, though you will lose the pool, you will gain something else (the ability to be outside?). The greenery there means that you will keep alive in this season as Covid's winter's wildfire begins to spark here. The greenery there, here, everywhere, making the air that we breathe. It speaks itself. Rumi listens:

Everyone talks about
greenery, not with words but quietly

as green itself talks from inside,
as we begin to live our love.

As green talks from inside. As we live our love. What is that, again? I think it has something to do with this aching book I carry, that I am afraid to love, afraid to believe in, afraid to put out there to be seen.

Whatever it means, I do not think I have been living my love nearly so often as I have been living my fear and my anger.

A portal from my own small world: where I walked among the fall foliage with a sort of a colleague-friend (when does one reach full friend status? Is it with the exchange of objects? Am I so much slower, warier than others of reaching that stage?). I met her at her on-campus house, both masked. We passed a few students along the campus path, also masked, and found our way round to the long woods trail. There she said, 'I'll take this off now, if you don't mind,' and undid whatever gauzy white thing she was using as a mask. I did mind, actually—I later realized, it is actually the law, to wear masks if you can't social distance—but I trusted in my own N-95 and pretended like I didn't. I was annoyed at myself for this, later.

And this is part of why I concluded, after, that the walk wasn't really worth it. Perhaps I 'built the relationship', but she certainly didn't offer me any kind of material help and indeed when I mentioned that my fellowship is up at the end of this year she became extremely awkward and quickly changed the subject. I left feeling that she'd simply been lonely, just as I have been. We talked of nothing much, but for a long time, so long that Micah, who never really relaxed about the idea of it, became anxious and called.

Unlike Mrinalini's playdate, then, it wasn't worth it. Yet, I find myself wondering if I will do it again.

And I suspect I will, unless I can find other avenues for fellow-feeling. I need something, other things, to love right now. How can that be, how am I not exhausted from all the love work I am doing? Yes, I am, every day, but also the opposite, exhausted from lack of love. I am engaged in the work of loving so few people, with so much force—as if by so doing I can keep them alive—that some of the inner greenery has died off.

Sometimes I find myself craving praise, I am craven for positive reflections of myself, for confirmations of other selves, other worlds that affirm the reality of my own. I feel I would debase myself for a kind smile from a stranger or some mild hallway warmth and flattery of the sort that used to cause me such anxiety, and pride.

You can see why I need a portal away from myself! It's a madhouse inside this skull! In particular I wish I could silence that nasty voice that waylays me in the night and scrapes my self-esteem to pieces. High-strung, that one, and so persistent once she gets going.

If these letters are a portal to future selves (selves understood as entangled organisms, fully but not-fully-consciously engaged in processes of connecting and differentiating, replicating and excising various of their sub-structures)—then let me leave that harpy here at this juncture. I don't need her for what lies ahead. Is there some riddle I can solve that will let me pass her by forever? 'What tells lies that look like truth just to stop you on your path?' You do, you self-critical beast.

I'm beginning to brace myself for the winter. We've assembled the swings and jungle gym and toys, we have our stock of masks and food. We have riches and riches upon riches of memories to draw on. Perhaps that is our most important, most invisible reservoir of privilege. I have made a list of ten-minute gloom busters and renewed my weekly exercise date with my sister, with cousins to perhaps join in. I will find (keep finding) something to love or learn about or simply divert myself with.

That's all for now, darling. Had to call the plumber on a Saturday to clear the mainline, which forced us out of the house for awhile, and it's cozy being back in. A sunny day, and tomorrow Areté's birthday. Oh! Thank you for the books, darling! So wise and funny and special! Areté immediately put the emoji stickers all throughout *The Missing Piece* which I thought was the completely perfect thing to do.

It might seem like I haven't responded directly to what you say in your letter, but everything is in direct response to you. Sending you air, water and light for everything that needs to grow.

Love,
C

OCTOBER 23, 2020 | *BACK TO SCHOOL*

C, dear C, the one on the other end of the line.

The feeling I have is of belatedness, because I have kept something from you this week, and every day I thought of telling you and then held back, and so this revelation-confession now feels overdue, even if it is right on time....

(I'm having a bit of fun here—building up a dramatic reveal—but also wondering if in the course of the pandemic, the trajectory of which we cannot foresee, this will mark a shift, a break, or a rupture in our shared timeline?)

We sent Shai to school. We really did. I told you that we were thinking about it and that we wouldn't do it, but when they announced that they were opening this week, and we looked at the local situation, and reviewed their procedures, and our own impossible lives, we decided to give it a go. We sent him to a little school that is no bigger than most people's 'bubbles'—one teacher, five two-year-olds, very large classroom spaces that are primarily outdoors—from 8.30–12. He comes home for lunch and his nap.

Today is his fourth day. He loves it. He is even using the little toilets there successfully (no accidents so far!); he wears a mask indoors; he has some friends, the only one whose name he will tell me is 'Jack'. The teacher, a pregnant woman whom I am quite confident does not wish to get Covid, texts us updates through a well-organized app.

Mrinalini has dealt with this cheerily, though she's the one who needs in-person school and friends. She seems to realize that it is out of reach for her. Her class went back in person this week as well, but with hundreds of children in a small building, there is no way we will send her, and so she soldiers on with miserable virtual school. She is happy for Shai, whose world has suddenly expanded.

It's both a major risk, and—I'm trying to figure out the words to explain it—doesn't feel that risky. I could tell you about my conversations with the school director and the teachers, but it's sort of beside the point. It's the safest school situation of any I have heard about. We are watching the local numbers carefully and are prepared to pull the plug.

In terms of childcare, well, I'm not sure how much it *helps* us. We still have virtual second grade going on here, and it's only three hours a day. But I will admit—and this is becoming clearer to me as I write to you—that we are also sending him as part of an effort to decrease dependency on my in-laws (in the short and long term), who have been back for a week and seemed exhausted by the kids on day one. Which, well, I both understand and don't appreciate at all!

I feel sort of wild and reckless and guilty and ambivalent about telling you, not because you will censure or judge (you are entitled to do both) but because, oh, I don't know. Maybe you will read in this confirmation that you and Micah are made of stronger stuff than the rest of us. Maybe you will feel a bit of what I feel every time I hear that someone I know has gotten a nanny or sent their kids back to school: incredulity, disbelief, some self-doubt, envy, some other ugly feelings.

We are still committed to survival. But its shape keeps changing.

It was an up-and-down sort of week otherwise. Mrinalini is doing much better after that stomach pain 'relapse' she had in the wake of my parents' visit (and no more talk of brain tumors or other random paranoias, thankfully!). I am making some slow progress on a couple pieces of writing. I read Natasha Trethewey's memoir *Memorial Drive* in one sitting yesterday— it's about her mother's murder by her abusive husband—and it was affecting and dark and sad. I gave you her poems, yes? She was my professor for a semester at Duke, and I so admire her.

I resumed swimming, even in the chilly pool. I am not ready to give it up.

I have lost interest in cooking and am trying to get back to the place where I can prepare meals with some enthusiasm. That place feels out of reach.

We are no longer sure how to entertain our children.

And something else new and risky is in the offing. My brother's long-distance girlfriend has booked a flight from Johannesburg to San Francisco. We have tentatively agreed to meet them all for a few days at the end of the year, in Southern California, about halfway between Tucson and the Bay Area.

And yes, all of this with record cases today, the highest ever in the pandemic, and every prospect that cases will only continue to skyrocket from here.

Clips from the dreadful presidential debate are circulating online. Eleven days to go until the election. Will it mean anything? 'Living with the virus' versus 'dying with the virus'. I believe that's the note they ended on.

I don't want to die of the virus. But I do want to have a life to live for.

All the love,
R

OCTOBER 29, 2020 | *HORROR SHOW*

Hi dearest,

Your buildup had me hurrying over your words and then reading the 'confession' with relief. I feared worse, I don't know what, the shadow of my own secrets, I suppose, the incognito tabs where I google the questions I don't speak out loud.

I'm glad for you, dearest, to have found such a safe situation for Shai, and that the new calculation of risk and reward is paying off for you. I love you and that's just another way of saying I understand. The pandemic is, I hope, softening me towards other human beings rather than thinking I am made of 'stronger stuff'. The main consolation of the path we've chosen is that, by deviating very little from it, we save ourselves the worrisome, repetitious work of the calculation you have just brought off. Kudos to you.

The weakness of my self includes an inadequate ability to work at the level to which I am being summoned in the Princeton class. I keep failing, collapsing, trying again. It might be an embarrassment, at least I frequently feel embarrassed. But it might be exactly that embarrassment that is teaching me something, teaching me how to exceed myself, how to soothe and escape myself, this particularly feminine brand of shame. I don't know.

I'm sorry this is so short, but I had little time and wanted to respond a little to the big news. The main development here is that Zia is reading. 'I see Sam, see me Sam,' that kind of thing, but I can see it happening and he does, too, and it is a moment full of feelings for me.

It's Thursday-feels-like-Friday, and time to go have dinner with the family. It might snow tomorrow, 'Halloween eve'. Zia is excited. We have a new horror show we like (*Lovecraft Country*), which pleasurably reprises the horrors of race relations in this country, and we repeat to each other the studies that suggest that watching horror might help people get through times like this. We cannot believe the election is on Tuesday (we both voted by mail).

I kind of can't imagine what happens after that.

So much love, darling.

C

NOVEMBER 6, 2020 | *ON SUNDAY SHE DIED AGAIN*

Hi dear C,

I am trying to think, but my head is full of the grating sounds of Mrinalini's virtual school. They are having an election for class mascot, which would have been fun in an actual classroom, where you put your head down on the desk and raise your hand, and they put the tally marks up on the board. Somehow instead it's just been an excruciating exercise, and Mrinalini didn't want to wear her headphones, and so we've all been listening to it. I'm a little too tired to put up a fight (headphones, dammit!) and so I've been sitting here staring blankly at the *NYT* front page, scrolling back and forth between *WaPo* and Twitter waiting for them to call the presidential election, while Mrinalini's second-grade class decides between penguin and panda and griffin and butterfly and whatever else, skydiving cats.

It is not even 3 p.m. and it's been many days today. Not just Friday but the fourth day of Tuesday, as they say. This morning before 7 a.m. I had already talked to my parents about their entire day in India: cremating my Patti and immersing her ashes, having lunch at her home, seeing various relatives, steeling themselves for many days of ceremonies ahead. My other grandmother, in Delhi, had yet another Covid scare and illness—coughing, wheezing, low oxygen levels—and though she seemed better by the end of the day (which, again, was early this morning), tomorrow they are going to do some tests. The doctor makes home visits, which is another mercy.

This is the thing about the time difference with India, which is a full day ahead (12.5 or 13.5 hours from Pacific time, depending on the time of year). You always have an experience of the future. Like how I talked to my grandmother on Friday night and she was dead on Saturday evening, which was Sunday morning, so when I woke up on Saturday she was already dead which meant I had lost an entire day, and when I woke up on Sunday she died again.

I have shed tears many mornings this week—of grief, of exhaustion. I've been rereading and writing about many years worth of emails from my Patti, roughly 2007–2015, which includes the years you and I were in graduate school. The years (roughly) before the kids. I've had a very keen and curious sense of encountering history through our exchange. Sure, it was just yesterday. But also: another world entirely.

Reliving that time has somehow also meant reliving all the stresses of the Trump years that followed. The Muslim bans. Brett Kavanaugh. Family separation. The Paris Accords. Covid. All his terrible shit. Covfefe. Being in Tucson and not wanting to be here in the Trump years. Narendra Modi being reelected during the Trump years. Mrinalini being sick during the Trump years. Losing both of Brandon's grandparents and my grandmother during the Trump years.

Who were we, before the Trump years? I have a new friend here in Tucson; we met on Zoom in a horrible faculty meeting. She's Navajo and appointed in Women's Studies, which she hates; we have a running joke that we should co-teach a class on 'Critical Indian Studies', though she says she 'crushes identity like a jelly bean'. She told me in an email today (or yesterday?) about how the person we are in the morning has to be translated for the person we become by evening. Yes.

It is a gray day here that is oddly also 33°C, a day when they just won't call the damn election. All of a sudden they've gotten very careful about the call; they would have been much more aggressive four years ago, or even two days ago. I've invited my in-laws over for dinner to celebrate what I hope will be Joe Biden's victory over Trump. But that means I have to cook dinner.

And then there's Covid. 120,000+ cases yesterday, and climbing, and the whole world seems to have given up on it entirely. Brandon and I have both taken advantage of the university's Covid-testing in the last couple weeks. They have made antigen and PCR tests available to the campus community, so he did an antigen test earlier this week and I did one today, just for kicks. I don't think we have Covid (the antigen tests didn't think so) but I don't like having this cold either. After the last however-many-weeks of tentatively trying to open up the world here—with the zoo, the desert museum, the playdates for Mrinalini, a little school for Shai—I know we're going to have to close it down soon, and I'm so sick of it all.

WWCD (What would C do?). Focus on the positives: Mrinalini's health is on the up for sure; Shai is demanding as all hell but cute as all hell, too. You: fellow traveler and path-lighter.

How are you, and yours? Splashing in puddles, I hope, and finding worms, and enjoying the jacket-free days, and getting ready to enjoy the jacketed-ones too, with a fire at home maybe, and hot chocolate, and movie nights. We have discovered the joy of real popcorn. A travesty to say that, maybe. I grew up with microwaveable bags of popcorn, and also pancakes out of a box. So the other day when I put the kernels in the pot and popped them: it was a revelation.

Be safe, my friend, be well, be you.

Big, big love,
R

NOVEMBER 14, 2020 | *REWARMED CHINESE*

Dear R,

Well, here we are. We: a simple word that I will now always associate with you, the pronoun's necessity and its impossibility and somewhere in between there, its many actualities.

Where is here? Here is 180,000 new cases today, and everyone as tired of it as we are. A vague promise of a vaccine ('hopium', Micah calls it), a promise of a new technocratic president. I worry both about a left-techno-authoritarianism that I would be tempted to welcome *and* about the more negative possibilities suggested by Trump's refusal to concede. Covfefe, indeed. The man has permanently altered our sense of the malleability of reality. He tells us what he's going to do (not concede, claim vote fraud, rig the courts), and yet still no one is sure exactly what is going to happen or how serious it might be. The firings of top ranking military and other officials is bad; the statement by a bunch of top business people that he has lost is good. For sure the US is in a precarious moment and an external attack right now would be devastating. Since 2020 is schooling us in worst case scenarios, and all.

But for me, there's the relief of knowing I have another year at Bard to figure shit out.

Re: Covid, though, I've been wondering if I could or should write you something that would encourage you to be vigilant, if you want that or fear it, if it would feel like judgment. If you imagine it happening silently already. If it would just be exhaustion on top of exhaustion. You probably already know women are at greater risk for Long Covid, which is disastrous in any line of work but would be especially painful to our intellectual pride. You probably already know that the new Danish mink strain of Covid is bad news for a vaccine. You probably already know any number of scary facts and statistics, but, like me, you don't know how much longer you can keep doing this, don't know how to just keep staying home, don't know if you are being overly cautious or a wimp if you do stay home ('We all die anyway,' as Bolsonaro said...).

I keep coming back to this one article on risk taking in the pandemic. The article basically underscores what we already know, which is that we are deeply affected by what we see other people around us doing. But there's this one image/fact in particular that I remember, which is that most people, sitting in their car in front of a train track with a train coming down it, will misjudge their ability to cross the tracks in time. To stay safe, they need either to a) go against their intuition, b) have been warned in a really memorable way by someone, or c) have a physical barrier in front of them.

Which seems like an apt metaphor, because the government has provided no barrier, and because the speed of this virus is so hard to grasp.

Today we let Zia watch as much TV as he wants, which is a lot, and did a ton of cleaning. I do not feel bad about it one bit, though I know we'll pay the price later. I'm looking at a big pile of cardboard, books to put into the little free library at the park, a huge bag of trash, and nibbling on a plate of Chinese delivery. The air feels a little fresher.

Are you reading anything good? I was reading Claudia Rankine's *Just Us* (why didn't I bring *that* up during our 'What is we?' event?) but it got to feeling...like a trap. She's so precise and subtle, showing this country's racism so deeply felt, and the unwillingness to confront it so deeply protected, that she tempts despair. I need the opposite of despair right now. But you would like, I think, her quotation of poet Erica Hunt, who defines love as 'a close reading' that 'help[s] me invent myself more—in the future.'

Wanted to write you something deep and smart and fresh but this is all I've got. Trash in bags and rewarmed Chinese.

Love you darling. This is hard but would be immeasurably harder without you. Sending so much love.

xoxo

C

NOVEMBER 21, 2020 | *INDIAN SUMMER*

Hi dear C,

It's a beautiful Saturday here. Global warming gave us the gift of a mid-November return to summer. Apocalyptic though it is, I took it. I swam twice at my in-laws place this week (they have solar panels and a pool heater). It helped with the seasonal affective disorder that I've been experiencing as the weather keeps threatening to change. I feel both grateful for this 'Indian summer' right before Thanksgiving and mounting dread about the inevitable arrival of the real winter.

I've also been sleeping more. I have stopped trying to wake up early to get in extra 'work' and I have failed to get involved in any book and have picked up and abandoned different ones each evening for the last many days. I am spending a lot of time *not* reading, in other words. Twenty pages in, it always seems like a better use of my time to just go to sleep.

Some sort of hibernation instinct? I feel the need to store up and gear up and protect myself from something that is coming. I've also started running again and that makes me physically tired. I am also spiritually tired from the year. And I am even more specifically tired from the year that started a year ago, in late September, when Mrinalini got sick.

So that's the other thing I'm focused on now: getting through 'the holidays' with my in-laws, which will be low-key, but also a major milestone for us, given how horrible last year's holidays were. Last year, the night before Thanksgiving, Mrinalini woke up at 3 a.m. pacing and dry heaving, panicking and telling me that she wouldn't be able to get through the day because she wouldn't be able to eat any of the holiday meal. I remember speaking to you by phone that morning from a Whole Foods in Campbell, where I was buying ingredients for Brandon's chocolate cherry pie (which, on the sugar free, gluten free, lactose free diet that manages her symptoms, she can no longer eat).

Over Christmas, she didn't eat a single meal with the family. Over New Year's, we went on a multigenerational trip to Cancun—my grandmother had come all the way from Kochi—and I spent the entire time researching Pediatric

Autoimmune Neuropsychiatric Syndrome and Celiac disease and tracking down antibiotics. Mrinalini subsisted on liquid nutrition supplements in the hotel bedroom while literally hiding from everyone in the family, depressed and anxious, reading the children's Ramayana and wasting away.

We have almost made it through one calendar year with no puking from Mrinalini. She is slowly gaining weight; the intense antibiotics earlier this year seem to have kept the bacterial overgrowth in check, and we've learned to cope with the rest. The trauma of last fall was far worse for us than the pandemic has been, and we are nearly through another fall, and I just want to focus on getting there.

So, this week was better than the last. Maybe because the Covid numbers are now so ridiculously high that we're feeling good, relieved, and strong about having gone back into the more locked down version of our lockdown: no school, no playdates.

In other words, this week we got to enjoy the feeling of having made the right decisions. It felt like we were returning to March, and in retrospect March was a joyous time, the time of discovering what we could do and be together.

Now, I want to soak up every last moment of the sun before the winter. I want to exercise and sleep and eat good food (I have regained some interest in cooking) and make cocktails and do puzzles with Mrinalini and laugh with Shai, eating raw onions and sucking limes. I want to get off Twitter, where I never see anything except things that shake my resolve to trust myself.

You were right of course. I'm glad we tried Shai's school, and I don't think we ever stopped being vigilant as such. But we have returned in the last couple weeks to a place of greater surety that we don't want or need to get Covid, and that we don't need to open up any more, and if that's what you meant by saying *be vigilant* then yes, and I was glad to read it from you, grateful for your nod, your taking of the hand, your vote of confidence, your reminder that we've got this.

Thank you love—always.

And all the questions, about you and yours.

R

FIRST WINTER: THE DARK

Hi, R.

Outside, the 18 inches of snow is still reflecting some slanting daylight. The snow is a good distraction. I have never enjoyed it as much as this year—I even welcome the shovel-sore-muscles. Something new to do with the kids, something beautiful and physically difficult and tangible. The fading sun reminds me that, though Christmas is in a week, Solstice is Monday. The shortest day, the day after which the light returns: ever since we moved to Oregon at that time, Solstice has been the more personally important holiday for me. And I missed whatever you did for Diwali this year, if you did anything, but you've been celebrating Hanukkah: this letter may be a kind of gift for the last day of that other festival of lights.

Christmas: I've been numbing my feelings buying lots of presents for the kids. Usually we feel pinched around this time, and falling short, and stressed about travel, but since we're not paying for childcare or airfare we had a Christmas budget that would've been unimaginable in previous years. So, the dubious turn to internet consumerism. Unsure how to teach the higher things about giving, and gratitude, and miracles, this year. But we have our daily routine and our yearly rituals and we are getting by; the kids feel loved, are learning to love one another—for now, that is enough.

Outside: my family members who are doctors have gotten or will soon get the vaccine. I read with disgust and zero surprise about the black market cropping up. Micah is distrustful about the vaccine itself, sending me articles about little-reported side effects (Bell's Palsy, which I had long ago and still feel the effects of, is one). Time will tell whether or how much too-good-to-be-true slants the vaccine storyline. But even now I sorrow over all the preventable deaths that the vaccine is too late to prevent (southern California at zero ICU capacity, nearly everywhere plunging towards the same nadir). The abominable concept of 'herd immunity' traces directly back to Plato's political (autocratic) metaphor of the people as animals and the leaders as shepherds.

But where do I want to be, how do I want to have grown, whenever this does end? I made a decision to apply for an opening in Bard Philosophy which I now feel bad about. I suspect they want to hire a person of color, and whatever tangible ways I have diversified my syllabi and would create space for difference (I dream about creating a forum to connect interracial families), however much I aspire to be a traitor to the white race (a far better concept than black-brown allyship, I think), I am myself not black or brown. (I am against the current fashion for capitalizing racial terms—I don't want to make Proper Nouns or Nations out of them.)

So it is probably a wasted effort, and an exhausting and humiliating one, and possibly slightly unethical, that I no longer feel I can back down from. That I always feel this way about academic job applications is not really a comfort, for I should know better, one way or another, by now. Whose approval am I trying to win when I try to win this prize?

So, I'm fine. Lonely, exhausted, sad, afraid of Covid and afraid of going off the rails, occasionally hopeful, loving towards the kids, fine. This afternoon (unable to work) I read a YA book I must've read twenty times as a kid, *In Lane Three: Alex Archer*, about a New Zealand Olympic hopeful swimmer. I cried in all the places I remember crying before. It was therapeutic.

Maybe I should leave all the scholarly pretense and intellectual confabulation behind, and just try to write like that?

What if?

Time to rejoin the family. Tell me how things are and seem to you. Take me out of my head for a bit. Remind me why it's worth it.

Love,

C

DECEMBER 21, 2020 | *THE NINTH MONTH OF MARCH*

Hi dear C,

I waited three days before reading your letter. I don't know what I was waiting for. It's a 26°C Arizona Winter Solstice day, and I am at my winter table, on my winter porch, on the other side of the backyard from where I spent my summer mornings, on a sectional in the shade.

What has changed, besides the weather? We are still here, aren't we, in the year of the never-ending spring break. Here in the year in which every day is a working Saturday. Here in the year that is closing with the ninth month of March.

Since you wrote: the new coronavirus mutation has countries scrambling to lockdown anew (not the US of course; we are Americans, with our god given rights to kill and die). It's Europe against the UK, Hong Kong against the resident Hong Kongers, Saudi Arabia against the world. You warned about this, after the Danish minks.

The new strain is in South Africa, too, but this morning my brother's long-distance love got on a plane in Johannesburg heading for Doha. After fifteen hours of worry that she wouldn't make it out, her plane took off. In Doha she will get on a flight to San Francisco and come to meet my brother in the plague nation so that they can begin what they hope will be the relationship to define the rest of their lives. I doubt the airport officials will even take her temperature.

And after she arrives safely—inshallah—and after all the rest of it this week (and hopefully after they get Covid tested), we are supposed to drive right into the belly of the beast, to spend a few days with them and my parents in Orange County in Southern California. The pictures of our rented apartment promise a jumbo Connect 4 set and a jumbo Jenga and other 'child-friendly' amenities for families like ours in which the kids have no cousins, no friends, and no playmates. There is a large backyard and outdoor eating space, as far as I can tell.

Will it be enough that we have been this virtuous this long?

The children are so excited. They are beyond excited about Christmas, of course, but even more about this road trip. We are rationally highly stressed in the 'no room for error'/'no room for a car accident'/'no beds in the ICU' sort of way. But it's still on the calendar and in the works.

That said: daily we are hearing news of new Covid cases, big clusters and little ones, all over the world. My friend in Reno said his brother's whole family in the Bay Area has it. Brandon's sister-in-law's aunt and uncle and family in Chicago. Brandon's cousin and husband in Mississippi. Today: Brandon's uncle in Virginia and maybe the rest of his family, too. Yesterday: cases at a private school in Napa, where a woman I grew up with sends her kids. Tomorrow: we get test results for my uncle's— how to say—butler/head of house/all-around-most-important domestic staff, who returned to Delhi from a wedding in the village with a fever. A family of five down the street: we waved to and chatted with them from across the road, hours before I read about their positive Covid tests on her Twitter feed.

Maybe that's why I'm pretty much off Twitter (sweet relief).

Tell me about the things you've gathered for Zia and Areté to delight and carry them into 2021? Here, Mrinalini is on the verge of acknowledging the non-existence of Santa, though she is sweetly resisting what she knows. She wrote a two-item wish list this year: 'Professional dream-analysis materials.' 'Some surprises.'

My mother-in-law is spending her first Christmas maybe ever without her siblings and without attending a Christmas Eve service. We feel the weight of needing to protect and preserve her holiday. And so we have committed to a little extra festivity: to a sleepover at their house; to Santa coming down their chimney, not ours; to a brunch menu set in advance; and multiple family Zooms.

And so it goes.

It's like nothing has changed, since everything changed.

C, I do wonder how much we will miss 2020. That I will miss it, certain things about it, many things about it: of this, I am absolutely certain.

Love,
R

JANUARY 3, 2021 | *WINTER COCOON*

Dear R,

By now you are home from CA, or almost—such a familiar thing, the return home, made strange by the rarity of leaving, these days. I want to know every single thing of your thoughts and feelings about the trip, the girlfriend, the parents, the return, the world out there through the car window. And happy new year. 2021. Pandemic Year Two.

Here there is little, almost nothing, to report. Busy, yes, but 'busy is a decision'—who said that? I have been busying myself today by putting away Christmas. First the ornaments, then the lights, the embroidered tree skirt, slightly mildewed. Micah hauled off the tree itself, and dumped out the tree stand with its needle-strewn water, and vacuumed up the needles, while I gathered up the snow globes, the storybooks, the black

Santa collection my mother-in-law started for us. I restrung the lights in the windows, however, having come to depend on their colorful twinkling, and am leaving up the wreath on the front door awhile longer. Areté bawled as I did all these things, making me feel quite Grinch-like (or is it Grinchy). Zia came downstairs after it was fait accompli and has said nothing. Perhaps the difference is that he's old enough to know that Christmas will return.

I was busy with the Bard application, too—until I let myself do what I wanted and quit.

For many days it was like I had two selves: in the sunlight, I would urge myself on with cheerful, practical, optimistic you-never-knows. In the moonlight, I felt only that I wanted neither to work on the application nor to have the job, but that the whole endeavor was at best a leftover goblin ambition from a world I'm glad to leave behind, and at worst, a load of lies. I didn't say that to my recommenders, of course.

When I decided to apply, I had in mind a line from the Desiderata that I often think of, about always pursuing your career. When I reread it (we keep a copy framed in our downstairs bathroom), I saw that it actually says: 'Enjoy your achievements as well as your plans. Keep interested in your own career, however humble; it is a real possession in the changing fortunes of time.' And I decided that I *am* 'keeping interested' in my career, precisely, by spending my precious time on things that interest me. Another small victory for trusting myself. I think.

It is supposed to snow this afternoon, nothing yet.

Almost goes without saying that I am not making any resolutions this year, beyond survival—the virus will continue to dictate the ways in which I will change my life. But I have naturally used the break to be a bit more active than I had been. Likewise I don't have any special hopes that 2021 will be better, globally speaking, than 2020.

Quietly, the media are starting to admit that a more

contagious strain of the virus is actually more deadly (in terms of numbers dead) than a 'deadlier' strain. Very slowly, more information about the vaccine is starting to emerge; at least one expert predicts that it will put pressure on the virus to mutate to evade it.

More than one person has said, it feels like March 2020 again. The March that lasted for several months. The March where we had an opportunity to work together with energy and innovation for the common good, and instead offered up our vulnerable and essential populations while the rich profited. Per usual. I'm no better than anyone else, on this count. I haven't stepped up to say anything or lead anything. I purchase 'morale boosters' for the family without regard for the limits of our planet.

But if I continue at the current rate, the house with all its possessions will be cleaner and more organized in 2021 than ever before, and perhaps that tidiness and discipline will eventually translate into something in my mind, affect and work. Eventually. Apparently Chinese bamboo grows its root system for five years underground before it suddenly sprouts 25 feet in the air. I read that in a novel so I don't know if it's true, but I like the idea of it. What might be growing inside me that hasn't leafed yet?

Miss you, dear R. I'm sorry I've been withdrawn. I'm not trying to, or I'm trying not to, but I feel it happening to me, a sort of winter cocoon. Felt good to poke out and write you, though. Praying you made it home healthy and safe.

Still no snow.

Or there wasn't when I typed the last line, but after reading it through just now, the flakes have *just* begun falling, thick and fast, like an invasion of tiny determined beings from the stars. Just like us.

Love,
C

JANUARY 9, 2021 | *DRIVING DISTANCE*

C,

Where to start? Or rather, how to begin again?

I'm wondering in this moment about periodization. The long-1990s, for example, stretch from 1989–2001. How will we periodize *this*? If December 2019 was the beginning of 2020, when will 2020 end? When will we bracket it off? (As if some human 'we' was doing, or could do, the bracketing.)

There are two new coronavirus variants this week (B.1.1.7 and B.1.351—names designed to be forgotten). The *New York Times* Covid tracker reports that at least 1 in 13 people in Pima County, Arizona, have contracted the virus since last January and at least 1 in 861 have died. Soon, it will be 1 in 10 that have contracted the virus. How low will the numbers go? How high? Arizona has the highest per-capita new-case number in the world right now and the highest per-capita hospitalizations in the US. The official count today is over 300,000 new cases nationally. Which really means what: 500,000–600,000?

Three days ago there was a literal attempted coup by Trump supporters who contest the election results and tried to take over the Capitol. Some were wearing Viking helmets and fur vests. They called for the vice president's head. They sat their muddy boots up on the desk of the Speaker of the House.

All of which explains the joke going around on WhatsApp: 'I'd like to cancel my subscription to 2021. I've experienced the free 7-day trial and I'm not interested.'

'Cognitive dissonance.' As with 'March again', I am conscious of how frequently I think this phrase, as I try to explain or justify myself to myself—and to you.

On the one hand, we are fine: we are holed up in our house. The university is its own vaccine distribution center and has pledged to vaccinate all us faculty and staff, starting in the next two weeks. We survived our trip to Southern California with minimal damage (and all the damage was of the frustration-with-my-family type). The children had their break from routine, my in-laws got a break from us; we all saw the ocean ('I want to move near the ocean', is a thought I had last week). We learned that the four of us can drive for seven hours straight with only one bathroom break ('nature potty' on the side of the road) and only stopping once for gas. I wonder where else we can go, what else is within driving distance? Albuquerque and Santa Fe; the Grand Canyon and Sedona; San Diego; the hellscape of Las Vegas.

So we're ok, and even speculating futures. But on the other hand, we're each teaching a full load this semester, which means for me anyway at least a 200 per cent increase in my official workload, and no change in childcare or school hours, and we (like everyone) were already stretched. I am deeply nostalgic for the earlier waves of Covid, for the summer mornings, for the not-yet-normalized-routines, for the satisfaction of pulling up weeds.

Need to get off Twitter, which makes me feel icky and jealous. I logged on a few times this week to track the responses to the Trumpist insurrection. Now, have had enough. I want to hold steady and recommit to what you rightly and beautifully describe as 'keeping interested' in that which is truly interesting, in holding fast to one's core and careers, broadly construed, and to defending all of that, maybe even before there is anything to defend (paraphrasing Kay Ryan).

A belated hug to Areté, missing her Christmas. Belated hugs to Zia, watching the seasons change with equanimity. Here the littles delighted in taking down our (fake) Christmas tree, because they were eager to examine certain ornaments more closely. We never strung lights outside our house, much to Mrinalini's dismay. Every year she asks, and 'every year you promise,' she says, accusing.

I told her that we are holding back so that she has something

to look forward to. Truth or lie?
    I can feel the engine sputtering.
    All the love to you four, and the strength.

    R

JANUARY 14, 2021 | *HAPPY BUTTON*

    Dear R,

    I made what felt like a radical decision on Saturday. I decided
to be happy. Just like that. It was such a small and simple thing
to do. Like pushing a button on the crosswalk. I don't know
exactly how I came to it. To be happy. To choose it. To 'wake
up each morning and take your heart in your two hands' (Grace
Paley). To take the silly giddy post-orgasm love I feel for Micah
and live all day long in that truth: I really am the luckiest
fucking woman on earth, I must make sure these three people
around me *feel* that. Not to worry about this dynamic or that
possible criticism. To cherish them (and you too) with all my
heart. Just like that, my heart grew a little bigger. Sometimes
it pumps with the creeping fear that I won't have all the time
I want to give all the love I feel.
    I wasn't high. In fact, since the holidays ended, I've been
abstinent from all my numbing vices (wine pot food Amazon
Twitter, in about that order), proving that they are mostly a
response to stress and social interaction. So maybe the joy is
hormonal, or maybe it's the effect of the herbal supplements I
started taking last month. Or maybe it's the cumulative effect
of the meditations I started in June or so, the slow effect of
silence settling deeper into me.
    I don't mean an audible silence, exactly. Plenty of times the
kids are howling or whatever. There is a certain winter quiet
outside, with animals hibernating, most birds gone south, fewer
cars zipping around. But that's not it either. It's the silence of the

non-presence of others. Faces, language, bodies, *souls*...missing from my life, and missing from Life.

Yesterday I saw a soul I thought I recognized walking on the street. We live on a dead-end street, you know, so we don't get too many stray walkers, even though we are near the park. This person was a young woman, hair so orange it had to be real, kind of mullety and unkempt, wearing a big black coat (of course, it's freezing). I could see her through the window facing my writing desk, from which I was trying to finish an essay for *The Philosopher*. She was walking slowly, gazing up and around, with a sort of half-smile on her face, like she doesn't get out much and was therefore really *seeing* the modest houses, the gray sky, or a friendly ghost. She could've been high, or just, like most of us, unraveling in some way. We are used to ascribing that unraveling to drugs or describing it as illness, but it can also be understood as turning one's face towards a different reality. As I say, it felt like I recognized her.

The decision to be happy, to turn to the reality of my loves: it's radical in the face of the statistics you recount, which are very bad and getting worse. The political news is, if anything, more frightening. Reports say that the Trumpists will try again before the inauguration. It is clear that they had/have tangible inside support from lawmakers, cops, possibly higher-ups in the military. Not clear that the key organizers of the insurrection have been arrested. Some corporations have withdrawn platforms or financial support from Trump, others are suspending judgment. He has been impeached by the House and may be by the Senate, too. Yet I don't see him and his ilk turning back now. Even if Biden takes office, he might have a civil conflict on his hands that would greatly hamper the pandemic response.

Which will start with the so-far miserable vaccine rollout. New York opened the next phase of candidates this week, so that I'm eligible, sort-of (they include in-person instructors, but I'm remote-teaching, but no one's checking). Like you, my inbox and WhatsApp were aflurry with colleagues' trials and travels to get vaccinated. I'm reminded of how people used to line up in front of the Cheeseboard in Berkeley on the night they made their corn-feta-cilantro pie, the queue stretching around the corner store onto my street, people colonizing the median to picnic. Hivemind!

I've done the research and the public benefit seems to outweigh the individual risk. Yet I'm content to wait-and-see. Why?

I admit it is hard to imagine voluntarily entering a shared indoor space. Mostly, though, I remember in my body that we don't know what we don't know, which predisposes me to let others be the guinea pigs. I distrust the reported numbers (95 per cent effective? *Really?* Like how 95 per cent of Iraqis 'voted' for Saddam Hussein??), and I do trust my behaviors to keep me safe. For now.

Right now, choosing happy means going to bed early—it's 8.45 now. Only one day until your birthday!

Love,
C

JANUARY 17, 2021 | *WE CHOOSE OUR OWN LIVES*

C,

I am in a noisy place. And in a bit of a rush. Hurrying to write, so I can hear back from you.

You wrote from a place of settling silence and the non-presence of others. I want to meet you somewhere there, but I am carrying with me (and within me) the considerable noises of others: the children, yes, but also my students, nearly two dozen crowding my inbox, and my colleagues, and our families. On Tuesday I start teaching two online but 'live' (meaning synchronous) classes. I just got off a tricontinental birthday zoom. And then of course there's the news, the Covid numbers, the data. Nothing has changed and everything is changing.

On January 26 I'm registered to get the first shot of the Moderna vaccine. My mother texted to ask if we can visit California for spring break and mercifully (also truthfully) I was able to answer that the university has canceled spring break this year. My brother is off to South Africa on Feb 6 to propose to his long-distance love, and my cousin just flew from New York to California to visit my parents, and my uncle is planning a trip from Delhi stateside to visit his granddaughter-to-be—so everyone is moving on, or trying to, or variously making plans to.

I wonder if you are moving deeper into the contented stillness, into the full and dynamic love, into the happiness, in part as an instinctive or unconscious response to the world spinning out of control. I have an image in my mind of a spinning top standing still as the world orbits around it. The top can spin, you see, but it chooses rest; it chooses balance. (So maybe the language of instinct is all wrong, actually. Maybe you would say, in the words of *Hamilton's* Aaron Burr: 'I'm not standing still / I am lying in wait.')

Did you end up seeing the movie-version of Lin-Manuel Miranda's musical? *Hamilton* will always be of this time for us, ironically so given the America we live in: the country bracing for inauguration protests, and the mainstream media glamorizing QAnon supporters. There are other things resolutely of this time that I worry I will forget. For months now I have been finding that all my shirts have holes in them, little holes, mostly in the same spot at my waist, and I have wondered why. Moths? But moths wouldn't bite the same spots again and again, would they? Only recently did I figure out that I am doing so many dishes these days, standing at certain counters at such lengths, that my shirts are getting cut on my jeans buttons. I can't tell you how many of my shirts. Like, all my shirts, with constellations of pandemic holes.

I've started writing about Mrinalini's sickness in fall 2019. She talks about it differently now that she has more distance from that time. When she was really in the throes of it, she kept a journal of 'clues': not clues about the sickness exactly, but clues about aliens and stars and the shapes of cars on the street. She would write them down during the evening walk she insisted on taking with me every day in order to avoid eating dinner, and which I indulged in order to keep her calm and happy-ish. I went looking for that journal the other day, and found only the clipboard to which it was attached. I suspect she destroyed the journal. Is she afraid to look back, of what she might remember fearing?

She is moving on, but Brandon and I are still living in the aftermath of all that. We are living with the decisions we made then when she was very sick, like taking her off gluten, sugar, and lactose. We still keep to the restricted diet, but as time passes we find ourselves wondering if and when we can begin to experiment, to open up her diet, to take some risks with it. Not so subtle parallels to other decisions we've made, and are making, with respect to Covid.

My winter porch is warming up. It's 26°C today. There will be colder weeks, but I can already feel us inching toward the spring.

And did I tell you? I had a lovely birthday yesterday. I channeled you and I resolved to be happy and I was. So many beautiful books to read now (thank you, for art, for *Agua Viva*). Coffee and cognac and creams and chocolates and a new comforter, too. I was spoiled and felt spoiled. My mother-in-law made a feast and a delicious apple tart (gluten free, no refined sugar). Is this what happens, if you resolve to be happy? That the world meets you with love and light?

We stayed up late, and so I didn't sleep well, but I still woke with a feeling of readiness to meet the day, a desire to trust my instincts, and the resolve to open the page to the page I want to open to.

Day before yesterday I spent my 'work' time reading Andrew Solomon's *Far from the Tree*. Did you ever read that book? It's maybe a decade old, about parents of children with disabilities and special abilities, about the interstices of identity and illness. About becoming ourselves in relation to our others.

Toward the close of the first chapter, Solomon writes this:

> We choose our own lives. It is not simply that we decide on the behaviors that construct our experience; when given our druthers, we elect to be ourselves. Most of us would like to be more successful or more beautiful or wealthier, and most people endure episodes of low self-esteem or even self-hatred. We despair a hundred times a day. But we retain the startling evolutionary imperative of affection for the fact of ourselves, and with that splinter of grandiosity we redeem our flaws.

I'm looking at the clock. Time to make lunch for the smallies and for Brandon. I am grateful I can choose to cook for them. That I can choose to write to you and to meet you in this space. I would do it again and again and again.

Thank you for ushering me into a new year with such love and heartening faith—

R

JANUARY 23, 2021 | *POLITICAL PAGEANTRY*

Dear R,

I always love receiving your letters, you know that, and whatever moment you wish to write is the right moment. I understand the urge to write sooner, not only to receive the gift sooner back, but also to write before events pile up beyond digestion.

This week there were two worth reporting, in my small world. One, of course, was the peaceable inauguration of Joe Biden and Kamala Harris. It's worth noting explicitly that the peaceableness was part of what was noteworthy. My fears of violence were overblown, or rather, they were blown to people in power as well, so that the violence was met with the legitimized counterviolence of the National Guard.

I watched the pageantry live, remembering watching such rituals for countries which have less hold on me. In particular, an image of a South Korean military parade kept surfacing in my mind. I remembered, too, an inauguration day protest in 2005, for Bush's second term. It was pointless and cold, but at the time it was worth missing the first session of my Fascist Europe seminar for it. There's a photo of me and my college best friend there, holding our signs in our mittens. Hers says, 'Don't cut my affordable housing budget—cut your war budget.' Mine says, 'Soldiers, desert!'

Fast forward sixteen years. I watched closely the official faces as they took their oaths with thrilling solemnity. My eyes as much as the Bible, I felt, were binding their words to their souls. The poet, Amanda Gorman, I watched after the fact, admiring her straight bearing and graceful gestures more than the jejune wordplay (We lay down our arms / so we can reach out our arms / to one another). But I guess I have more tolerance for state singers than state poets, because I grew emotional watching the singers, Lady Gaga and J-Lo, step out, visibly gather themselves into the moment, open their throats and sing out. That was the part that brought me to tears. I was ashamed to be taken in by such a discredited dream of America, but I wanted, all the same, for the dream to keep going.

And now, afterwards: the news no longer has the addictive tragic pulse of a telenovela. There were a few well-deserved parting shots at Melania Trump and her cynical greed, some soft stories about the new color of the carpet in the Oval

Office, the ever present Covid cloud, vaccine inequities. (Did we basically have a sex slave as First Lady for the past four years? I am in favor of removing the stigma from sex workers but really that seems like going a little too far. Also, where do presidents actually work? Like, where does the computer go?) Trump's punishment now, and our salvation, is mostly that he can be ignored.

That last may not be true, but I hope it is. There is something to say about Biden's shortcomings, the problem of elite capture, and the persistence of the swamp as well as of dangerous factionalism and untruth—but it can all wait. This week is for relief.

The second event is of the micro scale sort, worth reporting only to you and me. It happened the same day as the Inauguration: I rearranged all my books. They were unpacked haphazardly when we moved in here almost three years ago, and then further disorganized each time we rearranged our offices (at least twice since the pandemic began), and the books from my campus office just ended up wherever. It was a surprisingly emotional process.

To think I once read Kant! To pick up *Wretched of the Earth* and wonder if I made an ass out of myself teaching it last semester. To lay fingers on every book you've gifted me over the years, from *Golden Notebook* to *Martin Heidegger Saved my Life* to *The Mushroom at the End of the World* to Trethewey's *Memorial Drive* and the most recent *The Nothing That Is*. To restore a semi-wholeness to bodies of knowledge by putting all the Heidegger books together, between Nietzsche and Foucault, and by grouping all the books that don't fit anywhere else. It was like greeting all the people I've been. And then I put my current priorities on the top shelf, and staged my classical library for the Zoom background.

It feels good in here.

Many things I want to talk over with you, my dear. Your

writing about Mrinalini's sickness—a way of putting it in the past?—your first week teaching, the present that, presently, feels back-in-control (even as I know the Covid horrors are far from over). Your holey shirts, did no one replace them for your birthday, why did you not tell me to do that? I have not managed to find the happy button every day of the past two weeks, but more often than not.

So we go on, against the goblin odds.

Love,
C

JANUARY 30, 2021 | *FOR THE YEARBOOK*

Hi dear C,

What a weird week. The inauguration events all left me cold, and the feeling of indifference continues to build. I know this indifference is a kind of indulgence, and I am nursing it knowing how decadent, maybe even irresponsible, it is. I am aware, too, of what a bullet we have collectively dodged, even as the other bullets of the Trump years remain lodged in the national body—and elsewhere, in the corpses of the world.

Both Brandon and I got shot one of the Moderna vaccine this week, and this was an *event* for us, an 'occurrence of some importance' (thanks, dictionary.com). There is a part of me that feels shamefaced about having gotten the vaccine already since it is, in this moment, the object of widespread, even global, desire. It has been unevenly distributed and is inaccessible to many, or most. Nobody in my extended family has been vaccinated: not my eighty-five-plus-year-old grandmother in Delhi, not my uncle the politician who travels frequently by plane and is in close contact with scores of people, not my brother's soon-to-be-fiancée who is a working dentist, with her hands and tools daily in other people's mouths.

One day, we will find out what happened in India: their numbers are declining, their death rate is nothing to match ours. Is it just the fact of a younger population? Some preexisting immunity? Longstanding exposure to similar coronaviruses? Whatever it is, I hope it will be enough to protect my grandmother, my uncle, all of them.

In Arizona they clubbed teachers and staff from K-12 and higher education in with the over-seventy-fives. So we are in the second group, after frontline healthcare workers and nursing home residents. Should we be? When the registration opened up, and the emails started flying around my department listserv about how to sign up, we didn't hesitate, despite that nagging feeling of undeservingness. Most people I know here in Tucson have now started to be vaccinated, all our neighbors (who are old), and all our colleagues, and the teachers at Mrinalini's school, and Shai's, too…but not my in-laws, who are just under the age cut-off. Their goal is to be fully vaccinated by May, when they want to be able to leave for Maine. This I think will happen, but I am already feeling impatient.

The vaccination itself was a slow process. I waited three hours in a line of cars. It was our first (and likely only) 'snow day' in Tucson this year. Flurries for an intense thirty–forty minutes that morning, powder on the palms; it all melted by noon but slowed everything down. So I had a long wait. Then, the shot and the mandatory fifteen-minute observation. You wait in your car, with a post-it note on the dash displaying the time you can leave. A doctor comes by and introduces herself and says that if you feel badly, just honk your horn (I guess if your forehead doesn't hit it first). I raced home as soon as I could to teach my graduate class, five minutes late.

Afterward, my shoulder hurt like hell, I couldn't sleep on it, and the next day it hurt even worse. I took Advil, and that helped. To be honest, I was sore all over, had muscle fatigue—but was that my unusual attempt at yoga a couple days earlier, on a rainy day I couldn't run? Might have been. I was very tired that night, and my face and tongue felt swollen.

All the feels: Relief to have gotten the vaccine but embarrassment about getting it so fast. Unsure if it will do anything, like change our lives—or rather, quite certain it won't change anything in the short run, and not sure it will matter in the long run if the variants are as bad as we think? Moderna is already working on a booster, shot number three, to deal with the South African variant (and our family is likely planning a wedding in South Africa at the end of the year! Of all places...). How many boosters will there be? I am a bit nervous about getting my second dose, scheduled at the end of the month the day before I have many meetings and a talk to give. I've heard at least three reports of high fevers, vomiting, and other issues after shot two.

I attended a department meeting on Zoom yesterday; I am officially 'back' after being 'on leave' (ha!). A colleague I 'saw' at the meeting invited me to join him and friends at a socially distanced movie at the local independent theater. I politely declined, but it gave me pause. I've declined many invitations from this colleague, who is one of the few I like and admire, and I wonder each time I do: will there be any invitations left, on the other side of this?

I want to be there in your newly configured bookshelf, going through all those titles with you, turning the pages. Rearranging my books feels so beyond me, like a project for another lifetime.

As for the holey shirts: it's ok, I am still wearing them. I like to. They remind me of all the dishes.

This afternoon I took Mrinalini to take her yearbook photo—by appointment, solo, masked. Her mask was dia de los muertos-themed, patterned with flowers and skulls. We did her hair and put on tights, and the photo itself took about two minutes. She was so happy to drive up to the school building, much happier than I thought she would be. And then she came home and danced.

All the love,

R

FEBRUARY 7, 2021 | *AS IF NO ONE'S WATCHING*

Dear R,

It's snowing atop snow here. I want to hear and talk about it all with you, the humdrum happenings and the Event of Vaccination!

At a meta-level, the vaccine stands for the bet that it'll be easier or more effective to contain the virus by changing human biology—the immune system—than by changing human culture—our systems of interaction and exchange. Of course, no binary is so neatly divided. Neurotypical humans are hardwired to socialize, so the non-pharmaceutical approach also has biology to contend with. And culture is putting up a good fight against the vaccine on a number of fronts, from skepticism to pure incompetence.

(If there were a drug that decreased people's need to see one another in person, would that work just as well as the vaccine?)

And perhaps the greater force even than human biology is the capitalist market: which floods medical research with money, which needs people to continue to work and consume at ever increasing levels, which somehow profits from death. Doesn't the coronavirus represent Naomi Klein's disaster capitalism on an even more disastrous scale?

But at a personal level, I'm very glad you got some measure of protection, and your in-laws too, even as I wait out the first stampede.

It feels as though so much time has passed since I wrote last. The effect, maybe, of the start of the semester. The first week of class is off to a reasonable start. I found myself hoping not that it would 'go well' but that I would like the students, and that put me in a good frame of mind about it. Time in which more things are happening seems to move quicker. Does it also accumulate in higher and higher snowdrifts?

For me no Event has interrupted the winter monotony. My journal over the past few months is a consistent record of what intoxicants I used or didn't, whether I exercised or didn't (the occasional gentle walk); what I did for myself (today, writing you); what I did for other people (mostly the daily chores, the occasional heroic cleaning project, infrequently, something for someone beyond my small circle); the feelings that are going unexpressed in the bustle.

And I try to find one good thing that happens each day. Yesterday, it was re-arranging the living room. The new spaciousness induced an extra vigorous evening family dance party, complete with glowsticks. I love that this time has made dancing-as-if-no-one-is-watching (they're not) a regular practice. The kids haven't been schooled in their genders as thoroughly as we adults, and so dancing with them is also a way of exercising a certain fluid energy, being a body-in-motion rather than a body-with-breasts.

The monotony reinforces the lesson that my feelings have to do with me and my hormones and not the people or happenings I project them onto. I have been dreaming about our time in Oregon the past couple of nights, the blank ocean sky where I first really understood this truth. My period just ended again, so I am happy and peaceful again. We have been watching stand-up comedians Dave Chapelle and Ali Wong, which leads to huge therapeutic belly laughs. Also, an admiration for the social and intellectual freedom and courage that these comedians carry into the world, despite Chapelle's unfunny transphobism.

Today is my dad's birthday and we're due to Zoom soon,

so I'll break off here. But you know this dialogue with you is forever and ever.

Love,
C

FEBRUARY 16, 2021 | *NEWS FROM JOHANNESBURG*

C,

You wrote that the vaccine represents 'the bet that it'll be easier or more effective to contain the virus by changing human biology...than by changing human culture'.

You are so right. It is just that order of bet, and in that it is already the mark of a certain failure.

I've gotten over some of the self-consciousness of having been so far in front in the vaccine queue. My uncle and grandmother in India have now had the AstraZeneca vaccine. My aunt in London (a serious asthmatic) was called up by the NHS today for the same. Most of my colleagues and students got it. My cousin and his wife got Pfizer under the table.

To be honest, after I got the shot, the vaccination itself receded as an event of significance. Then I got two wake-up calls about how others are thinking about it. The first, in the form of a segment on *This American Life*. I listened to it while running by the Reid Park Zoo, next to the golf course, dodging pedestrians. See if you can hear how it would have sounded:

> David Kestenbaum: *There can be an intimacy to this moment of getting the shot, I think because there's a way in which getting the shot is like passing through a portal— out of this awful year. This other nurse, Amy Caramore in New York, told me she feels that way with every single shot.*

Amy Caramore: *I say, are you ready? I always say, are you ready, which is a little bit—which isn't just about, are you ready for me to put a needle in your arm, but is more about, are you ready for this?*

David Kestenbaum: *It's like, are you ready for the new world?*

I know you remember Arundhati Roy's essay, 'The Pandemic is a Portal', and so this invocation of the language of portal struck me. It was eerie, and telling, and it made me wonder anew where we think we're passing to, what we think we're passing through. Well, not *we*. Most of the world has not been vaccinated. And the joke of the radio episode was that they played clips of various people reacting to their shots with relieved laughter and tears and whoops, and then they all went to the observation room where they sat around on their phones, ignoring each other.

The vaccine as portal. The vaccine as failure. It may really be a failure, as new variants emerge, new recombinants and mutants, that could render the vaccines moot (at worst) or less efficacious (at best).

I was talking to a friend from Reno who is not vaccinated yet, and he said that after he gets the shot he's not only going to feel comfortable getting on an airplane but that he's going to lick the cabin floor.

So you think the vaccines are going to work? I asked.

He guffawed and shouted like it was the craziest darn thing anyone had ever asked him. *I wouldn't ask it to an anti-vaxxer,* I clarified. But I guess my point is that he really didn't believe I was serious.

I said two wake-up calls. The second is the not insignificant clusterfuck in the making of my brother's intended wedding. He got engaged this weekend to his girlfriend in Johannesburg. I am genuinely thrilled for him and hope he rises to the occasion of this partnership, which seems full of promise. But the wedding. If I just lay out the facts it's insane: possibly as early as July, 100–200 people from four continents, three days worth of events.

The wedding will be outdoors, they say.

Everyone coming from abroad will have been tested, they say.

All the adults will have been vaccinated, they say.

I'm not sure why I didn't see this coming exactly, because I saw it coming but I didn't see it coming quite like this.

And Brandon and I are the only ones who seem to think it's impossible, though it falls to me to make the case.

So this, I know, is going to be the defining conflict of the next couple weeks, maybe months, maybe years.

There is no world in which they go forward with the wedding and we don't attend, so how to get them to not go forward with the wedding? I am hoping that the AstraZeneca vaccine's uselessness against the South African variant might be enough. I am hoping that the borders close. I am hoping that South Africa bans weddings in Gauteng Province.

Equally, and in other parts of life, I confess a longing for a portal, for a bit of a way out. We're exhausted when we get into bed each night. Keeping up with our classes and colleagues and students is getting harder. Professionally we are itching to get new jobs, elsewhere, anywhere away from here. That feels impossible given the way our lives are structured, or if not impossible, then just too damn slow. Brandon is doing his part and just won a big award, which should help on the job market. Still, we need more time. The kids need to go back to in-person school. By that same token, I don't want to send them to these schools. Would any other schools be better?

And I know I shouldn't whine about the weather when you all are under snow, but we're missing the sun today. Although I don't want to die here and I don't even want to be here, I have learned to love the Arizona sun and its burn. I think I love it because it feels good. But then, it's also possible it's exactly the opposite.

More telepathically.

Love,

R

FEBRUARY 20, 2021 | *IMPOSSIBLE CHOICE*

Dear R,

What a dilemma you are facing: you can't go to your brother's proposed wedding in South Africa. You also can't not go.

I keep turning it over and over again in my mind, because it is an impossible choice. Because it has the structure of an impossible choice all of us keep having to make. As I keep turning it over, I glimpse 'the rivening' of our world, as it is called in one of N. K. Jemison's post-apocalyptic stories.

In the rivening, I see something about the social construction of reality that I never have before: that it lags behind material reality. Perhaps not as far behind as philosophy, but still behind. Because here is the material world of Covid, the catastrophe become ordinary days, and we have not yet built a social reality around it, a 'biosphere' or 'semiosphere' of meaning, that a majority can live in, but instead cling to the tenuous myth of a 'return to normal'. Here are two diametrically opposed necessities—to go or to stay. To hold onto tradition or to protect your future. And from such binaries, all of us must knit a reality that allows for many forms of life.

In another of Jemison's stories, a cyborg character comes to visit the slums of old-style humans who are maintained as a reservoir of human DNA to replenish the new hybrid race. He/it comes face to face with a young woman, who is faced with the choice of becoming a cyborg or being sacrificed. She asks him why he made the choice to cross over, give up who and what he essentially was. And he says simply, that was the way to go on.

In the Jemison story, one side chooses to change in order to survive, and the other side chooses not to. What I see from here is that both 'sides' (the pro-vaccine and the vaccine-hesitant, or perhaps the 'herd immunity' vs. Covid-zero strategies) are choosing one kind of change or another. And maybe from that choice, the world will fall into two classes: those with the vaccine passports and those without. Or just maybe, the sides will realize they need one another, come together in a doubly-changed form of life....

I'm telling stories, taking a meta-level, semi-compassionate tone. I know there's much I don't really know about the tangled family histories, the web of obligation and relation. And you know my true feelings: you can't go.

In no possible world do I not go, you say.

No one in your family is on your side, you say. Brandon will do what you choose but not help you fight.

So it falls to me—like you, trained 'to make the weaker argument the stronger', as Protagoras is said to have done— to tell you: it's okay to 'be the asshole'. To remind you, it's quite possible that the asshole move by today's standards looks different by future lights. If I were the type to give advice, I'd say you have got to insist on that reality-to-come, to shift from 'I can't promise I'll go' to 'I'm not going to go unless the situation changes dramatically.' To back up your current bluff by walking out.

What stops me from insisting on such things outright is knowing how much easier it is to say than to do. I, myself, never stop being surprised, and frankly, frightened, by the plasticity of my own brain, its ability to comprehend and consider diametrically opposed paths as equally my own.

What I will say unequivocally is that I hear you repeatedly

outlawing your own desire not to go. I just wanted to be an amplifier for that voice.

And I will also say, even more emphatically: be extra compassionate with yourself, as well as with your family and family-to-be. The conversations are long and beyond exhausting. But I trust some as-yet-unseen possible world will emerge out of love.

This has taken a long time to write and I have said nothing (very uncharacteristically!) of my life, of my own mini-dilemmas and the strange mix of feelings in me as we approach the end of our first year in lockdown. We have not seen Micah's (high-risk) parents since 2019—we worry we would bring the virus with us if we took the cross-country flight. But my family, whether we will see them or not or how, is a conversation landmined with old griefs.

But now, it's my turn with the kids.

Love you so much,
C

MARCH 1, 2021 | *IT'S MARCH AGAIN*

Dearest C,

It's March again—this time it's really March again.
Here I am.
Here we are.
March again.

After all our telepathic communications this week, I feel I am picking up many strands at once. The week before you wrote was the week of an impossible decision: how to go? How not to go? But at some point soon after I narrated the decision-drama to you, it became less impossible, simply because it became inevitable and therefore possible.

Right now, as it stands, we will go to South Africa for the

wedding at the end of July. Much may change, or not enough will change, or things will get much worse, or things will get much better, or some inscrutable, unhelpful combination, but in most scenarios, we will go.

I'll save the nitty-gritty for later: who else will come, who won't. From the US it really won't be anyone, just our family. That was a big part of the bargain: I forbade my mother from inviting any of their friends. But there will be the South Africans to contend with.

Oh, of course I dread all the obvious stuff. The flying for twenty-two hours in masks, in addition to all the other general discomforts of travel. But I'm also not terribly afraid of discomfort, having made so many painful trips with and without the kids.

October 2013. I remember weeks of travel throughout India with five-month-old jetlagged Mrinalini. She kept me up all night every night, so when I landed up for my aunt's wedding in London at the end of the month, I was literally hallucinating from lack of sleep.

July 2017. I flew to Chennai and stayed at my Patti's house in the dead of summer. She had no AC; there were mosquitoes galore. I crashed out of sheer exhaustion every night at nine, then woke up two hours later to face the rest of the night awake and alone, scratching, sweating, wearing so much insect repellant it was dripping down my legs and burning off my nail polish.

December 2018. Day after Christmas, I was awake all night at a shitty airport hotel in Houston after a missed connection. Shai was less than a year old, screaming and refusing to sleep. I remember I held him for twelve, thirteen, fourteen, fifteen hours until our tickets came through.

Could tell you many more such stories. The upshot is that I'm dreading the travel, but I'm also fairly confident that I know how to bear that kind of suffering.

Anyway, that's likely not what you're interested in hearing.

Covid, what about Covid? Well, they shouldn't be having a 'wedding' wedding, but they have to have a wedding for reasons that I understand and accept, and of course we'll be there at my only brother's only wedding, and I guess we'll be there even if it kills us.

But I don't think it will kill us.

You have said not to trust, not to trust these people or those, not to trust that others will have been careful, not to trust that they will be forthcoming. I have thought it many times myself and to some extent I am still with you. But there comes a point when you have to decide who you are willing to respect. The people who have managed (and had the privilege—that word again!) to keep themselves safe from Covid for a year...was it just luck? Don't trust them, sure, but respect the commitment.

More importantly: do you trust yourself? To what extent? How much? Where? Myself, I have been realizing that if I focus on whether or not other people's behaviors can be trusted, I miss out on the question of how much I trust my own judgment. Do we trust ourselves to assess evolving situations? Do we trust ourselves to act as required in the moment? Do we trust ourselves with the data? Do we trust our instincts?

We may yet step in it—indeed, I don't believe in luck, and I definitely don't believe that we are lucky—but Brandon and I, I think we feel that to some extent we have earned our own trust.

So I'm not terribly afraid, in this moment, about making a big decision or a bad one.

You quoted Primo Levi to me the other day. I wish I remembered exactly what you said, but basically it was that it wasn't kindness or empathy or taking chances or going on metaphorical flights to South Africa that enabled Levi to survive the Holocaust. What you said was more incisive, and colder. It was a perfect line. But there are other lines, like Elie Wiesel's words (maybe apocryphal) after Primo Levi's eventual death after the life he lived after having survived: 'Levi died at Auschwitz forty years later.'

Probably neither of us should be analogizing the pandemic to the Holocaust, but I think I know what you meant, and I think you know what I mean.

I would always choose martyrdom.

And I am not going to write everything I think or want to say about whether or not you four will see your parents (and other family, but centrally, I take it, your parents) in the coming weeks and months. Whether, and if so, then how. There's lots to be said, but I don't want to speak out of turn. And I know it's fraught.

I will say this though: at some point, you will have to decide whether they are your people.

With love,
R

MARCH 6, 2021 | *DARK CHASMS*

Dear R,

It's Friday afternoon as I start this, sunny and cold. My neighbor's flag, which periodically gets tattered from the rough handling of the tree branches it fronts, is waving fresh, intact, and bright. I thought it would be easier to write to you than to work on the essay coming due. But I find suddenly I am exhausted and without the words or wherewithal to respond to your news and your framing of my own choices. You'll go to the wedding. Inevitably, probably. Most likely you'll all come through just fine. I see the love in the choice and I love, so much, the person who chose love.

Rereading my last—now on Saturday—I think perhaps I was over-insistent, overly negative. 'I had passed judgment on people I thought were overly cautious, and I had passed judgment on people I thought were not cautious enough,' writes the Covid-afflicted AIDS researcher whose auto-ethnography you just sent me. You, with me, are always in a zone of suspended judgment.

On Wednesday I started to use the word 'depression' of my state of mind. It is accurate, though equally true to say an evil veil has fallen behind my eyes. I am functioning well enough: doing a good job, even, at teaching. But the happy button is not working. My thoughts veer towards magnetic precipices. I cannot stop peering into the dark chasms that hold only the euphoria of self-annihilation. I hate myself.

I know what to do and am doing it: have engaged a therapist, made social plans, recommitted to a daily walk. Attempting to remember and focus on dreams for my writing, my future. Attempting to be grateful for each day, for how easy it is to make Areté laugh.

A year ago, almost exactly, my family entered a quarantine pattern that has hardly deviated since. Micah and I argued and negotiated and finally agreed to hold ourselves apart from the world for one year, to learn what we could, with 'watchful waiting' our continual keyword. I accepted certain limitations, strove to be loyal and compassionate, found new depths of patience, acceptance, and capacity. Now the year is up, we are reviewing the facts: what do we know now about the disease that we didn't know a year ago?

We have agreed that it is no longer necessary to wash the groceries or decontaminate packages. We have agreed that outdoor masked social activity is fine and also that it is fine for him not to do it. In principle he has agreed to a family visit along the above lines, but in actuality there is a hard kernel of non-acceptance which holds me back from yet re-opening the subject with my family. I have raised the possibility of outdoor-masked summer camps but suspect having others care for our children may be his bright red line. It is also the core of the unsustainability of our current path. He sends me articles about the hikikomori in Japan and South Korea. I read them with a sad heart; is he saying this is his tribe? You wrote that I need to decide whether my birth family are 'my people'. It is more even than that, I sometimes feel—to live as Micah would want is to reject all humans as my people.

In the past weeks, we have both questioned seriously whether our union can continue. I find myself cycling among impossibilities. Impossible to change him, impossible to divorce him, impossible to go on as we are. Impossible to be myself as long as I am with him, forced always to become something other than what I have been, and *not* always an other I like.

Yet I love him, still, this impossible, sometimes awful person that no one else even likes. (I am awful too, I remember.) I respect his commitment to the things and people he cares about, and his disregard for the calculations of the majority. I remember when Mrinalini was in the hospital with what you would find out was Kawasaki's: you decided not to make any major decisions (like withdrawing from grad school) for the time being. So it is with me: pursuing separation is off the table until I'm in a more reliable frame of mind.

But in the meanwhile, I know that the tiny, invisible decisions count. To let him through the veil or not. To keep the divorce doorway open a crack or not. R, tell me—do you think the endurance of love always comes down to a decision? Or is there a line past which it is possible to truthfully say, I did all I could and I could not preserve the love?

I hesitate to write all this, knowing you have scant reserves for such darkness, and knowing too how things change. How my heart will sing for no reason as the weather warms—soon! How having the car working again—soon! after three weeks without it, the repair covered by warranty, thank god—will open up slivers of freedom and sociality that make all the difference. Even the return of the TV (also soon, also under warranty) will be the return of one small pleasure, one piece of our coping routine, one portal to a world out of reach. We might hire someone to build a treehouse. I might go ahead and get the damn vaccine along with everyone else. So, one way or another, these feelings will pass, in time. Already they are surpassed by the pains of others.

But I do choose to include them. Because as the AIDS ethnologist concluded, 'There must be a way to hold together a structural analysis of planetary catastrophe and the fear and fragility that lie at its heart.' These are the shadows of my fearful and fragile heart, today.

Love,
C

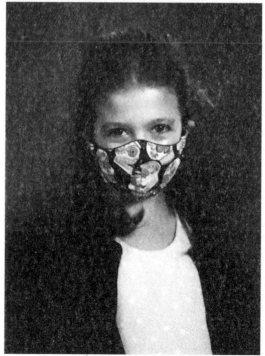

BOOK 2

THE PORTAL

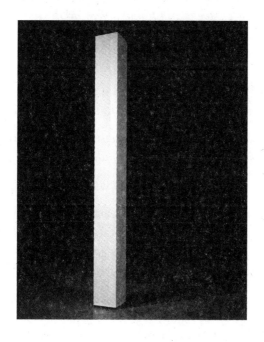

Where to start? Or rather, how to begin again?

Will you write letters back and forth with me once a week?

We say we are 'at war' with the virus. But what if it is trying to help us…evolve?

What do we know now about the disease that we didn't know a year ago?

Do we always have to balance safety and freedom in a zero-sum equation?

What to do with my privilege? What is essential travel? What is connection, now? What was it, in the before-times?

What is the word for when you are stressed but so is everyone you know, so there's little we can do to help one another?

Is there a God? Is God mad?

Where do I want to be, how do I want to have grown, whenever this does end? What might be growing inside me that hasn't leafed yet? What if, by giving form, and taking form, I invite counter-formations that I can't withstand?

Whose approval am I trying to win when I try to win this prize? Maybe I should leave all the scholarly pretense and intellectual confabulation behind, and just try to write like that?

If not now, when?

This is the struggle. Is it a beautiful struggle? Sometimes, when I am writing to you or reading you, I think it could be.

I don't want to die of the virus. But I do want to have a life to live for. What kind of wish is that? What sort of gift is this?

Will it be enough that we have been this virtuous this long?

Do I want normalcy, or do I want the end of the world?

*Remember when that was just a question, at
the beginning of our letters?*

Do you trust yourself? How do you trust yourself?

*Do you think the endurance of love always comes down to a
decision? Or is there a line past which it is possible to truthfully
say, I did all I could and I could not preserve the love?*

What if?

Some questions just have to be lived.

SECOND SPRING: THE RETURN

Hello dear one,

You wrote to me on March 6, sunny and cold. Now it's March 17, after the anniversary of the declaration of the pandemic.

After the anniversary of the Friday the 13th that my mother returned from India to the end of the world as she knew it (I warned her so many times that week on the phone...still, she didn't believe me).

After the anniversary of that first weekend when we knew there would be no more school or going to the office.

After the anniversary of our initial weeding frenzy, newly aware as we were of the garden, the yard, seeing everything in the house as if for the first time now that we knew it would be everything and all we had, and for who could say how long.

The days since the sixth have been a frenzy of happenings. Here we've got Shai back in his morning program. The teacher is vaccinated; he has four classmates in a beautiful big room with their own dedicated playground. He is delighted. Snacking too much and screwing up his schedule, and in general he is more difficult, cranky and willful, but he loves being back in school.

Mrinalini is as independent as ever. She's on spring break this week, and I enrolled her in two 'field' mornings at the university recreation center, with small masked groups, all outdoors. She was so nervous before Tuesday that she woke up four times at night calling out about bad dreams. But she had a great time, and that too despite an unseasonably cold Tucson day, rain, and the general drearies. I was so nervous that she would be unhappy, and so overjoyed to hear how much she enjoyed herself. She even made a friend, one who is miraculously our neighbor and lives just down the street! A prayer, answered. As for the rest of it: it's been one of those weeks where everything is breaking. A lamp we are totally dependent on with an impossible-to-find bulb. The bathtub faucet—this was a real disaster—stopped working, and Brandon tried to fix it, but his fix caused the faucet to run uncontrollably. We couldn't repair that, and so we had to turn the water off to the entire house for half a day, improvising bucket flushes for the toilets. He then gave up and called the plumber.

I am tired. I have been giving my students a lot—more, I think, than I knew I had; though not what I once imagined I might give them. Once upon a time I imagined taking my students out for drinks—like my advisor did, impressing me with her cocktail-savvy. I imagined having them over for a meal, like some of our professors did, inviting us into their private, book-laden homes. I imagined a big, wide open, robust academic sociality. Those days are gone.

Also, I am realizing again and anew how closely my moods track the weather. I was down for a couple days because it was cold (Tucson cold). I really have become a desert lizard creature who just wants to bask in the sun! There is so much I don't like about being here, but it's not the heat. Maybe it's as simple as what my colleague Derrais Carter writes: 'The desert is not my home.'

And if this desert is not home, what is? I don't know where we are, or why we're here. I am not sure *when* we are, either, or what I want to eat or what I want to drink or what I want to read. I have often thought that the question is not so much 'How are we going to survive the pandemic?' but 'What is going to be on the other side?' How are we going to get out of here, out of Tucson, out of this?

We can't stay here after this. We couldn't possibly.

So this is the new world and the new liminality.

Too much Twitter is also mucking up my mind. I was drawn in today by the news out of Atlanta of toxic and entitled white male on a shooting spree of Asian massage parlors. Feel inadequate to the moment but also feel the need to rise to the moment for my Asian American literature students and our Korean soon-to-be sister-in-law, who has been sending reports of hate crimes on the family WhatsApp for weeks and is particularly gutted. As I said to her though, with reference to the anti-Muslim, anti-Sikh, anti-Arab, and anti-South Asian violence in the wake of September 11: that violence didn't end then, and this violence didn't start now.

It all keeps on and on. Or, in Franny Choi's words, the world keeps ending, and the world goes on.

I want to say more but this will have to be it, my eyes are feeling so heavy. Let me pass you the baton then.

With big love,
R

MARCH 30, 2021 | *CHANGE IS POSSIBLE*

Hi R,

If I had to periodize—this continual urge we have, to try to historicize and temporalize what we are going through!—I would say we are in another phase, this one of acute cognitive dissonance. Or maybe it's just spring, is all, and I guess what is common to all springs—the sense of hope and possibility, tempered by the cold and rain—is taking shape in its peculiarly Covid way.

On the one hand, the tremendous hopefulness around the growing distribution of vaccines. Some of my students now have their shots, and all my professor friends have at least one. (We are the slowpokes. Unwilling to drive two hours for it, and unwilling to go indoors into a Best Buy for it, we're keeping our appointments at the county fairgrounds on April 12.) On the other, the CDC director's 'impending sense of doom'. A fourth wave is on the way, perhaps, driven by the new variants, probably, and perhaps new-new variants we don't even know how to see. Anthony Fauci holds out hope for summer camp.

It's a brutally busy time at work, grading and such. I have gotten roped into some unpaid labor, maybe a lot, and am kicking myself, my lifetime of gender training, because of it. I am struggling, as I've told you, to put a cap on this Liquid Philosophy column. I worry that I am not a good writer, which is silly, because that I am a good writer is the one thing I have consistently been told. Maybe it's symptomatic of a new low of self doubt—or maybe, of not knowing how to be a good writer at the new kind of writing I am trying to do.

My mom is coming this weekend for Easter. We will basically behave with her as we do with unvaccinated people: outdoors, masked or if not masked, distanced. Some seem to think the intimacy of family entails a right to infect one another—I see in family the obligation to protect one another.

Arranging this visit involved a frank conversation with my mom, about Micah's boundaries and his recently self-diagnosed neuro-diversity, and several with Micah, often ending in tears (mine). Plus a few cheery announcements to the kids. The weather looks okay. I did win an allowance around hugging. I fear another repetition of past interactions, painful for all, in which I see Micah retreat behind his wall and am unable to coax him out again. I hope that something new may be possible, equipped with new information and new emotional depths after the past year.

We arrived at this new label—neurodiverse—in a rush of conversation, research, and self-testing. It began when I read an article by an autistic woman about how much easier lockdown has been for her, socially. It was the author's description of preparing for travel, the way she pre-familiarizes herself with each step and stage, that reminded me of Micah. 'Caught my eye,' I wrote, and zipped it to him in an email, as we often do, with no intimation of the worms I was uncanning.

Isn't it odd, how unknowing can exist alongside knowing? I remember wondering, eight years ago in Oregon, if Micah was on the spectrum. Then as now, we were very isolated, outsiders in a small town of long-rooted insiders. Then as now, the isolation bothered me much more than it did Micah. I remember I brought up the possibility of autism with a fellow Occupier who'd come to visit us there. He dismissed it on the grounds that Micah makes eye contact and so on—a 'masking' habit, I now know, that a well-meaning teacher explicitly taught him in third grade. I mentioned my hypothesis to Micah, too. But he's worked so hard to distinguish himself from his brother, an even more isolated individual, that the idea was never allowed to enter the realm of the possible.

As for me, I feel like one big bruise, which is perhaps a sign itself that the pandemic is nearing the end, or that something is, anyway. Because just when you can't take it anymore, something changes. Right? That is what you told me about parenting, and that's what Rumi says somewhere, and I would like right now to believe that you are both right.

I am hanging onto these things: abundant kid cuddles, and today there was sunshine. My parents are vaccinated and Micah's have had the first dose. Micah himself is very kind and committed and a good communicator.

And we are newly insulated from financial worries. Although, after so many years of rollercoasting precarity, we don't yet fully trust this good fortune. A couple of months ago, Micah wrote a blog post on a new cryptocurrency music project that captured his obsessive mind. When he talks about this passion, I can see these obscure coins, tokens, and NFTs as a new philosophical language, summoning a subterranean riparian world onto the surface of the earth. Anyway, the insiders read the piece, and an American billionaire I'd never heard of DM'd him on Twitter. A few weeks later, Micah had a new salaried gig advising this man on his crypto investments.

It sounds too improbable even to recount. Like I said, I don't think we *do* fully believe in it, yet. It's the sudden and unexpected flowering of a seed of interest planted right after the Occupy times. And remembering this almost-decade of so many changes.... Dimly, I perceive that this stroke of luck is a validation that is enabling him to grapple with other equally long simmering knowledges about himself.

Going to try to sleep now. Sorry this is so short and squishy and self-indulgent. I like to see the pictures of Mrinalini and her new friends. Reminds me that change is possible, that relief can come in unanticipated forms.

Love,
C

APRIL 4, 2021 | *EASTER SUNDAY*

Happy Easter, dearest C,

It's a momentous one for all of you with your mother visiting, and I hope you will write to me about it. Indeed, I am in a hurry to hear your thinking through all of this. The reunion. The resurrection. The return.

I'm very preoccupied with return, as you know; it was the primary subject of my dissertation, and now I teach a class called 'Literatures of Return'. On return as a literary trope, return as life, return as birth, return as death, ashes to ashes, return on investment. We read the literature of economic reverse migration, deportation, return from internment, return to see *how much older [your] parents look.* Return through the cliches of diaspora ('You can never go home again'). Eternal return. Barred return. The impossibility of return.

Now of course we're in this bizarre pandemic moment of the 'reopening' and provisional 'return to normal' and we knew, didn't we, that this would be the worst part.

I will be saying like a broken record until we finally leave here that I don't *want* to return to life in Tucson, because I don't want to be here in the first place. But: I know now why we were here, why we moved here. We moved here for the pandemic. My in-laws moved here to help us, to save us, to save themselves with and through the kids, to carry us and us them. But now, our work here is almost finished.

And yet (and now I'm quoting Nicholas Dames' reading of *Anniversaries* from his brilliant essay on being left behind in New York in March 2020), I am afraid I am this guy: 'He thinks he is biding his time, will be able to fit through the door again with wife and child before it closes for good, but what he cannot bring himself to acknowledge is that while you are waiting, the conditions to keep you in place are hardening.'

Mrinalini is at the neighborhood friend's house, the only friend she has. I will confess to you that after my initial excitement I have cooled to this child and her sister. The hardness I feel for Tucson has crept in, and I am confronted with the fact that I, well—you're not supposed to be cruel about other people's children. This child: she is lively and smart and precocious. But also manipulative, and not very nice to Shai; she can be mocking and harsh, angry even, and messy, and bossy, and her father lets her, age eight, ride in the front seat of his car and she walks without shoes up and down the street. The feral bits I don't mind and even like, actually, but the hint of two-facedness I cannot stand.

I want to ask my parents: what did you do when you

didn't like my friends? Were my loner years, above all else, a profound relief? ·

In this moment I am floored by how very difficult it is to raise children, how many decisions you have to make, how much homework to supervise, how many unsavory friends to tolerate, how much heartbreak.

It's in the 30s here now. The kids were in the pool today. I jumped in myself after a run, fully clothed, and it felt miraculous.

We are completely over our heads with work commitments and tired (and hot). I feel disconnected from most everyone and entirely unwilling to reconnect with them (because, well, why?). I am worried also that even if I manage to get out of Tucson, I will not be able to dig deep enough to find the energy to make new friends, to build the community that we need.

Meanwhile, my motivation is low. I am giving too much to my students and feeling self-righteous, virtuous, and irritated about it. Mrinalini has finally outgrown the clothes she has been wearing for the last eighteen months. Finally, she has gained some weight, and she needs new stuff. So I'm cleaning out drawers and shopping for cheap shorts. It's summer now. A cruel summer, with a vengeance.

It was so much easier when we didn't have to have anything to look forward to. Now I realize that was one of the true gifts of the pandemic: the foreclosure of the future. We couldn't think about the future; we didn't have to. And now, we must.

There is more, but I feel my engine sputtering a bit. Sunstroke? The heat? I was waiting for it, C, and now it's here, and now I wonder what exactly I was waiting for.

All my love,
R

APRIL 13, 2021 | *WHAT TO WEAR TO A VACCINE APPOINTMENT?*

Hi, dear R,

As of yesterday, I have joined the 120 millions of fellow Americans with at least one shot of the vaccine. A sore arm, and—together with my growing determination to walk away from my academic job—a light heart.

It's spring, really spring, with mud giving way to newbright grass, gossipy daffodils, tall rays of forsythia. In this atmosphere how can one countenance the terrible news? The exponential growth of Covid worldwide, the current dark red hotspots in Brazil and Michigan and India and elsewhere. The pause of the one-and-done J&J shot, which represented the best hope for protecting poor and vulnerable populations here and abroad. From the telephone wire above, the cardinal and dove sing sweetly of unlikely possibilities, and I believe them.

The vaccination process itself I saw through the gaze of its dystopian filmmaker. Soldiers aiming at my forehead with a thermometer gun. Soldiers checking papers. Soldiers barking (but gently) to keep the line moving. Soldiers, also, swabbing the spaced metal folding chairs (a bit of hygiene theater that I for one welcomed, hoping it meant the powers-that-be had also considered a way to clean the air). A soldier guarding the entry, being told by a passing woman 'don't think this work matters less than what you did over there.' The woman reading the repetitive questionnaire to me, for the nth time, yet with care in her voice. The needle was administered, flawlessly, by a statuesque Melanie (could she have been trans, or is it just that I'm reading *Detransition, Baby,* to see what's all the hype).

I spent the fifteen minutes of mandatory observation time watching my fellow vaccinees (is that a word?). The most people I have been around for a year; fascinating! Even if all I could see were their sides and backs. What do you wear to a vaccine appointment? One older woman had opted for a sensible wool poncho thing that made it easy to access the arm; must have been her second dose, I decided. A young woman had rolled up in a floral velvet jumpsuit. Double masks were prevalent. Micah had brought goggles but in the end didn't want people to stare. Afterwards I did no work. Today, too, I can't really work on my article that is overdue. I have the week off from one of my classes, as my students collaborate on a syllabus for the last six sessions. And, on the horizon of more freedom, I am experiencing that thing an advisor told me once about sabbatical: that she spent the first part of it just becoming human again. I threw away holey and mismatched socks and, like you, ordered cheap shorts for the kids. I read a book about the Rwandan genocide, which unearthed hot memories of my short visit there, and sharpened the revolting feeling of how quickly the world can split open and reveal a face you denied was there.

I should tell you a little about my mom's Easter visit. About how numb I felt where I thought I'd feel pain and joy. How the children didn't move to hug her, but gathered close on the picnic blanket to hear her read new books. How the ninety minutes when she took them to the playground felt like it returned me to a new level of myself. How after she left there was a different current of energy among all of us: the small reality that we share, expanded by one set of eyes, body, heart.

And I should tell you how I've baby-stepped myself toward the decision not to renew my postdoc. Just a few weeks ago, I was psyching myself up for the career woman role, an administrative job at the center. Logistics, international travel, busyness, the satisfaction of being competent and useful. Stability, meaningful work and a boss. *Lean in!*

Then came some negotiations around the expectation that I would start the work now, for free. I was annoyed at that, and stubborn. But I'm glad now for that exchange, because it helped make it clear to me that I don't want any part of the job.

Despite liking my students, I have been miserable since the semester began, not really knowing why. I blamed Micah and the lack of childcare, even though I knew childcare would just come with its own set of worries and unhappinesses (remember the fights we used to have, rushing the kids out the door on time?!). Slowly it's starting to sink in that Micah's new job—he's a couple of massive-seeming paychecks, now, into his work consulting on crypto projects—means I don't need to earn an income. And as I realized that his growth and evolution demand mine...as I realized that all the problems that block what I want can be addressed...as I realized I don't have to become Virginia Woolf for me to justify devoting myself to my word-tinkery...I've become happier and happier and happier.

When I first started considering the idea, I didn't imagine that I would have the courage to do it. I'm too old for such leaps, I thought. Too practical. Too set in my ways.

But maybe it is not so much a leap as a *return*—to borrow your word. My happiness is its own proof-of-concept, returns its own strength to me.

So I've drafted an email to my boss. I won't send it just yet, because quitting always changes the relationship—and because I *have* been known to change my mind. So for now it is just my happy secret hatching plan, and yours.

Off for my childcare shift.

Love love love,
C

APRIL 19, 2021 | *THE LODHI CLUSTER*

Ah, C, well, what to say.

We've been ricocheting back and forth these last few weeks, you and me and ours. The mood keeps shifting dramatically; the tone has not been stable. How could it be? Or, maybe that is not right. Maybe, if I were to reread our last half dozen letters, I would find that it's all been building steadily, with a purpose and consistent beat, the steady onward march of homogenous empty time.

But I don't think so. I think it's all been dizzying and boomeranging and surreal: this bizarre extended period of Covid-anniversary, so-called-pandemic-exit-times, and wildly accelerating global crisis.

The news this morning: My mother who is in Delhi with her brother and mother, and who had two shots of the Pfizer vaccine before leaving for India, just tested positive for Covid after five–six days of being sick with a cold, fever, and stomach flu symptoms. My uncle and grandmother, age eighty-five, are also sick, and have just been tested, and we expect positive results. They've both had the Covishield/AstraZeneca vaccine.

Two-plus hours of WhatsApps and calls are ongoing. The entire extended family is involved, since it's a cluster now, in my uncle's house, where there are also vulnerable staff with children, parents, and extended family all living together in the compound. Have any of them been vaccinated? I'm not sure. My cousin just sent over a study saying that the AstraZeneca vaccine was 79 per cent effective at preventing symptomatic Covid and 100 per cent effective at preventing severe disease and hospital admission. Hopeful statistics as far as my family is concerned, and totally depressing, given how few people have gotten the damn vaccine.

It's impossible to keep the timeline straight, or the probable sources of the virus, as they've all had many exposures. When my mother landed up a couple weeks ago (I am losing track of the days, but I know she flew to Kerala after arriving in India, and then back to Delhi) various members of my uncle's household were already sick.

India is now experiencing, in April 2021, the crisis we all feared would happen last year. In Brazil some months ago it was 'gurneys in the gift shop'. Today, in India, there's no space even in the cremation ghats on the banks where the bodies would burn, if they could. (From *Reuters:* 'Gas and firewood furnaces at a crematorium in the western Indian state of Gujarat have been running so long without a break during the Covid-19 pandemic that metal parts have begun to melt.') There is no oxygen, and there are no beds in the hospitals. The variant known as the Maharashtra double mutant (which is also now in the UK, US, and elsewhere) is proving to be more contagious and virulent and, clearly, capable of vaccine escape.

Ay, it's not over. It's not over; it's not over; it's not over. Maybe, it never will be. We already knew this. I knew. You knew. I didn't want to know.

What to do, how to do it, how to raise our children? There is so much work ahead, and I feel inadequate to it. I long for April 2020. Today, the global numbers and infection rates are worse than they have ever been. Three million dead and (under-) counting. Surges in the US, too, on the East Coast especially. A group of my women colleagues are gathering on Wednesday morning for coffee and cake, attempting to herald the after-times. They are all double vaccinated, and I suppose I'll go for an hour. I don't think the Maharashtra double mutant is here yet, and most of these women don't have children. Arizona numbers are relatively low.

But it won't last. This feeling of relative safety: it's a mirage.

Am I worried about my mother? I just texted a friend who is planning to travel to India soon and I gave her the news of my mom's Covid diagnosis post vaccine. She called immediately, sensing that I would be stressed. And I am, I suppose, sort of, but it's a numb sort of stress, the fatalistic kind. I hesitated before picking up my phone this morning, knowing that my mum would have gotten her results.

Ninety-five per cent effective, they said.

Somehow, I had the foresight to plan an asynchronous class

today. I am not in the mood to teach. It is warm here, my arm is hot in the sun, and I'm back on the summer porch where I wrote to you last year, where I did all the writing that felt like a gift in the early months of the pandemic—and was, and is.

Are we still in the early months? Will we allow ourselves to be?

I am doing things that I wouldn't have done some months ago: I got my eyebrows threaded (the salon owner is not vaccinated, I was displeased to learn), I have been going in person to the grocery store, and buying half of what I would have bought before. In the early days, I would leave Sprouts with two carts full to the brim with weeks' worth of sundries (the guy behind me in line buying nothing but a loaf of bread would stare in stupefaction).

I went into a Target once, to buy water toys before a playdate last weekend, with our immunologist friend and his family (Mrinalini had such incredible, raucous, earsplitting-smile-levels of fun with their sons in the pool). And we have booked tickets to fly to Maine at the end of June.

I have started reissuing warnings to my brother and his fiancée about their end-July wedding plans in South Africa. The global picture is dire. There is no reason for optimism, not even of the will. Feeling heavy, and it's not just allergies. I probably should spend less time dreaming about leaving Tucson and double down on figuring out how to survive here. How can we refortify ourselves for the months ahead, and what can we do to bring others along with us?

You said it a long time ago. We'll be writing for some time yet.

With love,
R

APRIL 25, 2021 | *A HUG IN A LETTER*

Oh, dear R.

I want to send you a hug in a letter. How to open my arms wide enough to span the different realities, the ones each of us is 'in', the ones in each of us?

You opened your last similarly trying to get your bearings, I think, wondering whether there was any pattern to the ricocheting of moods over the past weeks. You closed on a grim note, 'There is no reason for optimism.' Just the week before, trying to lighten my own grimness, I closed with thanks for pictures of Mrinalini and her new friend: 'Reminds me that change is possible.' Before that, you wrote that you weren't sure where or when you were, or even what you wanted to drink. The week before that, early March, I remember as my low: 'I cannot stop peering into the dark chasms.'

The attempt to find a pattern leaves me feeling that it is impossible to contain all this reality. The crematoriums cannot burn up all the bodies; we cannot vaporize the image of them. Death overflows. Meanwhile we go to work, we feed our children and hug them and summon smiles for them and apply bandaids. Meanwhile we feed on their insatiable growth and receive their easy smiles and gather hugs from them and apply bandaids. Meanwhile, our credulence of horror is stretched again and again past its previous boundary. Will we become infinitely elastic and yielding, or be stretched until we snap?

Because the boundaries of reality/horror keep shifting (and will continue shifting), we are never sure 'when or where we are,' what we want to drink or ought to do. Uncertainty floods in and rises.

Well, all that is not a hug. It is, at best, the first step towards a hug by trying, impossibly, intellectually, to span where we are. I am thinking daily about your mom and grandmom and uncle with a part of my heart once known as prayer. That place in my heart tells me they will be okay. It also tells me of the many, in India and everywhere, who will not be, and how each death stitches all us survivors closer together.

I am able to let in some degree of this painful reality right now only because I have taken a vacation from it. I'm writing from a luxe vacation rental in the Poconos, with a hot tub and sauna and plenty of space—which someone else cleaned. Kids toys and a Nespresso machine and tea sampler packs and paper plates. Clean air and young stands of maple and alder, still bare, and a small lake with tennis courts and tiny playground. The house sits in a gated community, in a county which had only a few cases a day in summer, and a rate still a third of what it is in my county.

Most of all, I wasn't prepared for how much the kids would love the hot tub. They splashed around its perimeter naked and full of glee, making up chants and stories about water ninjas and volcanoes, and I, naked too, grinned until I ached as I sat in the tub with them and held out my arms and let my shoulders get sunburnt. If I could, I'd pour that joy into amber. It might need to last us awhile.

It is the first time we have spent the night away from home since January 2020. It is the first vacation we have taken as a foursome, just us four for ourselves, not for work or grandparents or some other obligation. The first that has not been stunted by silent, fearful accounting of pennies. It's strange and wonderful, a parallel privileged reality in which people own their own kayaks and do not skitter away from each other when they pass on the pier. The biggest dramas here are that no one wants to go on walks with me, and the neighborhood cat bit Areté. In the quiet, in the empty space, in the artificial hot tub heat, some small part of the year's excess burns away.

We are here to celebrate: Micah's new job, and my decision made. I handed in my letter of resignation to Bard. It feels good not to spend energy on the decision anymore.

Now the task is to write, and to repeat to myself, 'I can do this,' until I believe it or until it comes true or until I die—whichever comes first.

Love,
C

MAY 2, 2021 | *HOPE FOR WHAT?*

C,

Did I tell you I bought button covers for all my jeans? Covers for all the offending buttons that cut into my shirts, that created the constellation of holes that remind me how often these days I am standing at the sink doing dishes. But I can't get rid of the holes, you see, and so now I'm wearing ripped shirts over jeans with button-covers.

Too little too late, in other words.

Here's a recap. On Thursday, April 22, India recorded the highest one-day tally of new coronavirus cases in the pandemic to date. On Friday, it broke its own record. On Saturday, it broke its own record. And on. And on. We're well above 400,000 cases per day now, and it's a monster-undercount. In Delhi, the case count has been doubling every five days. Some are predicting a mid-May peak when India will likely record close to a million cases a day. Or more. Unofficially it's almost certainly already there. In Kolkata, where my mother grew up, positivity is something like 50 per cent. There are literally dead bodies in the bottoms of the auto-rickshaws and propped up between motorcycle riders.

Delhi has been for a couple weeks now the worst-hit city in the worst-hit country in the world. The city is 'a pyre'. Hospitals are out of oxygen; there are no beds in the ICUs; metal furnaces are cremating so many bodies that the metal itself is melting. The epidemic curves circulating online—curves that last year we in the United States talked about 'flattening'—indicate such unchecked exponential growth that the curve is essentially a vertical asymptote on its way to infinity. Observers are calling it a 'wall'.

It's systemic collapse. Arundhati Roy has called it 'a crime against humanity'. I am back in March 2020, glued to the news, reading versions of the same article again and again and again, clicking on aerial photos of graveyards and sari shops that have been turned into micro factories for the stitching of PPE, watching videos of last breaths taken in the backs of full ambulances in packed parking lots of overcrowded field hospitals. I am donating to whatever humanitarian funds I can, not sure my little contributions will go toward anything but administrative overhead.

I'm not tweeting about what's happening in India's second wave, because I don't have a public persona nor do I want one. But also, I am newly resigned to having not put myself in a position (in life, in the world) to be of any use in this kind of a situation. In other words, I didn't spend the last decade and a half of my adult life becoming a decision maker or a person of consequence at scale. I am just teaching my students (last week of classes next week, praise!). At best, if I allow myself to wax romantic about it, I am empowering them to think about the world, migration, identity, politics, literature. I might even be teaching them how to read. At worst, well, I taught my students *something* this semester. I have given them as much as I can for now, and it will have to be enough.

My mom got back from India in time for my father's birthday today. Surprise, surprise, nobody asked her a damn thing at the airport in San Francisco. No screening, no testing, no nothing. She got her negative test a few days ago. She's been so fortunate, I told her. Even her Covid was right on time, on a schedule that worked with her existing travel plans. I was partially joking, but also not. My uncle is still testing positive, and I think he's very fatigued. He was hospitalized last weekend with a dangerously low pulse of forty, which was for him about a thirty point drop. My grandmother is testing negative, but she's fatigued and feverish. Two members of my uncle's staff are positive. All of them so far are ok. As for long-term consequences, who can say.

It's not over.

Have you read Mohsin Hamid's *The Reluctant Fundamentalist*? It features frequently on syllabi as an exemplary global Anglophone 9/11 novel and I teach it in my Asian American literature classes, too. Anyway, the turning point in the book comes when the main character, Changez, a Pakistani-born Princeton graduate and management consultant who is in Manila on work, watches the Twin Towers fall and inadvertently smiles. He is seeing the American empire brought to its knees, and reflexively, he smiles. And then of course reality sets in, and he spends the rest of the book negotiating the painful new contexts of his interpellation as a Muslim in the United States.

I say all that in order to confess this: frankly, I preferred it when the US was on its knees, sustaining half a million casualties, and there was a dream/fantasy of cross-reactive immunity in the global South. I preferred it when the story of this moment was the end of America.

It was devastating, don't get me wrong, and yes, I realize that this empire is my sinking ship (I am nobody if not an American— well, I am nobody). But this current story is intolerable: vaccine apartheid, India's spectacular collapse and the rest of South Asia not far behind, South America in shambles while we're at it (though the American news media cares little), fears about what will happen if the new variants that have swamped India gain a footing in continental Africa....

Meanwhile, in the US, obnoxious, unforgivable debates about whether or not to magnanimously extend our humanitarian assistance (never mind break the vaccine patents, should we ship over our unused AstraZeneca stock?).... This is an overfamiliar, excruciating story that I don't care to read.

Also, I fully expect a fourth surge in the US, or maybe just dispersed fourth surges (already ongoing in Michigan and Oregon) because we are an impatient, undisciplined, and ignorant people.

I thought the reopening phase would be hard, the hardest of the pandemic, but I sense keenly now how much worse this coming year is going to be. Because now the US has declared mission accomplished, the schools are going to be open, the mask mandates dropped, and this year we will truly experience what it means to be on our own.

Thin and tepid fellow-feeling though it was, with its impoverished vision of collectivity, I am nevertheless nostalgic for the shared stakes we had in 2020.

The other stuff: 32°C+ here again, and this time looking to stick. My mother is booked to come for ten days in mid-May for the children's birthdays. My brother's fiancée is refusing to budge about the July wedding. I have issued a long series of warnings about the likelihood that my brother will have zero guests at the wedding if they proceed. We are expecting new surges and travel bans; the global picture will not improve in the next few months. You can imagine all the things I've said (very diplomatically!). I sense that my brother feels stuck and his fiancée feels stuck and there's all this stuckness, but also time is moving forward inexorably.

Will things get unstuck, or will we all just fall off a cliff?

My selfish hope: that my kids will be in school and camp in June. After that, who knows. Mrinalini's school is already dropping outdoor mask mandates, and I am not hopeful about what the new school year will bring. Hope. 'Hope is a lapse in concentration.' That's a line from a Manu Joseph novel. I said it to my mom the other day, and she thought I was making a joke. I wasn't though, not really.

Joan Didion was asked in a recent interview, 'Do you have hope?'

Her answer, peak 2021: 'Hope for what? Not particularly, no.'

Love,

R

MAY 8, 2021 | *WHAT THEY CALL FREEDOM*

Dear R,

I want to send you a shirt. Because those are the holes, that is the damage, that I can make whole.

You write of the loss of even the diminished form of collectivity of the first spring. Yes. From here, the global pandemic has become Othered again. 'It's over there, those poor poor countries, with their inadequate infrastructure. Tsk tsk, someone really must do something.'

I am amazed how quickly we (especially Americans, but possibly humans in general) forget. When it was blowing up in Italy, many people still didn't believe it was or would come here. And now that it is blowing up in India, and elsewhere, many people do not believe it will return. Such is the strength of faith in the vaccine—and the weakness of human memory.

Indeed, from where I am, I can easily see a general attitude taking hold in the near future: that we were/are wrong to be so cautious. *Coronavirus, it's just one of the risks of being alive, like you take every time you drive in a car.*

Are they perhaps right? With not much more effort, I can see in, ten or twenty years, people looking back on *that* attitude with horrified sympathy. *It was a symptom of adaptation to long-term trauma; mass death and shorter, sicker lives were simply accepted as the norm. It was the subjective attitude needed to shore up the economic reality.*

You also write of your acceptance of your own small part

in events. You felt, at that moment, resigned to having not devoted your adulthood to becoming someone who is useful or makes decisions of consequence 'at scale'. Hmmm. It's almost as though you're tempting me to give a screed on the value of literature, dearest, or of the significance of that butterfly landing in Jakarta just now. Acceptance is healthy and mature, but I worry your resignation was a mask for a detachment from or devaluing of your own vibrant, precious living. I was glancing back through our letters, you know, and it's not an exaggeration to say that your life has saved mine.

Because the worst side effect of the constant, wearing deaths (two *per minute* in India, I read) is that ordinary life *is* being devalued. Did you hear this anecdote? An aide was asked why President Biden was still wearing a mask at some outdoor event, after having announced new guidelines from the CDC that vaccinated persons need no longer do so. 'Well, he is the president, after all,' the aide replied. The implication was, to my ear, that *his* life is so precious—he makes decisions 'at scale'—that it is worth defending against every opportunity the virus might have to attack it.

His life has not been devalued. But the rest of us, and especially the rest of us *over there*—we're supposed to accept whatever probability value our respective governments choose to impose on the conditions of our lives. *Some X of the population will die or get Long Covid, let's keep it low enough that people don't revolt (or so high that they also can't revolt).*

This they call freedom? Freedom would be equal risk, equal right to decide, equal gains. Freedom would be revising rather than reinscribing the norms of gendered labor on this 'unprecedented time'. Instead the government prints money as a sop to blind us to their wicked, reckless injustice.

'We are on our own.' Yes to this, with respect to making our decisions of our life's worth independently from public health driven statistical estimates. And no to this, with respect to the other people of the world. If the cycles of surge come fast enough, if the case counts are high enough, maybe enough humans will be able to remember that we are a *we*.

Or maybe, it is time to countenance the reports that aliens are real!

In any case. Local conditions: I had my second dose on Monday. You've finished classes. I have a couple weeks to go. I think I feel strangely about it—it being my last class maybe for a while, maybe ever. But it's hard to tell because everything feels so strange. Haven't told my students that I've quit but I've started to think about how I will. I spent most of my week signing up Zia for some individual swim lessons and an outdoor masked camp and possibly tennis and he's very excited about it all. The summer camp still seems abhorrently expensive, but then I remember we can afford it now.

I'm trying to read Daniel Kahneman's famous *Thinking Fast and Slow*. I wish someone else would've already digested how his insights about the faulty nature of human intuition and faux-statistical reasoning apply in the time of coronavirus. This sentence of his I want to keep at the top of my mind forever: 'We are prone to overestimate how much we understand about the world and to underestimate the role of chance in events.'

It's strange, heading into our second summer. We are already thinking about renting an RV and driving somewhere sunny for part of next winter. Maybe to you?

Love you so much,
C

MAY 15, 2021 | *FUCK THE CDC*

Hi dearest C,

A lot has happened since you wrote: my mom's arrival; Mrinalini's eighth birthday; a colleague and her son came over on Wednesday; Mrinalini's neighborhood friends came over on Friday; our immunologist friend's family visited yesterday; in an hour, we have pool time with the poets and their little daughter who are moving to Colorado; later today, another friend of Mrinalini's, and possibly her parents; then dinner with my in-laws. Later this week, my father's arrival, then my brother's, more social engagements, Shai's third birthday.

All this socializing is because we're not ready for parties, but I wanted Mrinalini to have some friends over for her birthday. It helps a ton having a pool. We've got a kind of routine now: people come over and hang out poolside during the 3–6 p.m. pre-dinner window, I serve cocktails and snacks, the kids swim and play with water toys and build castles on the little fake beach, and everyone leaves before mealtime. It's getting easier, having people over, and when it's all vaccinated adults, it doesn't feel too dangerous either.

But in the middle of it all, Brandon is really struggling with his pain and frustrated with his lack of progress in physical therapy. I'm impatient. How many times do I have to tell him that his PT is not working? He was so happy to go back to it after getting the vax, but clearly it's not the answer to the problem of his persistent hip pain, his lower back pain, and how long it takes him to heal. 'Muscle weakness,' he keeps telling me—he has to correct 'muscle weakness' having to do with his arthritis—it makes no sense! I have learned over the years to ignore his various aches, though I know it's unkind of me to tune them out. Still, he's had these problems ever since I met him in 2003; he's always icing and using those rolling massagers on the floor, working out knots in his muscles with a tennis ball. Nothing fixes it.

My in-laws are getting ready to leave, in about ten days, for Maine. My brother's wedding in South Africa is still technically on the books. I have not booked our tickets. There is very little good news as far as the world picture is concerned.

Meanwhile, in the US, well. Fuck the CDC. They have been shit every step of the way, and this latest nonsensical premature edict on masks—'Anyone who is fully vaccinated can participate in indoor and outdoor activities, large or small, without wearing a mask or physical distancing'—is precisely what I meant a couple weeks ago when I said *we're all on our own*, going to be irrevocably on our own, even more on our own. Move to 'the honor system'? Really? So dumb and so dangerous. The big retailers like Costco and Walmart have dropped their mask mandates already. We're bracing for the airlines to do it, which will be infuriating. We're still booked to fly cross-country on June 28. Must invest in some really good masks for everyone. For myself, thinking double masking instead of N95s, which are too big for my face. But, anyway, there's time yet to plan all of that. For now, just raging against the CDC and the short-sightedness of this decision. Or, even worse, the sheer, grotesque calculatedness.

I've been enjoying these pool parties, C, but I'm not optimistic about the fall. And I was going to say more about us, about the summer heat, about the Indian variant and immune escape, about the likely next surge here, but, well, it feels not quite right for me to be worrying about these hypotheticals when India is still burning, when Gaza is being brutally shelled by Israel, when the news is full of stories of beautiful people, young and old, being sacrificed for, well, what? My small enjoyments unfold in the midst of so much brutality.

Reading you also makes me want to think more carefully and critically about freedom. What it means. How much it is worth. To what extent and when do I personally feel free? To what extent and how might I contribute to the freedom of others? What is the relationship between the pursuit of freedom for the self and one's responsibilities to others? Last night before bed, I had this image of being free of—well, I'm not sure what exactly—I had this vision of constructing a life around the pursuit of freedom, and it was electrifying, even in its absolute vagueness.

What else? My mother has been a wonderful guest. She always appreciates the food and my house; against all odds, she consistently deems me a stellar homemaker and mother. Isn't that strange? It feels strange. But as someone who spent so many years being a mother and homemaker (and really owning those labels, making them into identities), she has a lot of thoughts on both, and she always makes a point of celebrating and championing my own efforts in both areas. And so, I am taking a little extra pride this week in keeping the house organized, and in planning the meals.

Are you really going to rent an RV and drive out west?

Has Zia started any of his in-real-life activities? And what about for Areté?

Are you still enjoying those Friday playdates?

Are your classes winding down as you would want?

All the questions.

And big love,
R

MAY 22, 2021 | *SOCIAL CALENDAR EXPLOSION*

Dearest R,

This was the week my social calendar exploded.

It was the week people began to say to me, 'I'm just now realizing how hard it was,' as though 'it' is definitively over, after just one year.

It was the week I taught my last class at Bard.

Three farewell gatherings, two it's-been-too-long reunions. All outdoors, mostly masked. Back and forth over the bridge to Bard twice a day, listening to audiobook stories with the kids and Deepak Chopra meditations by myself. 'Today I will trust the unknown.' On the other side of the bridge, the Bard side, the parents of young children are still mostly masking up outdoors. On this side.... Not so much. And for how long?

I don't know if I can trust in the local lull or whether (most likely) the gods have fresh horrors in store for the cold months. As you say, it seems like an unnecessary question to ask, between the social frenzy and the global madness. Here we are, and now we are, and the horrors have taught us, possibly, something about this gift.

I find myself preoccupied instead, largely, with learning about Micah's place on the spectrum. His 'social allergies', as he sometimes calls them, are even more pronounced at this cusp of the return to normal. Indeed, when I come home from a social engagement he stands well away from me, arms wrapped around himself. He hesitates to touch me even after I have washed my hands. It would be offensive or hurtful if I let it, if I didn't know, through my paranormal pandemic-sharpened empathy, what he is feeling. It goes beyond germ-phobia. It is as if he can sense that the flowers in my field-of-being have been cross-pollinated with flowers belonging to other fields. For him the resulting explosion of pollen is almost repulsive.

ND (neurodivergent), HFA (high-functioning autistic), what used to be called Asperger's—in this case, the labels have allowed me to love him more. It has allowed me to see him better, feel more compassion, to stay calm when he goes on one of his rants. My parents' casual racism and annoying paternalism is real. So is their love. And so is his 'mind blindness', as it's called in the autism literature—his inability to weigh their love and intentions in his moral calculus. The situation still feels painful and probably irresolvable. But I have increased my capacity to hold conflicting truths without feeling crazy.

As for freedom...I am reading Maggie Nelson's *On Freedom* and I'm here to say that it's real. That, surely, is one thing the pandemic has taught us: that what we thought was normal and unquestionable is completely and totally contingent. We are free to imagine and create new paths, not just choose from the existing menu. That's what I mourn, that's what I fear about the return to normal: that it will also mean the papering over of that knowledge of freedom.

I'll tell you a secret. Early on, I somehow began to believe the absurd idea that the pandemic couldn't end until I had done the thing I was afraid to do—until I grasped my freedom to write, to be more than what academia makes of me. Now that I have done that, I'm also here to say, the fear of freedom (Sartre's 'bad faith') doesn't go away. It doesn't—unless I am actively working on the writing. Writing fiction is the most reliable serotonin enhancer I have ever discovered, because even if it is shitty, I enjoy the hell out of writing it.

How are you, who are you, R, in the new social world? Do you find yourself noticing that your expressions are unmasked, so to speak? Do you feel like the interactions are like some kind of drug, or like eating carbs after a fast? Something like this has been my experience.... And just when I had perfected, I thought, my ability to convey a smile only with my eyes.

All the love,
C

JUNE 1, 2021 | *REHEARSING RETURN*

Dearest C,

Let me start with today, which is where I suppose I'll also end up. June 1. The second pandemic summer is in full swing. 38°C in Tucson.

Last night Shai wanted to watch home videos from our first pandemic summer. We started with the music video I made for my in-laws before their departure for Maine, set to the King's song, 'You'll Be Back' from *Hamilton*. The kids looked so young. Brandon's pandemic hair was shorter, only chin-length, not inches down his back like it is now (I've always had a thing for men with long hair—was teased about this constantly in school—and now I've refashioned my nerdy husband into a cross between Tommy Haas in the early 2000s and Karl Ove Knausgaard at his shaggiest—success!). Mrinalini didn't have any of her adult teeth grown in yet, and Shai's curls hadn't yet come in.

It was an innocent time. We were still empowering ourselves to give up the old world, not clamoring like fools to get it back.

I'm sitting out on the summer patio now, on the couch where I wrote to you so many times last year, which feels like many years ago. Today, Brandon dropped Shai to school and Mrinalini to camp. It's the first time both of them have been away for the day somewhere other than my in-laws' place. Shai's school, which has thus far kept him healthy and safe, announced to Brandon at drop off that Shai will nap with ten other kids now, in another classroom. They have also dropped their temperature checks and wellness screenings, because—well, why exactly? I called the director to register my objections this morning and I had to remind her that the children are still not vaccinated, that the adults are feeling stupidly liberated and shouldn't—because, again, what has changed for the better? Anything? Thirty-six per cent vaccinated in a red state like Arizona and the number hasn't budged in days, maybe even weeks. I told her we have recently had three cases of vaccine-escape in my close family alone. I told her that I would like to be able to keep my kid in the damn school.

It all feels a bit futile. I am hoping for the best, but you know I don't do hope well, so my hoping for the best is closer to being resigned to the worst. We've had a lot of social engagements in the last couple of weeks—the routine with friends in the backyard, the pool and snacks and so on—but also one dinner with a vaccinated, childless couple who are themselves very generous about hosting, and so, I thought they'd be the first I'd call. That was new. No masks, indoors, and we fed them a meal. The kids were delighted to have new folks to show around the house and perform for. The grilled fish turned out ok, and the mojitos, and the vegan mint chocolate mousse. They overstayed, as childless people do (when the kids go to sleep, you leave! Doesn't everyone know this?), but overall it felt fine to have them over, not that risky, and like a thing from the before-times.

Which is not to say I want to do all that much more of it. (*I'm just not sure I want to.* Etcetera.) I suppose you could say we're 'rehearsing return'. Enacting a practice run, just in case.

And then there's the slow moving train wreck: the wedding in South Africa, the light at the end of the tunnel that is the freight train coming our way. Almost everyone else in the extended family has dropped out. My aunt and cousins in England are not coming because of the UK red zone; another cousin is not coming because of his US-visa reentry situation; two more are not coming because of babies to be born in July and November. My uncle won't come and my grandmother can't come unless he brings her. So now it's just my parents who have booked tickets, and I have pledged to go, but I am angry because all of these folks in the family were acting like they would come and working against me when Brandon and I put up our protest first in February, and then again in March and more recently in April.

Yesterday my mother woke up and asked my brother and his fiancée to postpone the wedding. Ha! Too little, too late, I said cruelly. We're all irritated with each other. How many times can one say 'I told you so?' (On this note, I've been wondering what you and Micah make of the recent brouhaha over the lab leak story.)

Everyone wants Mrinalini and Shai to attend the wedding, but I don't want to take them. It would be deeply irrational to take them. The pediatrician looked horrified when I mentioned at their recent well-check that this was even in the universe of possibility.

Anyway, plans are being made; reunions are in the offing. We are booked to fly out to Maine on June 28. It will be our first pandemic plane trip, hopefully not with too many anti-vaxxers and anti-maskers. Because of the South Africa mess, we booked only one way and have yet to figure out how long we'll be there, and what happens on the other side.

Meanwhile, bizarrely, my extended family that typically over-communicates and is generally over-involved is not actually all that much in touch anymore. In a way, I think what's happening with our family around my brother's wedding seems to be accelerating a process that would have happened anyway: everyone is fracturing, reentering the world (or not) at different paces, exiting the Zoom room for anywhere else, and leaving traces of our pandemic-produced closeness behind in the process.

There are so many people I haven't talked to at all during the pandemic who I was previously on and off in touch with and now I think we can never speak again.

There are some people I talked to more than ever during the pandemic who suddenly I haven't heard from in a month or two and now I think we will never speak again.

There are people I know we will meet on the other side of this and it will be as if the pandemic never happened.

I guess we're all just trying to figure out who we're going to be to each other.

Three and a half hours until I have to pick up the kids. Is this what they call a work day? Yeah, ok.

Tell me everything, please.

Yours,
R

JUNE 8, 2021 | *CAVE SYNDROME*

Dear R,

I am writing you in the dark of the night, by hand on the yellow legal pad I use for most of my scribblings. Not an unusual practice for me. I often wake at night and can only go back to sleep once I've discharged some consciousness in ink. If I can't sleep, I must write; and if I can't write, I must sleep.

It's summer here. Hot, Zia's online school has ended, travel plans simmering. Looking into private options for fall, since Governor Cuomo has already said public schools need not require masks indoors in the fall. Despite the increase in severe cases among the eighteen and under, despite the variants, despite everything. Learning what we already knew, again; everyone 'on their own' as official policy, and the least risk for the wealthiest.

People who are reluctant to return to social life are pathologized with 'cave syndrome'. What is the name for this sick and persistent collective delusion that the pandemic is over? 'cave syndrome' might as well refer to those who refuse to look outside the borders of this country. The World Health Organization has repeatedly said year two of the pandemic will be far deadlier than the first. America's arrogance is to believe those deaths will happen somewhere else.

Oh, I'm tired, too, of my own pessimism, I need to relax and celebrate too, I need to seize this small measure of ease, too. I guess it is a question of living locally without losing that global feeling, living in the present without neglecting the future. Locally, we're settling quickly into an outdoor sitter-share routine several mornings a week. It's not enough childcare, not by a long shot, but it's good for us and good for the kids, too. I don't mind wearing a mask for a few hours; I even like the privacy, the plausible deniability it affords. In a world that demands the labor of emotional expression from its female bodied half, I appreciate the break from the need to perform and emote.

(The cat sleeping in my office chair while I write you from my reading chair—resting is so effortless for him!)

The summer season begins in earnest this weekend, when my parents (negative PCR tests in hand) arrive for a couple nights. They'll stay at a vacation rental in walking distance 'uptown', which is downtown. We'll do some light hiking and creek-dipping. Micah will opt out or take breaks as his 'social battery' gets depleted.

Learning about autism in adults has become one of his 'special interests', to weird and sometimes exhausting effect. On the one hand, I'm grateful that he's embracing self-knowledge and growth, even if the direction of his growth is, 'I'm not willing or able to mask (as neurotypical) anymore, I just want to find out what makes me more comfortable.' So far that has included things like sunglasses to help with his light-sensitivity and sound blockers to help with noise-sensitivity. I'm hopeful that more knowledge can ease the relations all around. I feel lucky to live in a time where that knowledge is more abundant. And I happily credit autism for traits in him that I love: his capacity to stand apart from the crowd, his detailed observations and deep research, his sheer fucking brilliance. It is what makes him so good at his work in crypto: he's not caught up in the emotional waves that sweep people into the scam-du-jour.

On the other hand...

On the other hand, there's a new awkwardness in our relationship when one or the other of us recognizes an aspect of his 'condition' in real time. There's grief and mourning for all the things that will never be a part of our life together— spontaneity, couple friends, all the foreclosed possibilities of adventure and connection. There's fierce anger, as I learn about Cassandra syndrome, the loss of self-esteem and self-identity that plagues partners of people with Asperger's. There's plain old regret, that—having said for literally at least seven years that Micah was on the spectrum—I never delved into it enough to learn all the things we are learning now. There's the painful revisiting of old memories in a new light, all the fights, all the moments we almost broke up. There's doubt, of my own desire and ability to stretch, *again*, the borders of my self to accommodate his.

On the one hand, nothing has changed about Micah's character, except our understanding of it. On the other hand, understanding—re-learning—turns out to be almost everything.

And hope? That thing you say you are not good at, but which we cannot really live without? Whatever happens, I guess I can hope that I will turn out to be stronger for it. That, having learned to live without his emotional validation, I can also learn to create it for myself. That I might end up with the neurodivergent's strength of character along with the neurotypical's capacity for connection.

Really I have to laugh. To think I wrote my dissertation on difference and dis-ease! That I chose to meld the deepest layer of my heart with someone so painfully, irreconcilably different from me, from wiring to race to life experience.... Is there actually something wrong with *me*?

Grateful, I guess, again, to the pandemic, for giving me new unanswerable questions to live.

The first birds are chirping. It's time for me to try to head back to sleep.

All the love,
C

SECOND SUMMER: FOREVER

Hello, dear friend,

Dear friend, from my life, I write to you in your life.
That's the name of a book I haven't read. Isn't it funny how things like that come to us—things we don't know, haven't heard, don't own, can't remember—they're still there just under the surface, waiting to be unearthed. I've read another book by Yiyun Li, *Where Reasons End,* which is an imagined conversation between a mother and her recently deceased son. Li's own son died by suicide, but the book is fiction, not a memoir. Then again, what is fiction? In what ways is life a resource for fiction? What is memoir, if not the product of the fiction that life can be narrativized, ordered, made into story?

I didn't plan to write to you about Li. But those words— *dear friend*—they brought her to me.

Less than two weeks since I last wrote to you, but as always, worlds in between. I'll give you the mundane first. Mrinalini has settled into camp and seems to be enjoying all the various activities: archery, gymnastics, dance, art, ball sports, swimming. She doesn't tell us much about her days. But she's happy to go, and she's managing the gluten-free lunches I'm sending from home. I spend well over an hour each morning packing their bento boxes with little brie bites and cut strawberries and perfect circles of cucumber and monkfruit brownies (for Mrinalini) and vanilla-yogurt-raisins (for Shai), and it's exhausting and time-intensive, but I think we'll get through it.

Surprise surprise, having been moved to the larger nap room, Shai got a cold and we had to keep him home. Now he's on something of a food strike, finding watermelon and peaches 'too sweet' and refusing even to eat the jelly beans that I brought him as an afternoon treat. Covid and ruined taste? It's not outside the realm of possibility. But he's otherwise full of beans, energetic, and nobody else is sick, so I assume it's just willful little kid stuff.

It's sobering though, because I know that if I am genuinely concerned about Shai getting Covid from preschool, where all the teachers are fully vaccinated with mRNA vaccines, and he has only four other kids in his class, how am I supposed to take my unvaccinated kids to South Africa, where the third wave has begun in earnest and less than 3 per cent of the population is vaccinated, and of the vaccinated guests (60 per cent of the total, by my sister-in-law's count) many are only partially vaccinated and all the guests coming from India received AstraZeneca, which our immunologist friend calls a 'worthless' vaccine?

My thoughts on this subject have been shifting dramatically each day; we are living in a state of constant low-grade tension and decision fatigue. A week or so ago, I provisionally decided that I would take my whole family to the wedding. It felt worse contemplating not taking them. I didn't want to go alone. I couldn't imagine leaving Brandon behind in Maine to fly back to Arizona with Mrinalini and Shai, without me. I couldn't imagine being in Johannesburg by myself.

But then, as always, we read more, and the numbers kept going up, and the positivity rate, too. In particular, I've been following news of the Delta variant (the artist formerly known as the Maharashtra double mutant) and how much more virulent it is, how much more risky for children. The days of what our newly minted Pulitzer-winner Ed Yong calls 'vanilla COVID' are over; the days of the variants are here.

It began to feel profoundly absurd to even contemplate

taking the kids. Still, in an act of further self-flagellation, I decided that we would talk to my brother's in-laws directly, and ask about their planned Covid precautions. They, after all, are on the ground and making the preparations. I wanted to give them the benefit of the doubt, to do my homework before making the call (such a masochist and martyr I am—the combination of Catholic school and graduate school?). I heard many reassuring things from them: that all sixty guests would be masked, that they would wear red light/green light stickers to indicate openness to interacting with other guests, that the pre-wedding events will all be outdoors, that the guests from East London are driving the twelve hours to Johannesburg instead of flying.

But I also heard what they didn't say: that we don't know when the third wave will peak; that we don't know how much Delta is responsible; that many of the vaccinated guests are not fully vaccinated; that time is running out for the remaining guests who might 'get the jab' by the end of June to be fully vaccinated by end of July; that a lot of what they were describing to me as precautionary measures is what we would call 'hygiene theater'.

When I was pregnant, I didn't drink alcohol, not even one glass of wine. Not because I thought one glass of wine was going to do any harm. I'm confident, in fact, that it would have been fine. But I didn't drink. Because: why would I drink? Why take that risk, when there are so many other things you can't control?

I've been thinking of something Micah said at the beginning of the pandemic. I agreed with him then; I think we all did. He said it's better not to get Covid now. If we have to get it, better we get it in the second wave, or the third, or the fourth, or a couple years in, or five. Let's survive as long as we can without getting it. (Clarice Lispector's words: Let's not die as a dare.) It made sense then to imagine the treatments getting better (they have) and having greater knowledge of the virus (we do).

But: the variants. We didn't realize then—or at least, I didn't—that it would become far more dangerous for the unvaccinated (i.e., our children) to get Covid *now* than it ever was before. That the virus, what Timothy Morton calls this 'hyper-object' that is already *in* us, would only tighten its grip.

Yesterday, I booked my own ticket to Johannesburg, but I haven't told my parents or brother. I booked it in such a way that we could still all four of us choose to go. But I booked it knowing that it would push us in the direction of my going alone.

Then, we had friends over for dinner, a colleague of mine and her husband. I've texted occasionally with her this year, but would hardly call it being in touch. They are exactly the kind of people I was thinking about when I said there will be some people we meet again who weren't part of our pandemic life, and we'll just pick up casually as if nothing has changed. 'Time is meaningless,' she said in response to my 'Wow, it's been so long!'-type opening banter. They were warm and friendly, and generous about the food and the kids (who really do love having people over). They left right when we made moves to put the children to bed.

Neither Brandon nor I slept well after though. Shai didn't either; he woke up many times. And Mrinalini had a meltdown this morning when I told her the music on her headphones was dangerously loud. So, it's another mixed Sunday in pandemic times.

I'm grateful for you, as always, and for this.

Yours,
R

JUNE 19, 2021 | *WHY TAKE THAT RISK?*

Dear R,

Writing to you this morning from my parents' house in Arlington, Virginia, where I lived for short stints between the years in Egypt and Turkey (fifth and sixth grade), and another short stint between Turkey and college (eleventh and twelfth grade). I am here to see my sister and my nephew, who turns four tomorrow, freshly arrived from Jordan. I almost did not come.

The house, a far nicer version of our Kingston brick colonial, smells of Irish Spring soap and mothballs. It is lined with hardback books and ceramic plates and brass lamps and wooden figurines and inked calligraphy and curved conch shells and deep red wool rugs from the other places we lived. There are no cats or small children to smudge, smash, or shred these carefully selected, carefully placed items.

The house looks and smells different to me now, yet certain memories return every time, and return every time perhaps a little differently. Sneaking out this window at night to visit a boyfriend. Examining my thighs in this mirror inside the closet door. Drawing up a 1,000 calorie/day diet at this kitchen counter. Then 700, then 500. Making myself vomit in this toilet of the small *en suite* of my room. This was the adolescence that was prescribed for me in the magazines. Except for: the reading, reading, reading. I binged on books, but was anorexic about writing. I forbade it to myself, being not good enough.

But those are the same old memories I always touch on, because they are legible, because they have been made legible by those same magazines and books where I read them, because they've been encoded into a story I tell myself about myself, a self wild and restricted, seeking freedom yet falling into cultural traps. What if I dug deeper, to write a different past, for our daughters? 'I don't want to have children. I want to meet them. My child,' writes the writer-narrator in Mieko Kawakami's

Breasts and Eggs. To meet them, a different future past.

My roundabout way of replying to your perceptive questions about writing and living, perhaps.

Anyway, here I am, encountering an old past I haven't yet filtered through the pandemic present, and wondering if I will regret this trip in the future. Micah was strongly against my coming. I put it like that, as though it was a perspective he expressed in the course of a conversation in which I also aired my opinion and we worked it out, but it was not like that. To his black-and-white way of thinking, he *could not conceive* of anyone thinking it was okay to come.

I understand his reasoning: the CDC guidelines stipulate a seven-day isolation for anyone coming from abroad, vaxxed or not (my sister and brother-in-law both got Pfizer in Jordan, my nephew obviously is too little). And my nephew threw up on the plane Thursday, which can be one way the Delta variant presents (as you doubtless know), though he seemed fine when he woke up Friday morning. For Micah, visiting people just off the plane one of whom had some kind of illness is sort of like you and the not-drinking wine during your pregnancy: why take that risk?

Why take that risk? I think the risk is low. The positivity rate in Jordan now is about 2 per cent. The mRNA vaccines are still quite good against Delta; and we will lower the risk of transmission further by staying outside. If I have to go inside with them, I will be masked and it will be ventilated.

But mainly, I really wanted to come. I needed it. I was crying at the playground to my friend when, under his pressure, I had canceled my car reservation and didn't know if I could get another one. And also: I really did *not* want to spend Father's Day with him, after the ugly and condescending way he spoke to me. 'I just don't have anything for you,' I told him, sort of desperately trying to convey how utterly drained I am.

Am I being as selfish and reckless as he thinks? This one

time, this one drink, this one dose of giving myself what I want—
will it get me or my kids sick? Will it irreparably damage my
marriage? Will I die of something mundane like a car accident
on the long solo drive back? I don't know, of course. In this
moment I am glad to be here.

Dear friend, you had an eventful week yourself. (I have read
and not read those same books by Yiyun Li!) I'm glad all the tests
came back negative. I wonder how you are feeling about flying,
about South Africa, today. Tell me everything from your life.

Love,
C

JUNE 25, 2021 | *IS THIS THE TRUCK?*

Good morning, dear C,

Where to begin? I need a cup of coffee to make it through
this one. It's hot water for me now (very Asian, I know), a habit
I started when I was pregnant with Mrinalini. Two glasses of hot
water, a mug or two of coffee, then a banana and homemade-
yogurt smoothie. A humble liquid diet for a few hours. I haven't
deviated from this routine in months.

Of course this whole month has been a deviation from
routine, from the pandemic life we had established with my
in-laws as base and structure. Now that we're approaching the
end of June I can see the whole thing clearly: the four weeks
that were in front of us (and which are now behind us).

Oh, it didn't work out very well, not as well as we'd hoped.
I wanted us to prove to ourselves that we could go back to
something like 'our life' without being dependent on my in-laws,
but that long working Saturday especially that we used to get
from them...now I can say without a doubt it's what saved us
this year. And Tuesdays/Thursdays they would keep the kids
until close to six. Those extra three hours at the end of the

day will have made the difference, I suspect, if we get out of Tucson or get tenure, whichever comes first.

(How did you do without those hours? How are you still standing?)

The plan for June was four weeks of childcare for both children: Shai supposedly at school from 8.30–3; and Mrinalini at camp from 9–4. The first week was a four-day week anyway, and Mrinalini had a rough time adjusting. The second week, Shai was home with a cold. By the end of week two, he'd brought home a stomach virus (and gave it to the rest of us) and then we learned he had been exposed to Covid. We all had to get tested (three rapid tests at CVS, one PCR at CVS, and two PCRs at the university), and then he was home anyway for a week. Now it's Friday of week four, and this week we sent him for the mornings only (8.30–12) for four days. By the time we get through dropping him, it's basically time to pick him up.

'Four weeks of childcare.'

I'm moving Shai to another school in August. It's not just a matter of safety (though this remains the most serious consideration): the reason to send him to the school where he's been intermittently this year was that he had only four other kids in his class. That won't be the case in August, and so it's time to move on. I visited a new preschool, met the charismatic and cautious director, and despite the fact that they are scrambling to get set up on half of the deserted campus of a bleak-looking Tucson elementary school, I felt that I could invest some hope in them, and so we have.

I decided in consultation with my in-laws that Brandon and I will fly to South Africa for the wedding without the kids, leaving them in Maine, and I found a camp for Mrinalini for half the days we will be gone, to help them out.

After making these decisions (oh, how difficult it was to change the bloody tickets! Meanwhile, my parents' tickets to South Africa got cancelled! A cautionary tale about intercontinental travel in a global pandemic), a lightbulb went off in my head that we are not going to have the stomach to send Mrinalini back to her school in-person in August. There are 800 children in a small, differently bleak building and 32 kids in her class. And to quote the refrain that is building, here and elsewhere: 'This is the most dangerous moment to be unvaccinated.' All the pundits are saying it. They're saying it to shame the unvaccinated, of course, not because they care about vaccine apartheid globally or the inequitable distribution of vaccines in the US. And they never talk about the children who are not yet eligible to be vaccinated. Ghouls.

So this week has been about researching private schools and having long phone consultations with admissions directors. It's like when we moved to Tucson: we flew here on a Thursday, saw twenty-two houses, and bought one on Saturday. A punishing amount of research in a condensed amount of time. Can't say it's not efficient.

But all of this has been incredibly emotionally draining. Two major, contradictory imperatives undergird these moves I'm making to enroll the children in new schools. The first has to do with not wanting to go back to the way things were. I want to move house/city/job. Since I can't do that, at least there's this.

The second imperative is different. It feels like we have no choice but to move toward a different, better community here in Tucson. There's a big part of me that doesn't want to do it though, doesn't want to find new institutions and people to which and to whom we will have to connect. Not here.

For her part, when I asked Mrinalini how she feels about switching schools, she lit up. Yes, she said. Sure. Let's go.

Which tells me everything I need to know. Coming out of virtual school, I want her to be safer, I want her to have friends, a community, fifteen kids in her class, not thirty-two. I guess we're going to have to pay for it. We didn't want to send her to private school. But maybe this will end up helping us out.

Maybe we will not want to keep the private school going for too long and that will be another reason to get out of Tucson in a year or two?

This place is unlivable. Since I last wrote, we had a heat wave that broke many records. It was between 43-46°C every day for a week. Maybe I don't have seasonal affective disorder, but *solastalgia*: eco-anxiety, emotional or existential distress caused by environmental change.

Anyway, I realized one day recently while swimming (praise the lifesaving pool, bathwater-warm though it is now) that June was not just a single month that we had to survive before we travel to Maine and South Africa in July. June is August, September, October, November, and December (and only then will my in-laws be back from Maine). All of those months will be June, plus both Brandon and I will be teaching in person on campus.

Arizona governor Doug Ducey is tying the university's hands. No masking, no testing, no vaccination requirement on campus allowed. All prohibited. The university, desperate to fulfil its pledge to consumer-families, daily sends out threatening notes to faculty. Yesterday, the Provost said anyone wanting to teach remotely will have to get approval from her office.

Meanwhile, in India, the bodies are continuing to wash up on the riverbeds. In South Africa, the third wave is surging past the level of the first and soon will pass the second. Organizing our 'wedding outfits' yesterday night after the kids had gone to sleep, Brandon observed that the joke is going to be on us. With my parents' plane tickets canceled, my UK family unable to travel because of the red zone, and various of my sister-in-law's family unable to get visas in India, it'll be just the two of us there at the wedding, in the end. Ha!

And I spent months deciding whether or not to take the children. Unbelievable. You were right that I should have just said *no* on day one. I don't think my family would have heard me, and it would have been a different kind of torture. I did say no, in the end, but I nearly killed myself doing it.

The acute phase of the pandemic is over. The chronic phase has begun.

One last thing before I go to pack lunches: an image from this article that hit me (no pun intended—you'll see). It's by a woman who suffered a traumatic brain injury after a car accident. Her whole family was injured, but she has the lasting damage. She writes this:

> When we return to New York I take the subway to doctor appointments. I don't take out my phone, I just sit. My brain is quiet, which I find suspicious, but also soothing. Before the accident I went to yoga retreats and tried meditation. I said things like 'I just need to unplug.' Apparently what I needed was to get hit by a truck.

> Is this the truck?
> All the questions to you.

> And all the love,
> R

JULY 2, 2021 | *REUNION WITHOUT UNION*

Dear R,

Catching at some stray thought in the night again. You are in Maine, now, under the same longitudinal swath of stars as me, and perhaps with some measure of peace with the heat and the flight a world away. Though the South Africa situation is worsening by the minute (a second India, one headline you sent said)—perhaps they will have to call the whole thing off?

Here too we did the exhausting private school scramble. Just this week we found out that our school of choice has a spot in kindergarten for Zia, and a couple of days in the nursery for Areté. It's the best news we've had in a long time.

The school is small, progressive, Covid-cautious, lots of outdoor space, not far away. Governor Cuomo is not in the same league of supervillain as your Ducey, but even he has said schools can abandon indoor masking this fall! Thus the public schools will not be funded or prepared for the Delta-plus variant or its successors that are already making their ominous presence felt. I don't feel guilty about our 'privilege'. I feel angry that there is not the basic decency to provide this kind of safe and nurturing environment to every child.

But also, I am thrilled. I strongly suspect I will like the friends they make there and the parents of those friends. I have this vision for them, going off into their independent worlds and coming home to a loving listening lap and arms, having missed them, wondering at and enjoying who they have become in our time apart. I have a vision for my life in the fall, too, spacious enough for writing and slow reading and walks and yoga and more conversation with friends and perhaps even real political/community engagement. Imagine: the idea that I would have enough time that I would have some to give back! These visions are getting me through these summer months of still inadequate childcare and constantly shifting schedules.

Delta threatens these visions—almost, I fear another winter cramped up alone together more than actually getting Covid—almost—but I am learning patience. Feels as though the media are picking up the drumbeat of anxiety again. So at least that gives me the comfort of not being alone.

The visions—hope?—are new this week, a corner turned after a rather miserable trip to Arlington that I still haven't wholly processed. My nephew developed more symptoms while I was there, and I was anxious, despite his (unreliable) negative antigen test. It made it hard to have a good time, and my sister was frustrated and angry with me. It felt—how can I say this? Like a gulf between us. A reunion without union. I suspect she may be early stage pregnant (she wasn't drinking, looked heavy, had bought a strange balloony yellow dress), and was definitely jetlagged, and hot, and with some anxiety of her own about her son being sick. So I decided to overlook various unkind things that she said.

Then I arrived home after the long solo drive, and Micah didn't want to hug me out of fear of contamination.

It wasn't until the middle of this week that all that hurt, anger and anxiety expended themselves.

Despite all the feelings, I was glad to have the time to myself, glad to have found out that the Covid anxiety is indeed mine and not just Micah's, and am looking forward to next week's family trip to Virginia. I hope my sister will be in a better mood and that the kids and I will have a good time. I don't think that's a reasonable hope for Micah, but we have our own place, so at least he will have a place to escape.

And onwards we go. Despite the truck, onwards. And on, and on, and on. I took the kids to swim lessons this week and we all loved it. I did a successful interview for *The Philosopher*. I was relieved to finish a draft of a piece about Plato's cave that cites only women and brown people and worked through a problem that felt real to me. Writing stories longhand on yellow pads in the morning—no one could be more amazed than me at what comes out, at the simple fact that it comes out, one sentence linking to the next, and the next, and the next, until they find their own end. I have been upset about various things, but never about this: I am getting to know my muse and how to keep her happy.

Miss you more, dearest, knowing you are almost within reach. Tell me about your adventures.

Love,
C

JULY 9, 2021 | *CRUEL OPTIMISM*

Good morning, dear C,

Almost two weeks since we arrived in Maine. It's been gray and cold for the most part, and rainy, but the woods make up for it, the humidity, the greens. And we have had one or two sunny days. We've been out on the boat, in the canoe, in the kayak; I jumped in the lake more than once. We went tubing. For a few warm days, I swam, mustering courage in the face of the wilds, the fish, the seaweeds and grasses, the rocks and muck, the sunken boats and trap doors, and Ursula's cadaverous polyps, that I imagined were reaching up and grabbing for my legs.

It has been impossible to get anything done here. We've had a steady succession of house guests. Brandon went to Chicago for the week. I'm doing a lot of cooking, cleaning, and childcare. My in-laws do a lot, but there is much more to be done than they can do. I knew it would be like this before we arrived. I feel a kind of equanimity, a sense of my own depths and reserves, maybe like the lake.

Meanwhile, as we've been here, South Africa Covid numbers have continued to climb. It's possible they 'peaked' a couple days ago—too early to tell. On July 11, President Cyril Ramaphosa is expected to extend the level-four lockdown for at least another two weeks. In which case, my brother's wedding may be postponed by one day. A gamble. I will have to change my tickets and lose more money. We will have to go.

Equanimity, reserve, calm, resignation, acceptance, a healthy dose of numbness to go with.

I am working on yet another music video. The first, 'You'll Be Back', was for my in-laws' departure to Maine last September. The second, 'Wocket in my Pocket', was to mark my parents' and brother's visit to Tucson in fall 2020. The third, 'Here Comes the Whatsapper', was for my uncle's birthday in March

2021—it doubled as a finale for our year of extended-family birthday Zooms.

This new video is set to 'Call Me Maybe', redone with lyrics that tell the tragicomic story of my brother and his fiancée.

> Hey, I just met you, and this is crazy / But here's my number, so call me maybe / Coronavirus can't stop us baby / But here's my number, so call me maybe.
>
> And all the other flights got canceled baby / But here's my number, so call me maybe.
>
> We'll stop in Egypt for quarantinis / But here's my number, so call me maybe.

You get the idea. I have managed to get extended family on three continents to contribute little clips of themselves dancing with phones in hand. If we have to go, if there's something like a wedding reception, Brandon and I will be my brother's only backup dancers. Thus, the video.

Letter, interrupted: a call from Brandon, who returns from Chicago this afternoon. A visit from Mrinalini and Brandon's aunt, who drove in this afternoon from Rhode Island. *Oh, you're working,* they said. I'm sitting with my laptop up on the bed I've been sharing with Mrinalini. We're about to get turfed out of this room when both my brother-in-laws and their wives and multiple pets show up, but until now we've had lots of space, and I've enjoyed having my daughter and her hot breath in the bed next to me.

'Oh, you're working.'

It's pouring on the lake. Storms all over the East Coast—reports of tree damage in your area, too—and a heat dome back on the West Coast, 54–55°C predicted in Death Valley. All the fish and mollusks are literally boiling to death in the Pacific Northwest. The Tokyo Olympics will have no spectators. Delta is now dominant in the States. Nobody masks in Maine. Nobody, apparently, is masking in Chicago. The only people masking in Arizona are the vaccinated.

In the beginning we were reckoning with privilege, remember? Lately I've been thinking about luck. Brandon and I often joke that we are really unlucky: unlucky about the small things, if protected in the big ones. All my flights are always canceled or delayed. The one kid in Pima County who had Covid in June was in Shai's preschool class. The one time we had to go on a trip during the pandemic it was to Newport Beach when there were gurneys in the LA hospital gift shops. My mom went to India right on time for the Delta surge. The one and only time in a year and a half, maybe two years, that we ate inside a restaurant—for our tenth wedding anniversary on July 2, 2021, a dinner-gift from my mother-in-law—I got seafood poisoning from what I'm guessing was a bad clam, and I came home and puked my guts out.

One more: the one month in 2014 that we didn't have health insurance for Mrinalini between Brandon's postdocs in Princeton and Chicago was the month that she got Kawasaki disease and went into shock and almost died and landed in the PICU for two weeks. (My father-in-law started calling her 'million dollar baby' after that, though the ultimate cost was 'only' a quarter million...we didn't pay, because the saints at the Institute for Advanced Study received Brandon's panicked call from the hospital and actually rehired him on paper so that he was eligible for one more month of insurance. It's grotesque what you need in a country without universal health care: privilege.)

Getting lucky is never my plan.

Actually I think that's what optimism is: the assumption, the willed delusion, the fantasy that you're going to get lucky, that you're going to keep getting lucky, that history is on your side, that fortune is smiling on you, on us. Yeah, right. 'Cruel optimism.' Lauren Berlant died last week and the internet is full of tributes to their work. Ironic, because part of what is so obvious in this moment is how many people refuse to hear, to learn, what Berlant had been trying to tell us, about cathecting to objects that are obstacles to both our flourishing and that of others.

Luck. Crass casualty. Those purblind Doomsters. Hap.

There's more to say, but I hear steps and thuds and am bracing for what almost always follows: Shai's bumped head, his cries.

You are traveling today. All trips now are big trips.

Go safely, dear ones.

Yours,
R

JULY 16, 2021 | *VACATION IS EXHAUSTING*

Dear R,

We head back to Kingston tomorrow after a week away. From time to time over the week I have noticed with surprise how unreal that place seems. How can a place that contained our lives, so compactly for so long, vanish so completely from my consciousness?

One self-serving theory is that the past year has taught me to live more fully in the present. Noticing Kingston's absence from my thoughts is actually me noticing how much I am present, here, on vacation, with my family, swimming in lakes and pools after a very long dry spell.

Less generously put, it may be the case that my mind is so fully engaged in processing the myriad stimuli—the heat, the water, the social soup—that there is little room for much else. Vacation (with kids) is exhausting!

We have written and will surely write again of the strangeness of these times. For once, it is space and place that feels strange. Passing through blue states into red. Separating spaces we would formerly have shared. Sharing space, sharing food, with people who think Covid is over. Not strangers, mind you—my mother! My own mother, a PhD in molecular biology who works for the National Cancer Institute, this morning told me Covid is over. This very morning, when cases are up in all fifty states. This morning, when 1,200 scientists say that England's unlocking is a threat to the world.

'It's *so* not over,' I told her, but the crux of our conversation was not Covid, but whether or not she really ought to be working on a Saturday, as she has all week, shutting us all out and conspicuously not offering any of the childcare we desperately need. In the end, after I told her what message her behavior was sending to me, I shrugged and let her off the hook. Her life, her priorities.

We had this conversation from the threshold of what they call the Great Room (I am sure it is capitalized in their minds) of their new, still sparsely furnished home on the Eastern Shore. I had never heard of this area—Maryland's more affordable version of Cape Cod, I guess. The house has a pool and an aged dock jutting into the 'creek', one of those tiny spidery blue fingers on the map that connect to the bay. My kids love the pool, my parents favor the water view out back. I'm personally partial to the small bog towards the front, where frogs reliably startle the mossy water and me.

We're here for a couple nights to break up the long drive back to Kingston. The previous five nights we spent in a rental house within biking distance to my brother-in-law's family house on Lake Anna, Virginia. The kids have spent every hot available minute in the water, in the sun, in the fresh air. They are beautifully brown now, and covered in scabs and bugbites, and Zia's hair curls tightly in the way that I love, a secret code that black people will sometimes let me know they have read. They laughed at their Uncle Matt's jokes and read books with their nana and swam with their pa, and generally behaved themselves beautifully, asking to be excused from the dinner table and such. Areté suffered the small children's cruelties and exclusions from her cousin ('You're not big enough for this game!') and enjoyed the compensatory pleasures of the attentions paid to the youngest.

The adult layers of social reality—the ones I remember sensing as a child but not being able to name—are not as easy to parse. Autism, racism, family time as small-talk social-feint training ground, emotions (resentment, jealousy, hurt, bewilderment, judgment, fear of judgment?) as the dangerous underground. So much effort was expended on a surface-image that doesn't correspond to what I, at least, want family time to mean. There were no real conversations about how we've changed in this year+. Nothing about how to plan or parent or think at all about the insanely accelerating climate change (today, the floods in Europe). No consideration of what we should learn from the fact that our governments have reversed their position on everything that matters, from the masks to the lab leak theory...

I tried to ask what people are reading (emails, news, contracts). No one asked me what I was writing—which is to say, no one asked about the activity and project that is most central to who I am.

My favorite moment was this: I was driving the four of us over to the lakehouse for dinner after our afternoon quiet time. Everyone was talking at once so I asked them to take turns, starting with Areté. She spontaneously broke into a singsong: 'Dad is so special to me, mom is so special to me, Zia is so special to me.' Then Zia joined in (a break from his usual Zelda chatter). In the front seats, our hearts puddled into pulsing goop, and every single annoyance and hardship melted into a beloved part of our life together. I said, 'You know guys, everything we do, we do so that when you're grown up and you have the choice, you actually want to spend time with us.'

Micah added, 'And so you'll still tell us your secrets.' And they promised that they would.

Wishing you many moments like that, on the almost-eve of your South Africa trip.... Tell me everything, dear one.

Love,
C

JULY 23, 2021 | *THE DEAN AT MIDNIGHT*

Hi dear C, from across the world and time-zones, from the Amberhall Guesthouse in Randburg, Johannesburg, in Gauteng Province, where we are on a level-four lockdown—or so I've heard!

It's 3.30 a.m. Only it's not 3.30, doesn't feel like 3.30. Is it 3.30?

Wednesday morning Brandon and I woke up at the lake house in Maine, having learned the night before that our flight to Newark was canceled in anticipation of 'weather'. When the predicted storm didn't turn up, we managed to get a puddle jumper out of Portland. Then, with six hours to spare, we hopped a cab to Brooklyn to meet my cousin's three-week-old daughter, played 'bus' with her big brother at the playground (oh, how I miss the parks and playgrounds of Hyde Park, yet another thing missing in antisocial Arizona!), joined them for an early Thai dinner, and got back to the airport just in time to board our original flight to Johannesburg.

There were not as many fools on board as I expected, and so Brandon and I each had an entire row to ourselves. After fifteen hours of reading and dozing (painful but not anywhere near as painful as it might have been), we arrived, were met by my brother and his fiancée and mum-in-law-to-be, shepherded to Amberhall, greeted by my parents and their friends (old friends who refused to *not* be invited, and have come anyway to support the family—bless them!) with wine and Chinese take-out, came back to our room around 1 p.m. to shower, unpack.

At 11.30 p.m. I Zoomed with my Dean about a letter Brandon and I wrote to university administrators last week expressing deep concerns about the college and university's Covid-mitigation plans. We made a series of recommendations and requests (that will not be met). We went to bed without dinner at 6.30 p.m. East Coast time and woke up at one in the morning.

A knock at the door. Brandon is back from a bachelor braai with my brother and his brothers-in-law. He got his eyebrows trimmed at the barbershop, as part of the bachelor outing. Don't ask. He's cackling somewhat wildly and predicting a holly jolly Covid-wedding. My parents are taking maskless pictures in front of statues in Pretoria. In a few hours, I will need to be dressed and ready to make nice at dinner. It's Friday afternoon.

I'm still thinking about my call with the Dean last night. He wanted to Zoom because the Provost has forbidden him from responding to our letter in writing. Apparently, if the administration is caught via public records request writing to faculty about vaccination, testing, or masking, the Arizona state legislature will accuse the university of politicizing Covid and then use *that* as pretext to further withhold funds.

Oh, it's bad, C, I don't even know where to begin. The *New York Times* Covid tracker is showing 170 per cent, 180 per cent—one day this week I swear it was 195 per cent—increases in the '14-day change'. Delta is surging. Pediatric cases are climbing. After denying and denying and denying that Delta is more virulent (they would only admit 'more transmissible'), pundits and scientists are finally starting to read the anecdotal evidence (which is, to be clear, *evidence*). The 'hard' scientific studies will follow. To adapt Teju Cole's words from another context, the danger of Delta has been 'a secret only because no one wants to know about it'. Indoor masking is a topic of debate again. Meanwhile, as you know, Governor Ducey in

Arizona has not only banned testing, masking, and vaccination mandates at the university level, but he's banned mask mandates in the K-12 schools and is going after quarantine requirements. I have been diligently filling out the admissions and enrollment paperwork for Mrinalini's and Shai's new schools. I have been scrutinizing the university's classroom layouts online, looking for windows and exits.

The Dean told me that nearly every student living in the dorms last year got Covid. That nobody died. That his hands are tied.

The 'Tokyo 2020' Olympics started today, with no spectators, multiple cases in the Village already, and various high-profile withdrawals. The Bootleg Fire rages. Hundreds of tons of dead fish in Florida are washing up with the red tide. Hundreds died in flash floods in Western Europe. India's current Covid toll is estimated at four million, and counting.

As you said a couple of days ago, 'that was a short summer.' Hot vax summer. Ha!

Scrolling through my phone right now, I can see the titles of the articles I texted Brandon this week, in a long thread consisting of screenshots and links: 'The Age of the Great Dying is Beginning'; 'FDA will attach warning of rare nerve syndrome to J&J'; 'Almost 25 per cent of COVID-19 Patients Develop Long-Lasting Symptoms'; 'Summer camps hit with COVID outbreaks—are schools next?'; 'Delta is Driving a Wedge Through Missouri'; 'In this summer of covid freedom, disease experts warn, "The world needs a reality check"'; 'It's time for the FDA to fully approve the mRNA Vaccines'; 'COVID-19's Effects on Kids are Even Stranger Than We Thought'; 'Coexisting with the Coronavirus'.

Brandon rarely responds to these texts, but I know he eventually reads the articles, and heeds them. Everyone else— my in-laws, my parents, the world—nobody wants to hear it. The collective appetite for thinking Covid is zero. At the grocery stores in Maine during these past three weeks, I have consistently been the only person wearing a mask. I experience these unmasked crowds as incredibly violent and aggressive, and it doesn't help that in Maine nearly everyone is white.

We're giddy with the ridiculousness and stress of it all. I couldn't tell the Dean that I was Zooming in from Johannesburg with a straight face and expect him to take my Covid concerns seriously (my mother-in-law's dressy rain jacket camouflaged my pajamas). We're going back to Arizona in a week and hoping that by some miracle the kids don't get Covid. The miracle would be pulling them out of school and going into lockdown. But we can't do that; we won't do that. Are there any other miracles to be had?

Hap. A few days before we left for South Africa, Mrinalini had a terrible fall, a terribly silly and unnecessary fall, while playing a game of 'restaurant'. She bashed her face on a dining bench in Brandon's parents' house and broke her nose. Racoon eyes now. A whole day spent in the ER. Every time I think about the fall—the sound of the impact, the way she howled and cried out that she couldn't see, the way she groaned on the way to the hospital, then fell eerily silent for the rest of the drive—I feel like I just had my own head bashed into the wall and my whole body aches.

And yet. And still. It was beautiful this morning, crisp and clear, when we stepped out of the Guesthouse. My brother is getting married and his in-laws are lovely and warm and already fond of him.

When we came back from the ER with Mrinalini fixed up, my father-in-law, who had driven us, was depressed and exhausted and spent. He put his head down on the table, and looked like he couldn't get up for a minute. Then he looked at me. *This is the good stuff,* he said, *even when it's bad.*

Isn't it though.

All the love,
R

JULY 28, 2021 | *COVID FOREVER*

Dear R,

You exert such gravity in my cosmos that your trip is tilting my own orbit, even as I stay in place.

Or it's the virus.

All I know is I feel quite strange. The news that is not news to you and me is hitting the mainstream in a big way.

The fact that (counter what they told us) vaccinated people can and do transmit the virus at an equal rate to unvaxxed.

The fact that 'fleeting transmission' is possible, and outdoor transmission is possible.

The fact that the CDC is now reversing its position, again, recommending the masks we should never have dropped.

The fact that Delta, scary as it is, isn't even as bad as it's likely to get.

Are we really going to send our kids to school in this, Micah and I ask each other, at night after we've given them their last kisses for the day. Maybe just until Thanksgiving?

I keep thinking about this: 'The horrible reality I don't think people have really got to grips with yet is this is a new, nasty disease, which is going to be here forever, probably. It's just an additional burden that all of us will just have to cope with.' That's Martin Hibbert, professor of emerging infectious diseases at the London School of Hygiene and Tropical Medicine.

Forever. Covid forever.

Dr Tedros actually has a good plan that no one is listening to, that would mean Covid free instead of Covid forever. Vaccinate the world, aiming for 10 per cent by September, 40 per cent by January, 70 per cent by spring 2022, wearing masks until we get there…no one will listen.

So, yes to school, whatever that looks like—masked, part time, outdoors, all of the above? Because I can't keep them home forever.

I'm glad we pivoted last year, and we're doing our best to keep reorienting to ongoing disaster. It might mean getting a puppy for my birthday. It means dreaming about land, and a passive house on it that can withstand the extreme temps, the fires, the floods. It means thinking about what I can do and write in the time I have.

It means trying to stay awake to what seems like a nightmare.

Over the past couple of weeks I inhaled Ted Chiang's marvelous collections of stories (*Stories from your Life and Mine, Exhalation*)—excellent concepts, excellent craft. In one of them, a sentient robot opens the back of his own skull, sees its workings, and comes to understand that he and his entire robot civilization are destined to run out of ether, their vital nutrient. When this becomes widely known, there are the sorts of reactions we see today. Denialism, miracle-ism, technological innovation-ism.

Chiang explains in his story notes how he learned from a physicist that 'we are consuming order and generating disorder; we live by increasing the disorder of the universe. It's only because the universe started in a highly ordered state that we are able to exist at all'.

In other words, humans are entropy machines. And so human civilizations end. They just do. It's not necessarily a moral failure (although in the case of ours, it seems to be). I remember thinking about collapse early in the pandemic, and telling myself I was exaggerating. I remember how the extremity of the crisis was mediated into the new horrible normal. In that sense, it's March yet again.

So again I write to understand, to accept, to preserve, to endure...to love you and this broken, breaking world. Chiang's stories celebrate the tiny miracle of free will, the tiny acts of kindness, how these become habits with a gravity of their own. How each ion and iota—the Greek *i*—counts.

Including the tiny bones in Mrinalini's poor fractured nose.

Miss you, I miss you, tell me everything, dear god I hope you are safe and healthy and sound.

Love,
C

AUGUST 5, 2021 | *BE CAREFUL WHAT YOU WISH FOR*

Dear C,

We're back in Tucson.

My brother's wedding was not a super-spreader.

I realized yesterday afternoon that my most serious and sustaining relationship might be with the pool. It literally holds me, transforms my body, skin, and hair (already I'm bronzer after three days back in the water, already my hair has that chlorine-coated thickness that masks how much I am losing with age). You know that feeling with little babies: how you could just *eat* them, their chubby feet especially? I could just *drown* in my pool. I think I wish it would swallow me.

Mrinalini starts at her new school on the 13th; Shai at his on the 9th. This whole week has been intake forms and assessments and noting down school holidays on the family calendar and signing up for new tuition management systems and ordering uniforms and masks. All the 'good' mask websites are overwhelmed; all the shipments backordered. Docile, tractable, I am checking these things off my list. But right under the surface is despair and resignation, an undercurrent of sheer terror. I don't actually want to send my kids back to school because even with the masks, even with the reasonable levels of vaccination in their particular school communities, I know that it's not enough, that it's only a matter of time. Please, fates, let them just get vaccinated before they get Covid.

The public schools went back today, and Tucson Unified had the stomach to defy the governor's order against mask mandates.

There's a bit of fight in our district! Meanwhile the university has been pathetically silent. I am teaching online this semester, again. I am dreading it. I feel sick thinking about it all. My throat is sore, sinuses hurt. Allergies? Covid? I've been tested twice this week and just signed up for another test because, well, I'm not sure why. By the time you test positive, it's too late, so why sign up? Brandon is constantly looking at me like I'm out of my mind, but I can see him spiraling, too.

Shai is on his way back from a doctor's appointment right now; he's been diagnosed with something called a spitz nevus which is a mole that looks like a melanoma (but probably isn't). To be sure, it has to be removed and tested, and they want to do it under sedation. Apparently the dermatologist started telling Brandon about the process for pediatric sedation, and he stopped her with a dark laugh: this is not my first rodeo, he said.

We've done it all with Mrinalini. General anesthesia, local anesthesia, for multiple scopes, for the nose procedure. She's had an MRI, MRA, CAT-scan, EEG, ECG, spinal tap, blood transfusion, fluid resuscitation, two rounds of intravenous immunoglobulin therapy (IVIG)…I don't know if you remember this part, but when she was in the PICU with Kawasaki Shock Syndrome, she didn't immediately respond as expected to the IVIG. Her doctor came to us worried that maybe she had lost too much oxygen when she went into shock and suffered brain damage. She hadn't, and I knew in my heart that she hadn't—but there was a moment before I knew, when I didn't yet know.

I don't know why I'm writing all this—maybe in an effort to contain it—but mostly it makes me want to scream.

I meant to tell you about my brother's wedding, but already it feels like a lifetime ago, another world. Were we really there, playing drinking games with the in-laws, telling childhood stories and breaking bread and toasting to the new extended family, planning for a trip together to India, warming our hands by the braai, drinking gin and tonics and doffing our masks after the first two have gone down, scrubbing lipstick out of those masks, pushing through the jet lag?

It was surreal and intense at the same time, especially watching my brother with his wife, who has taken 'his' name—especially watching their first dance to a song he sang and recorded in advance. How can I explain how moved I felt watching them, hearing his voice. I love my brother best through music, through his singing, through all the CDs he has burned for me over the years, through all our duets and shared lines. I felt that his dream of finding a life partner had come true. It felt like a beautiful, happy ending. But it was tinged, too, with the terror (yes, that word again) of beginning again in this world, now, here. There is nowhere else to go, to be. No way out but through.

My sister-in-law has left her family back in Johannesburg and is moving to the States. She can never un-move. She can never go home again.

I am so happy for them, C, truly I am. And I am so worried for them, for everyone, for all of us.

My cousin flew from New York to London last week and got Covid, possibly in transit, post-Pfizer. My mother's dear friend flew from California to New York yesterday and arrived to a positive PCR, also post-Pfizer.

Yesterday, we had brunch with a colleague of mine and his family. They spent last year in Vermont and will spend this year in Berkeley. They, like us, keep trying to get out of Tucson. They've been here since 2013 but have never found a community, never felt at home. What is it about this place? The underfunded and devastated public schools, maybe. The awful, isolating sprawl of a Sun Belt suburban city. The lack of playgrounds. The boomer-snowbirds who don't pay taxes, not even to refurbish a habitat at the zoo. The enervating, punishing heat.

Oh, and I wanted to tell you about the neighbor's children.

They are the friends I wanted for Mrinalini ('I have my first best friend!' she told me yesterday, with glee) and as soon as she got them, I realized I didn't really want them; I can't handle them in our space; I haven't been able to warm to them at all.

Be careful what you wish for, I've been telling myself this week. As I look up job postings to get out of Arizona. As the kids get ready to go back to school. Be careful what you wish for.

My love to you and yours. You feel close by, but I wonder where Zia and Areté are? It's been too long.

Always,
R

AUGUST 11, 2021 | *THE FLOODING OF ATLANTIS*

Dear R, dearest R,

You are right to be worried for all of us. I wish I could say you weren't. The other morning Micah and I had an exchange something like this:

—'Did you hear the news? The gulf stream water circuit is collapsing, another sign of the end of the world...'

—'Just get the kids into the car and to camp on time.'

The retort was mine and I wasn't proud of it. It's as if I (you, we) are stretched between two temporalities: the timeline of continuity (get the kids fed, get them to camp, get them to bed) and the timeline of collapse (living through the endless end of the world). And you (I) feel sometimes that you ought to stop all the activities in the timeline of normalcy and reproduction, to devote all your intellectual and material and emotional resources to coping with the unevenly distributed collapse that is past, present, and future. It is popular on social media, you've probably seen, to reference the idea that there are multiple timelines or possible realities, and we live in the worst one. We do; but no one can live in it all the time. Hence the various forms of numbing.

In the continuity timeline, we are having a fence built. It is an extravagance and a wonder to see it go up, board by board, by unstinting immigrant sweat, between me and my unvaccinated neighbor, erecting our own small refuge. I found a new book I love, Ben Okri's *The Freedom Artist*, a distillation so simple and rich that I almost don't mind the insomnia that's been dogging me. New York's Governor Cuomo resigned this week over a sexual harassment scandal, in the latest bit of political theater, and if I was surprised then, I now fully expect the Swamp to swell and disgorge more foulness. Zia's final day of camp is tomorrow, and then we have almost no plans and no childcare before school starts September 10.

The thought of the first day of school—the moment you are now in!—triggers my re-entry into the collapse timeline. This week the thought of catastrophe surrounded me like a pincer, on both personal and impersonal vectors.

On the personal side, this week my uncle, the infectious disease specialist in Boston, had some startling things to say to Micah. After a year of silence, Micah has started communicating with other advocates for stringent Covid-elimination, and this week on his substack he floated the idea of organizing Covid-free communities. In response, my uncle seemed to advocate for a benevolent dictator and the incarceration of the infected. In Massachusetts, where he lives, there are laws on the books about this for recalcitrant TB patients. Flaunting his connections to Anthony Fauci and Rochelle Walensky, he intimates that they haven't even told us the worst of it; that what we've seen so far is just 'the tip of the iceberg'. About that much, I believe him. All the CDC's actions bespeak a lack of faith in, and desire to manipulate, the American people. And this distrust of government reminds me of Okri, and reminds me of the places the timelines touch.

On the impersonal side, beside the gulf stream news and the stream of ominous Covid news (children's hospitals filling up, more about the prevalence of Long Covid in even asymptomatic cases), there is a new report out from the Global Sustainability Institute identifying the six nations most likely to be able to retain 'nodes of persistent complexity' in a time of 'global de-complexification'.

Translation: where might civilization persist during collapse? Over the next few decades, the 'de-complexification' is likely to proceed unevenly, in sudden spurts (tsunamis, earthquakes) in some places, and in a more leisurely way (famine, drought, pandemic) in others. It's been documented but still rarely admitted that the 'propensity for humans to destroy forests' (to borrow another phrase from the report) exacerbates the risk of pandemics, among its better known negative ecological effects.

Could they be wrong? It's happened before in human history—I think about Plato's myth of the flooding of Atlantis, possibly based on the disappearance of an important city called Helike in a combined earthquake/tsunami—but not at such scale. At some level I admit I don't know; at some level I wonder if our stories about collapse will be as unbelievable to some future ancestors as the stories of Poseidon or Apollo's anger are to us. It is the continual labor of creating continuity that makes possible the headspace to confront collapse. Or, in Walter Benjamin's formulation, 'that things go on is the catastrophe'.

What is the question I should be asking? What work is worth attempting? Loving the kids is (how to love the kids?), writing these letters is (how to write these letters?), that goes without saying—because that level of joy needs no further justification. But what else is really worth doing?

My unvaccinated neighbor, who lends me his ladder, who harbors conspiracist views about the virus, who is registered Republican, who rides a noisy motorcycle—in short, my neighbor with whom I disagree on many subjects—agrees with me about the importance of that question. He retired from the utility company about the same time I received my last check from Bard.

(Did I tell you they asked me to fill in for an elderly professor who's probably freaking out about Delta, on an adjunct basis? No thank you, I said quickly and politely.)

Anyway, I wish I could say that it is these existential questions that keep me up at night. I confess it is really a fixation on imagining and re-imagining the placement of my garden beds, an eventual patio, how to design an attractive, permacultural edible front yard. I will keep reading Okri, and keep reading you. Maybe in time, if there is time, on one of the timelines, these literary dialogues will elevate me beyond myself.

Love always,
C

AUGUST 19, 2021 | *WHERE'S THE LIE?*

Hi sweets,

What time is it? Meaning also: what timeline are you in? I hear your formulation of continuity and collapse, the constancy and rivalry of both. The impossibility of the present. The politics of the meantime. The unthinkability of the future (also: no future). The necessity of getting the kids in the car, with their shoes on; playing the same old games; keeping the dance party going; being enough for them, even when we aren't quite enough for ourselves.

Here are some things I said in my letter on August 5 that didn't turn out to be true:

My brother's wedding was not a super-spreader.

I am teaching online this semester, again...

My mother's dear friend flew from California to New York yesterday and arrived to a positive PCR, also post-Pfizer.

'I have my first best friend!' Mrinalini told me yesterday, with glee...

The day we flew out of South Africa, July 27, my sister-in-law's nephew was playing at the house of a cousin (who had been at the wedding), was exposed to a Covid-positive housekeeper (who got it from her other employer, who lied to her and concealed having the virus), and started a chain of transmission. The count now is appalling. My sister-in-law's mother, father, aunt, brother and his wife, their two kids, the cousin, cousin's wife, their kid...not to mention the maids and nannies and their children and their classmates and their teachers and their families and...whoever didn't get counted, but of course counts. Everyone is ok-ish, with the significant exception of an unvaccinated sister-in-law, who is in her early thirties and had to be rushed to the hospital yesterday because she has a history of blood clots and couldn't breathe ('Feels like breathing through a straw,' she said). From afar, I listen and don't know what to say. *There but for the grace of God I go*, and so on. A total mess.

I thought I was set to teach online when I wrote to you. Afterward, the Provost overturned my department's and college's decisions to let me back into the Zoom room. I spent an entire day on the phone and email with my Department Head, Associate Head, Dean, Associate Dean, HR, the Disability Resource Center, Faculty Senate, the Registrar, all of them. I fought (channeling a little Micah-versus-landlord energy). I wanted to effect some larger policy change, and send a message to the Provost about equity, but ultimately I could only save myself. I got to keep my class online on the basis of the fact that our Undergraduate Program Coordinator had already notified my class of the switch to the 'Live Online' format. Blessings on you, Undergraduate Program Coordinator, for jumping the gun and saving my skin.

(Truly saved me. A couple hours ago I opened an email from the Provost to all faculty with an invitation to a webinar with the offensive, noxious, patronizing title: 'Keep Calm and Carry On...' about creating 'a safe and equitable learning environment in classrooms'. It was followed by a university news alert saying that we've just admitted and welcomed to campus the largest first-year class in our history: 8,700 students. Our total student body is 46,932. Yeah, there's no vaccine mandate.)

My mom's friend was sent the wrong test results. A close call, remedied just in time for her to celebrate her 60th birthday with her children in New York.

Mrinalini's neighbor-friends: that's another story. I'm not sure what happened, exactly, but Brandon took them all to the park last weekend, and it ended badly in a fight between the kids and since then we haven't heard from them. Mrinalini is still talking about the girls, but asking for them less, trying to keep the relationship alive, but entirely on her own. Or maybe it's that the older child texted me on a Monday (I hate that! I would never let Mrinalini send direct texts to the parents of her friends) and I didn't reply until Thursday. Or maybe it's that Mrinalini has new friends now, at the new school. Maybe the neighbors have Covid.

Be careful what you wish for. I wanted them gone. Now there's just us to fill the void.

So all that stuff I said on August 5? It was true but it also wasn't quite true, not the whole truth. And this is also what we've been living through: the slow release of half-truths (by pundits, by the CDC), taking a year to acknowledge and make official what we already know, refusing to accept the now-truth of the stories, waiting for the too-late-truth of the peer review.

This is the most dangerous moment for our children. I've been saying it to Brandon for months, many months, since the CDC unmasking-debacle in May, since before the wretchedly short summer. Delta is more dangerous. Delta is more transmissible. The vaccines don't work the way people think they do. Something worse than Delta is coming. There are too many breakthrough cases for this to be explained by statistical probability. I (we) kept saying it and saying it. This is the most dangerous moment to be unvaccinated. No, it's not time for 'Stage 4: Normal Operations' at the university! Where's the lie?

Slowly, the story gets revised. A few weeks ago it was: 'Everyone is either going to get vaccinated or get the virus.' Now, it's turned into: 'Everyone is going to get the virus; better hope you're vaccinated.' Well, shucks. Guess who can't get vaccinated? And yes, I'm asking this from the vaccine-hoarding ground of the US of A, collapsing-and-taking-everyone-down-with-us empire, where adults are soon to be eligible for boosters, while, as of July 5, only 2 per cent of people on the continent of Africa have been vaccinated. Today, Afghan journalists, interpreters, translators, activists and artists watched US military planes leave them behind in Kabul. Where exactly does the US think it is going, leaving everyone else behind?

You're reading Plato and Ben Okri, high cultural stuff. I'm thinking about a moment in the silly yet satisfying apocalypse movie I watched on the airplane back from Johannesburg, *A Quiet Place*. There are these crazy sightless monsters about to kill everyone, and Emily Blunt is looking at John Krasinski in desperation—they've already seen one of their children eaten alive—and she says, 'Who are we if we can't protect them? We have to protect them.' Pure, delicious cliché. But that's what's in my head as I spend $350 at Best Buy to snag the air purifier you recommended and now I'm going to give it to Shai's school to use in his classroom. Maybe the other parents will want to join up, to raise funds to outfit the rest of the rooms.

Yet another thing, like the pricey masks, I'm buying to try to take control of a situation that I can't control. Maybe it'll be enough. Will it be enough? It can't hurt. It's better than nothing. If I do every single thing I possibly can, and if we take everything else out of our life except the schools, maybe....

Yes, I know it's called bargaining. Yes, it feels like flailing.

This week, I reviewed a book by a friend, J. Daniel Elam, on the politics of anticolonialism. It's one of many books these days that is trying to think about the impossibility of revolutionary change and the necessity of keeping going anyway. He writes, 'To think consequence and inconsequence together, to imagine a future and to imagine no future at once.... These are not paradoxical practices for people whose lives have been deemed irrelevant.' I am a so-called postcolonialist, finally learning the lessons of colonialism. Where's the lie?

Clock is ticking. Entering the school pick-up timeline.

Tell me the things, you haven't been telling me?

Love,
R

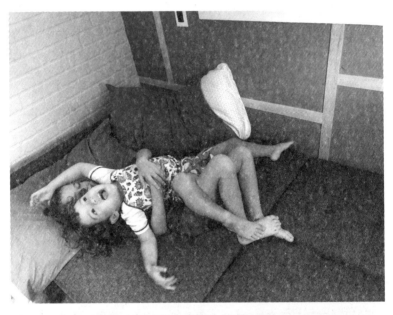

SECOND FALL: THE BOTTOM LINE

AUGUST 26, 2021 | *A DAMN GOOD DISGUISE*

Dear R,

It feels like I'm writing you from another place and another time entirely. Well, it feels like that because it *is* that. Yesterday I turned thirty-eight, and today I'm writing you from a tree platform above a happyswift river where we celebrated. In this instance, I hold a justified belief that is also a true belief, though the analytic philosophers would be quick to point out that the two don't always coincide. These months, your last letter, are rich proof puddings of that. That kind of philosophy never was my field, though. This, maybe, is my field now: the study of new words, new feelings, new temporalities, of what a river can create.

The new place is Fallsburg, New York—only an hour away from Kingston, but someone else's home and decor and amenities, and right on a river that feeds my soul. So much for the new place.

The new time—that is the new year of life. Despite everything, this might actually have been the best birthday of my life: I celebrated myself with real gifts, the things I really hold sacred. I got up early and worked on the story I have cooking, which is the practice that allows me to sleep again at night. I spent most of the good hours of the day in the rental's separate writing studio, logged into a free writing workshop with the philosopher-novelist Lars Iyer. The workshop was very familiar philosophy wise, but creatively productive. And

I let myself open your gift during the seminar break, and felt thoroughly seen and spoiled by the notebook and Naipaul's *Enigma of Arrival* (and how have I been living without that divinely scented handcream? I felt like the queen of the harem at night when I worked the rich unguent into my hands and then Micah's deserving feet; his exertions and orchestrations to make the day so beautiful I have not mentioned but did not go unappreciated).

The new time also has come about, I think, because the collapse timeline and the continuity timeline have been brought into alignment. Meaning, we've more or less decided to homeschool the kids again. There will be no 'get them off to school on time' to clash with the sense of living through a situation of extremity.

No one who knows us will be very surprised, including you—we homeschooled last year, we read the damn news, and, most importantly, we have the time and resources to devote to it. And it works. Somehow or other, Zia can read. He's playing chess and once in a while beating us (or the computer). He wants to start a tea business selling the special anti-nightmare blend he's created. He wants to learn Spanish, so I put on Spanish language playlists and found him someone to talk to on Zoom. We will let them play as much as they want, like in Finland where they don't start formal school until age seven, and do our best to help them connect with others outside and masked, or over Zoom. Honestly, I'm not mourning it as much as I thought I would be. The main feeling is relief.

I do worry about the loneliness of winter, and whether our kids will turn out awfully peculiar, and resent us. Because eventually the curve will drop—may already be dropping?—and we will wonder if we should have stuck it out. But winter is always hard. And it's not such a bad thing to be peculiar. And the kids will, inevitably, fault us for one thing or another. So I kiss the kids goodnight and tell them that the pandemic is a blessing in disguise, that I get to spend so much time with them when they are this age. Most of the time, I mean it.

I just don't tell them what a damn good disguise this blessing is wearing.

The river is calling me, dearest. Thank you for the gift of true friendship: you are a gem of this life.

Love always,
C

SEPTEMBER 2, 2021 | *THE OPPOSITE OF RELIEF*

Hi, hey, hello, C,

I have to ask. Are you still in that place you wrote from a week ago? It was a hell of a place. *The main feeling,* you wrote, *is relief.* I had to squint through muck to see you there. Thank you for giving me a taste of that relief, for enabling me to touch it for the time it took to read your words.

A week ago I was feeling the opposite of relief. My life had been hectic morning lunch-packing and school drops, non-stop stress about having the kids in school in the first place (do those Sono-masks even work? Are the Enros truly washable?), no time to do all the work like getting ready to apply for academic jobs I might not want, but think could be one ticket out of a daily-more-unlivable Arizona since the kids are only out of the house from 9–3, cooking and cleaning and cooking and cleaning and cooking and cleaning and swatting flies and mosquitoes that are everywhere thanks to Tucson's record monsoon, teaching again and dealing with my rightly traumatized students, being dragged into the continuity timeline again, chafing against moments like clueless interim department head starting last week's meeting with: 'How is everyone feeling being back after Covid?' Frantic, frantic, frantic, frantic.

And that was before the complete collapse in Afghanistan.

Before Hurricane Ida and dead bodies in the New York subway. Before the Caldor Fire and evacuations in Tahoe. Before Trump's Supreme Court declined to stand by *Roe v. Wade* at midnight on the shadow-docket (two nights in a row). Too true, the bit going around Twitter: '*Preventing measures to stop COVID, restricting the right to vote, defending the right to carry weapons of war, forcing right wing school curriculum, prohibiting the right to choose: Texas GOP is a window into the minority rule Republicans want to impose on all of us.*'

Commentators are straining for analogies. Is the bounty now imposed by SB8 in Texas like slave-era bounties for hunting escapees? What does the history of abolition teach us? Is GOP minority rule like white tyranny in apartheid South Africa? Does anybody give a shit?

Well, nobody gave enough of a shit when they forced migrant women in Krome Detention Center to give birth against their will, when they denied abortions to rape victims in prison. Meanwhile, the kids are still in cages, battling RSV; Sandy Hook meant nothing, so no point feigning surprise that all our children have been left to the vagaries of Long Covid and the likelihood of lifelong disability. (New variant of concern: Mu.) Actuarial science says to the stock market maniacs: collect quickly, before the bill comes due, and don't worry, you can stick it to those other guys on your way to your winter home on Mars.

Do you feel some version of what I feel? Angry, disgusted, nauseated, fed up, exhausted. I've been mentally reliving the non-stop assault of the Trump years: Muslim bans, gutting the EPA, Russia, family separation, Jared Kushner unleashed, the violence of Brett Kavanaugh shoved down our throats, non-stop-ever-present white male mediocrity and evil, the stealing of Ruth Bader Ginsburg's seat, January 6. That's not even the tenth of it—why am I even trying to write it down? My point: how have we even made it this far, trying to pay attention to all this shit while carrying on with the mundane demands of daily life? Why did I go and have a second child in the middle of it?

I know you remember the days leading up to the first lockdown. I did all the stockpiling you urged me to do. The raids on the pasta and lentils at Sprouts grocery, laundry detergent and Mucinex at Target. I made multiple trips to the Indian store for dosa batter. I went to Total Wine for vodka, gin, whiskey, mixers—bought enough to get us through pandemic spring and, it turned out, summer (I restocked, curbside, in fall).

Brandon got just three things: a wheelbarrow, a big-screen TV, and a vasectomy.

How I love him for that, for taking up residence on 'V Street'. Yeah, it was planned in advance, but it was so perfectly timed that I like to think it was the product of his uncanny, end-of-the-world foresight. This is a man who loses his glasses between the bedroom and the kitchen, and once parked his car at Sweet Adeline Bakeshop in Oakland and walked home to South Berkeley and didn't notice for three days that the car was gone. Somehow, he knew what was to come and that he'd better do his part to make sure I never got pregnant again.

I've been pregnant by choice, and I've been pregnant by accident, and I've been pregnant on purpose and then realized my mistake. Two kids, one miscarriage. I've used Plan B. I've had two abortions: one at a Planned Parenthood in Chicago, and one at Planned Parenthood in Southern Arizona. The first was what they call surgical (a five-minute procedure with local anesthetic); I got hot chocolate in the 'recovery' room and relaxed for twenty minutes before driving myself home, picking up wine and ice-cream on the way. The latter was medical (mifepristone and misoprostol pills taken at home); that's when I binge-watched *Made in Heaven* on Netflix, bleeding in relief.

Because of Arizona's TRAP laws, I had to go back to the Tucson clinic more than once. I had to deal with the transvaginal ultrasound, the mandatory twenty-four-hour waiting period, the do-you-want-to-see-the-ultrasound-image and I-have-to-describe-it-for-you and I-am-required-by-law-to-ask-you-again-do-you-want-to-see-it. State-funded medical schools in Arizona are actually prohibited from teaching medical students (including those specializing in gynecology and obstetrics!) how to perform abortions. But to perform an abortion in Arizona, to dispense the pills in the brown bag, you have to be a licensed physician.

Eighty per cent of Arizona counties have no abortion providers, but I only had to drive ten minutes. I took the week off. I could pay the $400.

A curse upon them all, who are trapping women inside their bodies and then sending children into virus-infested, gun-vulnerable classrooms to die.

My mother arrives tomorrow. I wrote to my in-laws last week and told them they have to fly back from Maine to help with Mrinalini and Shai in October, when they're home for Fall Break. I didn't leave them any room to say no.

Neither of us is thirty-five anymore. But I'm holding on to some lines of Ishmael Reed's 'The Author Reflects on his 35th Birthday' today. Or at least this one: *make me as hard as a rock.*

Pressing send now.

There's love here, too,
R

SEPTEMBER 8, 2021 | *A NEW FRIEND*

Dear heart,

I hope you are not still in the same place as last week—emphasis on you, emphasis on hope—dwelling on the hard, asking to be made harder. If life makes you harder, will living it become easier? I think the opposite might be true, pace Reed, even if you've got his dark humor spiking the punch.

Yes, I'm tracking Mu, and Ida, and Afghanistan—*I told you so, Dad*—and the Texas abortion law, at least a little, as much as I can bear. The Afghanistan news shook me the most, maybe because the 'war' (occupation) there was the start of my adult political consciousness. Or because my parents served there for a time. Or because it is so much the symbol of the collapsing empire, however much the media want to moralize it as either the right move, or the right move in the wrong way, or the wrong time, or the wrong move altogether. But none of it shook me out of my groove.

Here the timeline is only: five days until Zia's birthday. He'll be six. He requested a surprise party on Zoom, a version of what we did last year. And so your party kit with snacks and balloons and items to scavenger-hunt is on its way, and per Mrinalini's suggestion, costumes have been recommended for the guests. We are overcompensating for the in-person party we can't give him—Zoom party, gifts, horseback riding, a trip to the farm with the gigantic 'jumping pillow', which is like a temporary release from the gravity of this earth....

And the universe has presented him with the best gift of all: a new friend. We met them at the park just on Monday, a family newly arrived from Brooklyn. They were wearing the coveted Happy Masks also, they are mixed race also, they live in walking distance of the park also, the boys would've been classmates at High Meadow also, had we not opted out (the daughter is a bit older than Areté, having just turned four). The kids match up roughly in age and more importantly, in kindness and temperaments. They came over this morning for a masked backyard playdate—painting, tree climbing, cardboard box play, freeze tag, beyblades, chess—and the dads dropped by to meet up as well. So, it's our turn now to dance with that dream of the neighborhood friend.

And it is a dream in more ways than one.... In one of those bizarre workings of the universe, the mom is of Indian descent, like you, and the dad is, I kid you not, named Brandon. How much of life is just repeating patterns and templates? They remarked too how much I look like their friend 'Julia'. Don't worry, no one is going to be able to catch up to the thousands of friendship-hours you and I have logged. But for Zia, and for Areté... I wish for them friendships like the one we have. I see with my mom-sight that in this respect Zia is like me—his heart has decided at once, already, intensely, that this person is his beloved friend, and I am nourishing the bloom of that love with all I've got.

After the playdate, though, I had to take a shower *and* a bath. Not just to wash away the sweat (it's still warm here) or the social residue, but simply to bring my nervous system back down, down, down, in order to be able to sit and compose coherent sentences. I read about half of Sally Rooney's latest in the bath, refilling the hot water twice. It says, I think, the same as us: that it's these friendships that make the catastrophe worth living through.

Hope the news from in here can counter the News out there.

Love,
C

SEPTEMBER 16, 2021 | *THE PLEASURE-PAIN DIALECTIC*

C! Hello, dear friend.

I heard this bit on NPR the other day that got me thinking about our various exchanges around happiness. You don't want me to be hard, you say. But you know I don't have what you call 'a happy button'.

The interview was about what we might call the pleasure-pain dialectic. (The interviewee, a neuroscientist, didn't use the word 'dialectic' but you know what I mean.) The same parts of our brain that process pleasure also process pain, she was explaining. But, and here I'm quoting from the transcript:

one of the governing principles regulating this balance is that it wants to remain level... It doesn't want to be deviated for very long, either to the side of pleasure or pain... when I eat a piece of chocolate, immediately what my brain will do is adapt... by tipping my balance an equal and opposite amount to the side of pain.

Yes, we know this is how addiction works, that the body builds up a tolerance to whatever substance and so we need more and more and more, to keep getting high, to keep feeling good. We need more pleasure to outweigh the pain. What I liked about the discussion, though, is that it was not just about addiction but about pleasure and pain more generally and much more broadly defined. It was about the fact that the body, chemically and physiologically speaking, doesn't want an excess of pain— *but it doesn't want an excess of pleasure either.*

This makes a hell of a lot of sense to me. I get why the pursuit of happiness is important (personally and societally), but the pursuit of *balance*, I think, is just as significant. The pursuit of *clarity*. Of *equanimity*.

I think my resistance to 'happiness' as an ideal or goal, like my investment in Lauren Berlant's critique of cruel optimism, stems in part from my distrust of the (neoliberal?) demand that we—any of us—must engage in the production and espousal of good feeling, and that we—mothers especially— must perform all that work on ourselves in order to present happiness and create an 'optimistic, positive affective disposition' (recently heard Catherine Rottenberg give a talk on this). In Barbara Ehrenreich's words, 'the relentless promotion of positive thinking' has undermined us all!

I say all this slightly tongue in cheek, of course, because the terms of the discussion on neoliberal feminism risk conceding happiness at the outset.

Still, for me: balance, clarity, equanimity. A belated response to the challenge you once threw me that I offer up something as worthy as the pursuit of happiness!

Which is not to duck the responsibility of writing to you from this moment. You said you hoped I was not in the same place as before. Well, I'm not, but also, don't worry about that place, love, that place of hardness. I needed it. It fortified me for the days after, which have been about teaching and drafting materials for the job market run and writing emails to recommenders and spending time with my mother who was here for a week filling our freezer with chicken curry (Mrinalini's favorite) and twice-cooked karela and malai shrimp curry (mine).

I didn't spend all that much time with my mother, and I rebuffed some of her attempts at 'conversation'—I admit, I wasn't on my best behavior—but I think she knows how very much I appreciated her coming. I called a few weeks ago and told her I needed her over the long weekend, and she booked her flight that same day. She knows that I know that I can rely on her.

She's off to India soon, hopefully with an unauthorized Pfizer booster in her system.

My brother and his wife (his wife!) are coming to visit us for Halloween. Before that, my in-laws arrive for fall break. We need all the help we can get, and I'm trying to be better about asking for it.

As for the job market, which is what I'm mostly occupied with this week: I'm applying widely to jobs I want, and jobs I'd be afraid to have, and jobs I think I'd never take. I'm applying the way I applied in 2016: like the future depends on it. In 2016, I knew that if I didn't get a job, I wouldn't get out of graduate school. My advisor had just asked me to start my dissertation over from scratch. I said no. I said I was going to market the dissertation (however abject it was) and get a job and move on. And I did. Now, I have a different but related certainty, which is that if I want to get out of here (not just the university, but Tucson, and Arizona), I need to get a job somewhere else.

As I've drafted all these job applications, I've come to understand that it's not just that I don't like my job and don't want to be here in Tucson. It's that I'm *done* being here. It's over. I've done what I came here to do. This phase is coming to a close. This chapter must end. There is no future here—but that doesn't mean that there is no future.

Maybe it sounds like word play, but to me in this moment it is profoundly important that I be able to distinguish between: *I need to leave because I'm not happy.* And: *I need to leave because my work here is done.*

Disconnected-connected thought. You know that saying: friend for a season, or friend for a reason? I never really understood what it means. Isn't a season also a compelling reason? I just googled it, and it's actually *friend for a season, a reason, or a lifetime.* I still don't know what to make of the distinction between the first two terms. Perhaps I've had it on the brain because I've also been thinking about the changing seasons. Here the pool gets cold before the days. This morning's air was chilly (20s, to be clear) and I started longing for autumn. I am looking forward to running again, even though that means giving up the swimming that I love so much.

I'm grateful for all the changes and thoughts of moves and turning seasons, even though in so many other ways life looks and feels like more of the same.

Officially, 1 in 500 Americans have now died of Covid. And unofficially?

You're between birthdays at your house. New chapters, new years. Bless those babies.

All the love,
R

SEPTEMBER 22, 2021 | *HAPPINESS DEPENDS ON BEING FREE*

Dear R,

I can't remember now exactly what Aristotle says about true friendship. Is it that, if I am a real friend, I would want for you what you want for yourself? Or is it that I should want for my friend what I want for myself? I'm wondering because I find it impossible to want hardness for you. And I can only wish 'balance' and 'clarity' for you through the mildly arduous process of transmuting an abstraction into a feeling. But to wish happiness for you, your self's true joy, is just like breathing for me.

As for pleasure and pain, that neuroscientist makes sense to us partly because she's repeating an ancient wisdom. Hours before Socrates is slated to drink the hemlock, just after he feels the relief of his manacles unlocked, he remarks on the copresence of pleasure and pain:

> If somebody chases the one and catches it, he's pretty much compelled always to catch the other one too, just as if the pair of them—although they're two—were fastened by one head!

Wild image, right? And delivered just after Socrates asks for his wailing wife, Xanthippe, to be taken away—as if clearing the emotions in order to make way for philosophical talk. But the upshot is not balance, or equanimity. There's a difference between describing a biological or even metaphysical principle of balance, and setting balance as one's life goal. In *Phaedo* (unlike the earlier *Protagoras*), the 'hedonic calculus', or the calculations involved in minimizing pain and maximizing pleasure, are not sufficient to the good life. There needs also to be the pursuit of justice—which he enigmatically defines in *Republic* as 'doing one's own things' [*to ta heautou prattein*].

Not that Plato gets the last word. What worries me about the balance sheet approach is the way in which I know I have used such calculations to justify the contraction of my heart, to talk myself into doing things which I don't really wish to do, to minimize rather than experience the painful parts.

Having tripped into subjects I used to think I knew something about, I'm anxious not to write an essay accidentally! I always admire your pragmatism and your fortitude, even as I'm inclined more towards vulnerability and expansion. You remind me of another ancient maxim, pithier and more apropos to your circumstances: 'Make up your minds that happiness depends on being free, and freedom depends on being courageous.' That's Pericles, praising the Athenian democracy and its wars.

I see you similarly girded for your battle to get free of a state that makes war on its citizens (and those who would cross its borders), to escape from work that you no longer recognize as your own. The cynical quip that today only the rich are free. Maggie Nelson would say that freedom is always a matter of navigating degrees of constraint, not escaping them absolutely. In entering the bog of the job market, you are angling for a place of greater expansion, more in line with the life mission you're creating and discovering. I celebrate you for that.

Isn't it a lark to be a member of the only species which doesn't know how it is supposed to live, 'never really at home in the interpreted world,' as Rilke puts it? I'm laughing a little, yet I'm often saddened these days because so many humans have agreed to accept the unacceptable costs of Covid-19. Just the latest of the totally avoidable, human-made, travesties of history.

Remember that vision, that clarity of sight granted by the real nightmare of the early pandemic, with which we glimpsed the possibility of another reality...? That dream which we keep alive through the continuity of these letters...? It's been buried and the grave lost again in fog, for most.

For some reason—to be precise, out of profound gratitude

for the love and joy and freedom I've been granted, and fearful awareness of its fragility—lately I've been reading the Bible. Literally incredible, these stories, this language, this total disregard for generic divisions—and shocking how much is familiar to someone who quit going to Church even at Easter at a very young age.

'Naked I came from my mother's womb, and naked I will depart.'

'I am the voice of one crying in the wilderness, make straight the way of the Lord!'

Job, St. John.... But the story I find myself thinking about the most now is Noah and his ark. Forty days of rain, and forty plus days of waiting once the ark lands on Mount Ararat, in eastern Turkey. I summitted that mountain, the summer before I turned thirty. Now as I approach age forty, the gods rain down their fury on a populace who refuse to open umbrellas, while Micah and I are scraping together the wood to build a tiny ark that can float through whatever lies ahead. I think almost daily about what books should be included in the apocalypse library. It's a long list (and more varied than today's citations would suggest).

Here too the season is shifting. That first small golden leaf that catches your eye in its graceful descent...its bright transience shining on the treasure of lifelong friends and loves. My 'babies'... these days I find delight in how much I get to know them, how I get to blanket them with love and learning. One day they, like you and me, will keep their mother at arms' length *at least*. Zia's birthday celebrations went off well enough. I think we'll retreat to the woods somewhere for Areté's next month. The day after he turned six, we formally began homeschool, with the help of tutors on Outschool.com, and extracurriculars like karate at the park, and horseback riding lessons, and apple picking on Sundays with friends.

Sometimes it comes home to me how peculiar, how weird

is this path we've chosen. But it's happier, less lonely than I feared. I remember the etymology of weird: from the old English *wyrd*, for fate or personal destiny, with roots further back in words meaning to turn or rotate, to become. In this mystical mood, my weirdness is how I'm fated to turn out.

Love always,
C

SEPTEMBER 30, 2021 | *OWNING IT*

Hi my dear philosopher friend, friend of my heart and adulthood, fellow traveler,

Let me set the scene first. The weather has turned, finally, and we've lost the pool. But this means we've gained the mornings. They are beautiful and cool, and all the windows and doors are open. It's sunny; the roses in front of my office window (which is to say, the window in the closet) are blooming again. The mosquitoes are finding it a bit too chilly for comfort—praise!—and so I've been out back again lately, sitting on my summer couch.

I've started wearing socks and ankle boots, too, when I go out to drop the kids or pick them up. I love boots, I remember now. I wear them with my 27R 'curvy true skinny' GAP jeans, the ones that I have worn so very many days during this pandemic that they are ripped at the knees, in the back pocket, at the sides, and in the crotch. My grungy second-skin jeans; I love them so. I wear them to Mrinalini's Episcopal school just to mess with everyone, and as the right pairing with our filthy, bumper-stickered Prius. I wear them with my mother-in-law's expensive hand-me-down tank tops. They are the only shirts I have now that are not constellated with holes, and they are far nicer than anything I would ever buy myself.

I won't quibble more about balance versus happiness, except

to say that I do think clarity and equanimity are not necessarily about calculating ups and downs in what you called the balance sheet approach (ouch!), but more about accessing a mood, tone, and rhythm that are sustainable and sustaining. I'm willing to concede that underneath all my equivocations about happiness, and resistance to self-help doctrine, and diminishment of what adrienne marie brown calls 'pleasure activism' (a dear friend gave me this book; as far as I can tell, it is an extended response to Audre Lorde's 'uses of the erotic', and skimming it the other day I felt like quite the prude!), there is of course a desire to find a rapprochement with all of these terms, on my own terms.

Of course, that means I have to do the hard work of figuring out what 'my own terms' are.

It means reckoning with the fact that I am the child of two martyrs, each of whom, in their own way, values sacrifice, suffering, and the integrity of hard work above all else.

It means having to confront the fact that I live with someone who is—and who has always been, ever since I met him—in chronic pain.

And it means I need to create the conditions in my life to hear whatever my terms might be, find them, access them— even if it turns out they are overdetermined, and not my own terms at all.

Instead of grading last night I read 'the cannibalist manifesto' ('Manifesto Antropófago'), trying to understand how and why I insist on metabolizing so much of what I also want to oppose and reject ('I am interested only in what is not mine').

That said, I am allowing myself to more fully inhabit my promise to myself (and my promise to Brandon, and his to me) that we are not going back to this university next year. I am going to teach online in the spring semester, and he is not teaching at all. If for some reason we haven't created the conditions to leave for new jobs next summer, we will either go somewhere abroad for a stint, or I at least will find a way to take a leave of absence.

This job: I don't want it. I have to own that. But I am not ready to give up my academic identity, work, and profile, and I have to own that, too.

People sometimes say that academia is a cult, with very narrow and rigid values, hierarchies, and norms. I think that's right. When you're in, you're in. When you're out, you're out. And it's hard to leave a cult because the people there are your people, the people you know, the ones whose respect you have been trained to seek. There's that for me, of course. Even more significant, however, is that Brandon and I have made the university, and our joint inhabitance of this profession, really central to our social and communal lives, fragmented and tenuous though they are.

What other community would have us? Brandon grew up in an interfaith Christian-Jewish household, but his is the religion of mathematics. I grew up in a culturally Hindu household, but mine is the religion of literature, philosophy. The result is that we belong to no religious community (and never will).

Neither are we part of any ethno-racial group. I think often these days about the fact that I grew up in an immigrant enclave of diasporic Indians, and how central that experience of ethnic and cultural belonging was for me, though in so many ways I have left it behind and am not trying to reproduce it. Consciously, unconsciously, we seek out other mixed-race families. We make kith and kin of them, but it is not the same.

We have no home to go back to: no hometown, no home city or state. We will never live in Toledo, Ohio, where Brandon grew up, or the Mississippi Delta, where his ancestors are buried, or small-town Pennsylvania, where his father was raised. We will almost certainly never live in the Bay Area, where I grew up. And though we might one day pursue a sabbatical in India, it will never be permanent. We might 'go home again' but we will inevitably 'also leave again', to riff off Suketu Mehta.

The academic diaspora is our primary community, and community is something I want not so much for myself but for Mrinalini and Shai. If we belong nowhere and to nobody, how will we model and create belonging for them?

Which is why I am ready to leave Arizona, Tucson, and the godforsaken English department, but I'm still applying for academic jobs, still working on the tenure book, still provisionally committed to this perhaps irredeemable profession, though daily it betrays itself, its students, and the future.

I am not sure which off-ramp to take.

I want to acknowledge Covid. I want to acknowledge that we all are trying to change our lives, because to do any less would be to not take the challenge, opportunity, and occasion of the pandemic seriously. Some people managed transformation after year one of the pandemic. They moved states. They quit their jobs. They began again. Do you feel that you are on this timeline?

For myself, I know the change is slower-going. But by not going back (back to work, back to teaching in person, back to socializing, or back to traveling), by not returning to normal, I am trying to protect the conditions through which I/we are going to be able to transform our lives. That's part of the holding pattern. What the finger-pointers call 'cave syndrome'. It's to protect the possibility of emerging into a world made new, having fortified oneself for a different life, having learned at least some of the lessons that we were given to learn.

I feel that possibility today. Against all odds.

School pick-up time again. I'm already in costume.

All my love,
R

OCTOBER 8, 2021 | *WILLING TO FIND OUT*

Dearest R,

I have to apologize if—okay, that—my words in my last letter stung. Sometimes ideas sweep me along and I forget how clumsy are the footfalls of the words I put them in. Of course balance and clarity are not only a matter of calculation. All I can say is that in stinging you, I sting myself. That one word (*ouch*) stayed with me this week.

Attached to it, somehow, is your question: *if we belong nowhere and to nobody, how will we model and create belonging for [the kids]?*

It's the proper pairing with your question about finding your own terms or your own way to metabolize the terms we absorb daily. And it's a question towards which a number of my experiences rush. Growing up an expat kid. Writing my dissertation in a small town on the Oregon Coast. Neither philosopher nor Classicist nor anything else. Looking for community in all the wrong places! It's the sort of question that summons that well-worn advice of Rilke's (*love the questions, live the questions*). Unfortunately, that line is more threadbare than your jeans and tanks (and not as sexycool as you at school pickup). But maybe some of the original force of it is in the attitude, *be willing to find out.*

Which you are. Boots and all. Resistance and all. The W. S. Merwin poem you sent me once when I was late with something or other feels like it will always be appropriate:

Again again you are
the right time after all

not according to
however we planned it.

That kind of timing is the timeline of transformation. Indeed, the next stanza, which you hadn't sent but which I searched out just now:

> unforeseen and yet
> only too well known
> mislaid horizon
> where we come to ourselves
> as though we had been expected.

It's easier to write to you than about me, lately. I've been reading the Portuguese poet Fernando Pessoa's *Book of Disquiet*, which he sometimes calls a 'factless autobiography'. Pessoa was someone who did not belong. And who had many personas, in various stages of development, that he wrote and perhaps existed as. I read him because he often touches on that feeling I have too, of not being oneself, but not necessarily with pain or alienation:

> All that I've done, thought, or been is a series of submissions, either to a false self that I assumed belonged to me because I expressed myself through it to the outside, or to a weight of circumstances that I supposed was the air I breathed. In this moment of seeing, I suddenly find myself isolated, an exile where I'd always thought I was a citizen. At the heart of my thoughts I wasn't I.

From the way Pessoa elsewhere describes the presence of other people as a debilitating prison I think he might have been autistic—etymologically, as you know, a deficit or disorder of self.

And despite important differences, I sometimes think I am too.

The possibility first came in my dream, a couple of months ago now. Earlier that day or week, I'd taken the kids to a playdate with people I was only acquainted with by email, genderqueer artist types. The summer afternoon passed pleasantly. But afterwards I experienced a kind of recoiling from myself, a toxic shame at the person I'd performed as, a deep anxiety about my likeability and self worth. For me, this is a pretty normal response to social outings, not a pandemic specific response. In the dream that occurred some days later, I was speaking over our fence to someone, and one of these artist types told me, 'Stop sucking on your hair. It's so autistic!' I was taken aback. 'Could I have caught it from my husband?'

That's the comic punchline of the dream. The emotion of it, though, was deep, sobbing relief. Like this was the answer to all my seeking about why I don't fit anywhere. Any relief in real life has been slow and intermittent, mixed with resistance, confusion, skeptical appraisals of the research on autism in women, criticism of the flatness of current labels. I didn't come out as autistic on the online quiz I took together with Micah, back in the spring. I don't fit the predominant male-researched, masculine-based stereotype. But when I look at the checklists specific to autism in women.... Well. It's an awful lot of checks.

I guess it is a question I'm willing to find out about. Is this question-answer related to Covid? I think it might be—one of its lessons I have to come to terms with before it can be over for me. One of the ways the virus is here to help me, to go back to one of my earliest letters and convictions.

A quote from epidemiologist Michael Osterholm making the rounds: 'We still are really in the cave ages in terms of understanding how viruses emerge, how they spread, how they start and stop, why they do what they do.' I appreciate this reminder of the 'unknown unknown', in the middle of what can seem too often these days like a settled question for most folks. Not that I think anyone is going to change their basic attitude toward Covid at this point.

But maybe there is still the potential to shift away from the alluring narratives of victims, villains, and victors that give us our certainty. Indeed, that might be the one change we need most.

Another change may be coming too, I think. Micah's regular paycheck has put us in a comfortable place since March, but one of his bets has the potential to put us somewhere even past that. Past replacing the car with only three working doors with a (used) Tesla, not to mention the chipped dishes and frayed towels. Past paying off all six figures of our student loans, our debts to my parents, past absorbing the cost of relocating and caring for his fast-aging parents and dependent brother. Beyond gifts to the people and institutions that have supported us.

The bet in question is a carbon-backed coin called Klima. It's a complex project, activist and financial and technical. The aim is to make carbon offsets so expensive that mega-polluters are forced to change their ways, and others are incentivized to find ways to put or keep carbon in the ground. A revolutionary coin, in other words, so maybe not as off-brand for the co-creator of Occupy Wall Street as it might initially seem. The world of crypto is *highly* uncertain and volatile. But just possibly, it's time to stop thinking about how money could change our lives and to start thinking seriously about how it can change the world. To dream harder about creating a Covid-and-climate-refuge… our ark. You're invited aboard, of course.

Though I don't blame you if you're hesitant. Like my potential neurodivergence, I haven't totally embraced this potential wealth, yet. I have a lot of weird feelings around it, including shame. If it happens I'm sure I'll get over it.

In the meantime, I want to know: what would you do, R, if you had financial freedom for yourself and your loved ones, and then some, to make and give things to others? It's an important question to dream about—and not unrelated to the conversation about happiness.

Love always,
C

PS: Are these letters getting longer as the days get shorter?

OCTOBER 13, 2021 | *BREAKING THE FOURTH WALL*

Hi sweetness,

A funny thing happened on the way to writing this letter. I thought I knew exactly where I was going to begin, and indeed, I sat down with the feeling of having already written to you, and needing only to transcribe what had been composed in advance in my mind, and then I reread your letter, and I found that it wasn't what I remembered. Not the letter I'd responded to in my mind, anyway. The same words, sure, but not the same letter.

I'll try to get back to that. But for now, let me begin again where I'd planned to, which is in saying that your letter made me uneasy, but not for the reasons you might think. It raised for me more profoundly than before some questions about the purpose of this writing, about our addressees (present and future), about the selves on the page. I don't normally write about our letters in my letters—I try not to get too meta; not *here*, of all places, where I strive for a record of the pure inhabitance of thought and feeling. But if you will permit it, I might even break the fourth wall this afternoon.

First, that 'ouch'. It wasn't a serious ouch; it didn't mean to sting you because it didn't reflect my being stung. Or did it? If I were to write to you and say, *Hey, I was just being playful; your description of bean-counting cost-benefit calculation in the balance sheet approach to life was provocative, not hurtful, and of course appropriate in response to the language of 'balance' that I had in fact used,* would you feel that I wasn't invested enough to be hurt by what you'd said?

The possibility of misapprehension is a condition of all communication. You and I both know J. L. Austin's felicitous take on infelicities and misfires; inevitably, our words get away from us and can be taken up in any which way. Your opening lines (on ouch!) made me wonder how many times we've done it to each other in these pages. How many times we've gotten away with it, to quote Austin, 'like, in football, the man who first picked up the ball and ran'. He goes on to say: 'Getting away with things is essential, despite the suspicious terminology.' Normally, I suppose, we just let it go; we let it get away. This time, it gave me pause.

And then there was your self-description as autistic. Which immediately made me nervous. It made me want to talk directly to the other you—*you*, not you C, but *you* whoever you are who might be reading this (Mom, is that you?)—and to say that you (you, C) meant it only figuratively, that you (you, C) know that not every brilliant and introverted woman is autistic. I wanted to defend you against the charge of appropriating as an identity what to someone else might be a medical diagnosis reflective of far more disabling struggles (I use these words advisedly—what is disabling is not autism, of course, but the societal norm of neurotypicality—is that maybe your point?).

But then, what the hell do I know about the spectrum? I did read that very long checklist. I wondered about my impulse to explain you (you, C) to *you* (whoever you are) and why I thought such explanation was warranted, when *you* (whoever you are) have been reading you (you, C) alongside me, all these days, weeks, months (if only a few hours, for *you*).

And then I wondered what the affordances of autism are for you, C, what it means to you to write or imagine yourself into this identity through which you have most recently been thinking about your husband, with whom you are of course deeply involved on so many levels.

And then, you followed with an announcement of impending wealth, which at first I found funny—only because you made it sound so deadly serious! But then, as I sat with your letter, it started to sound to me like an extension of what had preceded it. In other words, that impending wealth, to use your term, was an impending transformation at the level of subjectivity, of identity. And this, again, to use the same phrase as before, gave me pause.

Should I try to make you feel less self-conscious? Should I respond to your question about financial freedom? ('Financial freedom' is not a phrase that resonates with me much, probably because of my own privileged—that word again!—disinterest in money.) Should I try to give you some language with which to talk about a potential windfall, some language other than that of 'sudden wealth'?

Here's how I would describe Micah's bet on Klima and the money you may now have or soon. It would not be sudden. It's more akin to a company going public, or getting bought out. Micah has been interested in and learning about cryptocurrency for over a decade—I can attest to this—and now his own private firm is ready for the IPO.

I grew up in the Silicon Valley in the 1990s. What this means is that I have known many, many people who have made, earned, or fallen into big money, sometimes slowly, sometimes all at once. (I also know many people who have lost money in various ventures and crashes, including my parents, but that's not the story I am telling right now.) I have been to the parties convened specifically to toast to the purchase of the first Mercedes Benz. I have been to a wedding where there was a ten thousand dollar bottle of Dom Perignon spinning in a block of ice. My brother flew to Las Vegas for a sixteenth birthday party on a wealthy birthday boy's private jet. Etcetera.

And yes, I will admit that part of my resistance to going back to live in the Bay Area—against my mother's hopes, and knowing that this means I have left the community I grew up in behind forever—is because I *don't want to raise my children around those people*. Money produces many kinds of loss, whether you consciously let it or not.

Of course, I know that making money stands to transform your relationships to your families in significant ways, given the material (and other) entanglements you have (or will have in future) with both sets of your parents. I want for you to pay off your debts and to continue with the world-making and changing that you are dreaming about. But I can't imagine what difference it makes to our relationship whether you have a million dollars in the bank, or fifty, or fifty million. I can't imagine it, because I don't want it to make a difference. (I guess if you get Bezos-level rich and fly off to outer space that's another story.)

I hope this isn't a violent or intrusive letter. I don't mean it to be. I think your letter made me uneasy because it made me realize both that I don't always enjoy being read (ouch!) and that I was going to have to respond to what you'd written. I hope you know that I am writing this out of the love that moves me to try to meet you where you are.

And then of course, there's the philosophical money question. I will admit again that I have a comfortable—vulgar in its own way—middle-class disinterest in and disdain for interest in money that is rooted in not having had to worry about it or think about it all that much, coupled with not having spendy tastes, and the perverse reverse-snobbery of someone who wears everything (yes, with the holes!) until it is unwearable. I will still be using the chipped dishes until they slip from my hand and shatter on the kitchen floor. This is my own private ecology. Use up everything I have, and go with nothing.

In that spirit, when I think about lessons I strive to impart to my children, I think of Natalia Ginzburg's elaboration of the little virtues: 'not thrift but generosity and an indifference to money; not caution but courage and a contempt for danger; not shrewdness but frankness and a love of truth; not tact but love for one's neighbor and self-denial; not desire for success but a desire to be and to know'. I am not saying I rise or cathect equally to each of those little virtues, but I recognize in her words much of my own orientation.

I said I'd try to get back to the transformation. When I reread your letter this afternoon, it had lost what I had earlier read as self-consciousness. It had gained a quality of integrity, lightness, and earnestness that outshone whatever it was before that had left me out of joint.

So I'm sending these words back to you with the acknowledgment that they might be all wrong and infelicitous. It is a deep commitment: speaking and being heard, writing and being read. I think it's not the writing that's the hard part.

Some news from here: a chilly day, in the teens, I'm genuinely cold. I enrolled Mrinalini and Shai in a CDC-funded Covid study called Arizona HEROES which is being administered by the UA College of Public Health. Weekly tests, which I FedEx back to them, and antibody tests before and after vaccination.

And I'm plodding on with job applications, what I call 'designing lottery tickets'. They may be tickets to the future. But they might not be. I'm willing to find out. (A wise friend once told me that.)

Love always,
R

OCTOBER 19, 2021 | *PERMISSION TO BE*

Dearest R,

The kids woke me hours ago and I haven't been able to fall back asleep. I'm distracted by the hum of a strange refrigerator, in this small woodsy rental house where we spent Areté's third birthday, yesterday. It is the minimalism of these places that is both restful and annoying. On the one hand, no baskets of small plastic parts of miscellaneous toys cluttering the surfaces. On the other hand, no stepstool for small people to handwash and teeth-brush. We leave tomorrow, or I guess today; I'm scratching this out in the semi dark, kept company by the shadowy masses of our half-packed possessions. I hope the cat is still alive. I hope the cleaners remembered to lock up after they left.

I drove us here in the slashing rain in the new-to-us Tesla. Or rather, I mostly sat at the wheel and paid attention. Have you ever played Mario Kart, or those quarter-slot games at the arcade? Driving a self-driving car is like the opposite of that. In those video games, there's all the skilled control and adrenaline of driving, without the embodied experience of it. In self-driving mode, you nominally retain control or at least responsibility. There's no skill and little adrenaline, but all the sensual pleasure of sitting still at great speed in a well designed vehicle. It's a strange thing, to learn to trust the intelligence of a machine. It is Micah's dream car, not mine, but I am curious to drive and ride in it with him.

So, today we return home. Tomorrow, Areté begins at Forest School, a three morning/week outdoor masked program, run by the same socially progressive folks who hosted Zia's summer camp. It runs until Thanksgiving and resumes in Spring. We're trying to make outdoor plans with my folks for wintertime. That means trying to bypass the 'scientific' and geopolitical debates around Covid. This was my script: 'Given that we're not going to agree about this, how do we move forward in a way that centers family connection?' I thought I almost saw my dad smile when I brought out this pre-prepared line, as if he recognized the structure of this move from his diplomat days. (I didn't play defense.) They're off in a couple of days for a three week trip to Egypt and Jordan, where they'll see friends and visit my sister, whose baby daughter is due in mid-February.

Socializing outside is *our* new normal, I'm trying to tell them. Can you accept it? Can you accept me? Am I allowed to be different, or do I have to conform to your ideas of what's normal in order to be loved?

Re: your last, I'm left wondering what you would've written had you responded to what you read the second time! I will note the irony of being called out for reading your 'ouch' too literally—a classic Aspie mistake—while being dissuaded from locating myself somewhere on the high-functioning end of the spectrum. I really don't think anyone with ASD would mind if I want to join the club. But you ask a good question—one the Jungian therapist I saw over the summer asked, too: what would that label do for me?

I answered her: self understanding, and permission to be. Maybe a trained clinician would dismiss my hypothesis, or maybe not. But the possibility has helped me understand my sudden awful fits of rage, which I'm told occur as if with an on/off switch. It's helped me understand my lifelong practice of inward rehearsal before the most elementary encounters, and the deep fangs of my fatigue after the social pleasantries of a yard sale. It's helped me understand my obsessive, looping, sleepless thoughts on certain topics, and the often inappropriate intensity of my feelings in my relationships. And of course people on the spectrum are also apt to be seen, and publicly laughed at, for being overly serious, as you did (ouch).

But the clue that stops me in my tracks is the reported lack of self among high-functioning autistic females, theorized as the result of successful 'compensatory mechanisms'—that is, the use of one's intelligence to camouflage one's neurodiversity. That's the kicker for me, the trait I have trouble explaining away as a coincidental resemblance to the brilliant introverted woman writer I'd love to be.

If I felt mildly misread and extremely exposed, though, it just reminded me of the ways you're still mysterious to me, even though I've loved you so long. It reminded me of all the things we're *not* writing about, when we write about Covid or what's occupying the conscious brain.

Covid is less and less on normal people's brains, I take it. 'Normalized catastrophe,' I wrote to an acquaintance. Mass death, 1,500 Americans/day, get back to work. News is really quiet, and Joe Biden's ratings suck anyway. 'America, world leader'—in Covid cases! At some level, do people know it's unconscionable, to blithely transmit a disease that might permanently disable? Or do they genuinely think it's an okay trade-off, to harm the immune system for the economy's sake? Are they not able to see/imagine that going down this path of 'living with the virus' means a *fifth (sixth, nth)* variant of concern that outcompetes the Delta family of variants?

The lab leak theory is more broadly accepted now, but the critical window in which that hypothesis could have shaped people's attitudes and policies is long gone. I also can't find the study I saw on Twitter, about how countries that controlled Covid better suffered less economically as well as having fewer fatalities. Shocking, I know. That thing is happening/has happened, that thing that happened with the Iraq War when the war was declared over and only the dedicated cranks continued to churn out the useless critiques with additional supporting information that changed absolutely nothing.

About the money—maybe somewhere between a million and a billion, maybe somewhere between three months and three years from now—and whether it's better described in terms of continuity or change, in terms of an IPO or a windfall, whether the appropriate virtues are Ginzburg's 'little ones' (you gave me that book, I loved it), whether I have those virtues or some other ones—all that I think is best to let go. I think I was asking, if I become part of the 1 per cent, will you still be my friend? And I think that you said yes. The rest we'll have to be willing to find out.

Love always,
C

OCTOBER 28, 2021 | *THE EGG AND THE CHICKEN*

Hi dear one,

I don't have Covid. That's what it says anyway, when I log onto the test portal on the university website. After dropping Shai to preschool this morning, I popped over to campus, parked not too far from the office I never go to, which is filled with multiple shelves of books I apparently don't need because I haven't yet gone looking for them (all that Foucault from graduate school!), and showed my QR code to get an antigen test. It was quick and efficient; I was back to my car before the half hour that would have tripped the $2 parking charge.

I went because I had a cold yesterday. Sneezing, congestion, a bit of a cough. It wasn't bad, but it was definitely a cold, and thus bizarre. Nobody in the family has had it, and I don't ever see anyone else. I slept it off. Now it's gone, and it wasn't Covid. I suppose it was one of those viruses that sits dormant in your nose, throat, chest. I remember hearing a podcast about something like this very early on in the pandemic. It played like a mystery. *How on earth did X get sick when he hadn't left the house, and nobody had been to the house, and all the mail was sanitized and brought in with gloves?*

It's been a long week. On one sleepless night or the other, I must have nudged that cold and woken it up.

So I don't have Covid. But Covid still has me. It still dictates my movements (or lack thereof). It is still my alibi (for not going to campus, for not accepting a student's gift in person, for virtual office hours, for welcoming a new hire on Zoom). The daily numbers still hit my inbox. Some months ago, I wrote to you that the local numbers were, oh, maybe one in twenty-five or one in twenty. Today's Coronavirus tracker from the *New York Times* says one in seven people in Pima County have been infected, and it's one in six in Arizona. One in seven is the official US count. We know these are undercounts (Brandon's estimate for the national figure is one in three).

When I dig around the news or Twitter, I see that there are reports of new variants, and research on Covid as an Alzheimer's trigger, and evidence that Covid will likely cause future reproductive harm. Some scientists are estimating that over 40 per cent of American children ages 5–11 have already been infected. And yet the news this week of the FDA's approval of the vaccine for children in this age group—Mrinalini's and Zia's age group—was met with relative silence by the mainstream media. For all the reasons you said, and because the vast majority gave up or stopped reading (stopped caring?) a long time ago.

We have become rather freakish. The invitations I suspected would dry up have in fact dried up. Not just in person but even on Zoom. The few friends we used to regularly chat with online have disappeared back into their own real-time, face-to-face lives. We are continuing to do just enough outside, by way of school events and playdates, that Mrinalini and Shai don't quite know how stilted this life is. Well, Mrinalini knows. But she doesn't seem to mind. Or maybe, she has decided to forgive us.

We are not going trick-or-treating (again) this year. We had been testing the waters with Mrinalini's sugar consumption; she had ice-cream with no issue for the first time since fall 2019, but then a couple Starbursts the other day seemed to set her over the edge. She was pale, upset, worried, distracted from her food, unsettled, a fog behind her eyes. So, we pulled the plug on the dietary experimentation and she seems fine now. She has an intense gut-brain connection, clearly. Likely also a heavy auto-immune load and genetic predisposition toward inflammatory conditions.

So, we're skipping the trick-or-treating, but we've promised a family party (my brother and sister-in-law will be here, dressed as Thing One and Thing Two), complete with carving jack o'lanterns, homemade ice-cream (made with coconut milk, dark chocolate, fresh mint), costumes, and dancing. Like Areté,

Mrinalini is going to be a witch. She has royal purple witch's robes, with a fabulous multicolored pointy hat, and a cheap broom I bought at the Spirit store. Shai is going to be '999'— or what I call 'the Incredible 999' because I snagged him an 'Incredibles' costume and have fixed it up with the number 999 at the chest, in bubble-letters on a cloth napkin, pinned on like a running bib.

You know, I'm not sure I intended to write any of that when I pulled my laptop onto my lap and decided to write to you. It strikes me that I am channeling the mood and tense, the style and tone, of our first letters, from early pandemic days. There is a comfort in this. And I'll confess, I am a bit wistful about it, too.

Maybe I'm not ready to let go of Covid. Maybe I am still in the cave, groping around. Maybe I am not ready to walk through the portal. Or maybe I am already on the other side, but just blinking in the light.

It's been a strange few weeks. In the past couple of months, Brandon has gotten deeply into the study and thinking of chronic pain—books, meditation, podcasts, cognitive behavioral therapy (CBT). He is working to understand how he has reinforced his brain's pain channels over the years—how he has cultivated a sensitivity to hurt that is out of proportion to any actual harm that befalls his body. We are starting to understand, in other words, that his chronic pain may be significantly 'neuroplastic'. That he might well have arthritis in his back, but that doesn't actually have to cause him any pain. That avoiding certain activities the whole time we've been in Tucson (like biking and running) has only reinforced his suffering. That his obsessive over-stretching and icing and massaging and physical therapy have only served to over-attune his brain to the possibility of pain, even in its absence.

All of this has led us to some challenging conversations and provisional insights that have been a long time in the making.

For instance, the question of whether he is unhappy because he is in pain, or if he is in pain because he is unhappy?

I am having to unlearn many of my rehearsed narratives about him, and in the process about our relationship. *I have many complicated friends, and I am complicated, and I chose Brandon because he is uncomplicated. I have female friendships full of drama, and by contrast my relationship with Brandon works because it's drama-free. I don't write about Brandon much, because he's not a problem in my life that I need to work out.* Do I not write about Brandon because he is not a problem and he has no problems, or because neither of us have ever confronted the problems he has—that we have?

At the risk of over-personalizing his current journey, this also has me wondering about my radical aversion to the desert. Is the land in fact hostile, or have I imbued it with hostility?

These are chicken and egg problems. A couple events this week had me asking similar questions. I gave a guest lecture in a graduate seminar in Social, Cultural, and Critical Theory (you can guess the whole syllabus, I'm sure). It went very well. The students were appreciative and even deferential and admiring, and I was reminded that I am actually quite good at being a professor, strange job that it is, with its various competing and often irreconcilable parts ('40 per cent research, 40 per cent teaching, 20 per cent service').

The next day, I spent ninety minutes on Zoom with a new, eager assistant professor who wanted my advice about adjusting to the tenure-track. As much as I could, as casually as I could, I warned her about my vantage (critical, negative, done with it all—if not in those words). Still, I had a lot to offer her. I came away from that meeting again reminded of how deeply steeped I am in this work, how well suited I am to it in many ways, and also how very many good people are actually here. But I also came away from the conversation newly sure of the fact that I am done with this particular institution, its culture, this place. That it has served its purpose, whether season or reason.

Am I just repeating the same things I've been saying all year, going on two years? Probably. I wouldn't fault you at all for tiring of it. My constant repetition with a difference, in perverse Derridean fashion. I'm thinking about Trinh T. Minh-ha today, how she used to tell us in class, deadly serious and enigmatic, 'When you come to the impasse, it is the pass.' I am thinking about my deep-seated tendency to sit at the impasse, to revel in it, and yes, to wallow sometimes.

As for my last letter. Well, the tricky thing is, that *is* what I wrote after reading you the second time, isn't it? I can tell you now what I suspect was at the heart of my unease: your serial becoming away from me: non-academic, autistic, wealthy. I could feel your hand slipping from mine, and I might have held too tightly in response.

It has meant so much to me that we have been in this struggle together.

Always,
R

NOVEMBER 5, 2021 | *PRODUCT REVIEWS*

Dear R,

I'm relieved you haven't got Covid. I guess I'm also relieved it's got you, as you put it. There's evidence, as you know, that the virus affects the brain in various ways that are not yet well understood, and often it seems nearly everyone's lost their mind, or gone to sleep. Then I remember that this head-burying is 'normal' human behavior. Conscious and self-aware beings— but not quite enough to override the desire for normalcy or the propaganda effect or whatever the heck explains this mass abdication of responsibility. I sent a large gift and sincere regrets for my doctor-cousin's very large indoor wedding in Minneapolis on New Year's Eve. They're asking for vaccination and PCR tests, but let's be real. *Someone's* going to have it, whether guest or staff or hotel bellboy, and that person will pass it on to someone else.... Neither of those people will be me.

A funny thing happened on the way to reading your letter. I was waiting and looking forward to it, more so even than usual this week, yet somehow I missed the notification that it had arrived. Eventually, late last Saturday night, I checked in, thinking perhaps that the very thing which *had* occurred might've occurred. But when I loaded the doc on my 'smart' phone, it did something weird. The first line of your letter flashed up—'I haven't got Covid'—but then the screen offered up my last letter. It acted as though you'd never written, even when I tried refreshing the page. I didn't know if I'd dreamed it or what, but it was late, and I shouldn't look at my phone late at night, so I gave up, and half-worried through the night about why you would have to say you didn't have Covid, or why you hadn't written.

The next day, Sunday, I finally accepted the imperfect resolution Micah and I have figured out for a winter visit with my family. Not indoors, which my parents wanted, and not the warmer Charleston, South Carolina, which I wanted, but outdoors (which Micah wanted), near their home in Maryland (which they wanted), and all together (which I wanted). We booked a fancy rental house with some hammocky chairs around a firepit thingie. I hope it'll be nice. I have a lot of repair work to do there which I don't know how to do. It occurs to me, not for the first time, that the tensions in the family—race, Covid—mirror at the micro scale the larger conflicts at the national scale. That does not make them easier to resolve.

Only after I accepted that the difficult three-way negotiation was in fact resolved did I open my phone to find the belated notification of your letter. It was like each question was a lock in the damming of a river, and the resolution of one opened the lock so that the water could flow into the next lock, which then opened and let the water flow into the next.... That's no kind of causality or even relationship that science would recognize— maybe it's more on the plane of Lispector's egg logic—but it was the case.

So your/Minh-ha's line about the impasse being the pass... struck me as correct.

Today I spent most of the morning looking at climate maps and properties in Maine, for the multi-generational, net-zero climate ark we're dreaming about. It feels far away. I like that we have friends here. I like the like minded people at Areté's Forest School. I'm feeling my age as a kind of stubborn immobility. We used to move around at the drop of a hat. When we were younger, three years in a place was a long time, we'd be itching to go, as you are from AZ.

The maps say my local area will be hotter, and at high risk of flooding and storms, likely to be overwhelmed by climate refugees from NYC and NJ, likely to be a breeding ground for amped up versions of Lyme, Zika, and other insect-borne diseases... In my head I replay the scene in Amitav Ghosh's *The Great Derangement* (thank you, dear, for sending), when his mother looks at him like he's crazy for suggesting she move out of her ancestral home because the World Bank reports it's at high risk for flooding. It's a calm afternoon and he drops the idea. 'Contrary to what I might like to think,' he writes, 'my life is not guided by reason; it is ruled, rather, by the inertia of habitual motion.' I think we will end up building our dream here, too.

So who's normal, and who's 'crazy' or 'freakish': the ones who heed the warnings or the ones who listen to their hearts' tradition? The conflicting demands twist us all into strange contortions. When I saw my sister in the summer, she told me, angrily, that the way I've been living this pandemic is 'not normal'. 'Well, maybe I'm not normal,' I said, hurt but calm, 'and definitely these are not normal times, so I'd say "normal" isn't a reasonable expectation.'

My sister's barb still sticks in my heart. Yet it is one of those ambiguous gifts of the pandemic to make it clear that those questions—who is normal, who is crazy—are so ultimately unanswerable that we are free, and obligated, to make up our own way. I think we're all very much in the portal, my dear. Even if it's that part of the flight where the crew asks you to lower your window shade for the comfort of the other passengers.

I imagine a plucky historian of the future telling the story of the pandemic through the enormous archives of product reviews from this time. Reviews of masks, obviously ('good size, breathable, and cute designs. I felt better about flying because my 2 year old daughter actually keeps this one on'). But also foldout couches ('we haven't really used this for guests, since the pandemic happened right after we bought it, but my kids like to unfold it and build forts'), felted slippers ('the rubber soles mean I can wander outside when I need a Zoom break and think about how insane this world is'), aromatherapy machines ('great for a little pandemic self-care!'), and all of the too, too, too much stuff we humans cannot stop desiring.

Love,
C

NOVEMBER 12, 2021 | *WALK THROUGH LIGHTLY*

Hi dearest C,

'I think we're all very much in the portal,' you wrote back to me last week. Well, that depends, doesn't it, on what we mean by *portal*.

If the portal is the time-space of opportunity for transformation enabled by real-time living in world-historical crisis and confronting the very real, near, and certain end of the world wrought by climate change, ecological devastation, neoliberal finance capital, the failed liberal state (choose your culprit, there are many more), then of course there is a case to be made that we will always be in the portal. Our task will forever be 'learning to die in the Anthropocene' as Roy Scranton would have it, and learning 'to unsuicide', in Richard Powers's words.

But if the portal was the discrete time-space of collective Covid reckoning, then in some ways we have all been ejected from it already by the twin happenings of escalating Covid worldwide and the widespread, increasingly intractable commonplace that 'the future of the virus has arrived'. Europe's fourth surge is very much underway; closer to home, Arizona is number one again, this time in being the only state in the United States in which Covid is the leading cause of death.

What does it mean: the future of the virus has arrived? On the one hand, it is a species of the gaslighting that has been going on all along. On the other hand, I think it is also qualitatively different in that there is no longer the salutary possibility of storyline. Not only will this story not be resolved ('Covid forever'), not only have we been denied our end ('endemic Covid'), but there is no further *eventness* to collectively record and process. We have all been spun out into the narrative temporality of perpetual denouement.

To put this more simply: we have moved from the temporality of 'no future' to the temporality of 'no plot'.

This is the way in which I am suggesting we may have been ejected from what Arundhati Roy called the portal in her April 2020 essay. I think (and hope) that you and Micah are on a raft (a swanky, decked-out raft!) to the ark, elsewhere. I think we too may be standing on the other side of the portal, though for the moment, I'm visualizing us covered in the gunk of a storm drain, ejected onto the bank at the end of an industrial sewer (it is not as swanky as your raft!). We are blinking and scrunching our eyes in the glare, having not yet made up our minds which way to go.

I know, I'm mixing and muddying metaphors. I'm probably also assuming you can read my mind and between the lines. I guess my point in dwelling on this is that to some extent we all already know what we are going to know, what we were willing to learn, even if the task will now be to know it and learn to live it anew.

I reread Roy this week. Here, again, is what she said then, at the close of her essay:

> [The pandemic] is a portal, a gateway between one world and the next. We can choose to walk through it, dragging the carcasses of our prejudice and hatred, our avarice, our data banks and dead ideas, our dead rivers and smoky skies behind us. Or we can walk through lightly, with little luggage, ready to imagine another world. And ready to fight for it.

We already know who has walked, is walking, will walk through the portal weighted down with the carcasses of dead ideas. We know who is walking through lightly, with little luggage.

Or trying to, anyway. Every day now, I am dropping bags, and Brandon is, too. Belatedly, perhaps. ('Belatedness is possibility,' the postcolonialists say.) But also just in time.

Yesterday, I submitted the last of my job applications. I had to get it over with while I still had the enthusiasm to do it. So far, all I've heard back are desk rejections and crickets. But I feel liberated by having put in what I genuinely believe is a good faith effort to present my professional record to date and not consciously undermine myself. I am willing to give a version of this job (which is to say, this life) another go, somewhere else. And so, I put this effort out into the world.

What I'm *not* willing to do is stay in the job I have, or

to live any longer in this desert. Three cats have now taken over our backyard; they have made themselves thoroughly and inexplicably at home here, appropriating various of the children's toys, cuddling up against the rotting pumpkins that have been out back since Halloween. They curl around our majestic, devastated palo verde tree, into which the children flew so many paper airplanes these last two years. They shed so much hair on the couch that I can no longer sit there without sneezing. The cats are telling me that our time is up.

I feel a new warmth even for those would-be friends whose absence I have been resenting. I feel like Tucson is not just the scene of a crime but also a sphere of missed connection. And that's ok. Like labor pains, this too will end. I feel confident that we will leave here, and when we do, it will be in the knowledge of what this place has been and meant. We will know why we were here. And why we had to leave.

Since I last wrote, I got the boost. Mrinalini got the vax, shot one. My brother came to town. My mother returned from India. I cut off most of my hair. I am working on my daily yoga practice. I am learning to say more no's. I am unlearning some of what I believe has been holding me back from the equanimity and clarity that I am seeking. Maybe the word I was looking for is *truth*. You know how I shy away from universals.

In a moment, I am going to close this letter with love. I'm going to grab my watch and head out for a four-mile run while it's still cool.

It is a genuinely beautiful, sunny day here.

In more ways than I have said, you make it possible for me to see that.

All my love,
R

NOVEMBER 18, 2021 | *SUBTRACTION*

Dear R,

I didn't know I was going to write to you today. I went for a walk, and the surprise of the warm sun coaxed some words out of me (into me?). On the wooded gravel road back to the passive house that we're renting, now with some sense of what I might say, I met the house's owner in his rugged electric wheelchair. What beautiful day—a last reprieve, he said. I could only echo him—such a beautiful day. I hoped a smile would make up for the sentences I couldn't think to say. In these letters, on the road, even in my nightly journal, I've been feeling like I'm running out of words. Like there is nothing that I have to say. It's a hard feeling to describe, except maybe by absences. So I guess that's what there is to write about: subtraction.

What happens when you subtract the academic calendar, the social calendar, most of the bodies. When you subtract the noise of the bodies, of the machines, of the calendar. What happens when you subtract the need to steer the car. What happens when you subtract the limit on dreaming? Minimalism—the aesthetic of subtraction—is still the dominant design trend, despite the criticism that its ideal of beauty is classist. For example, the white-tiled kitchens that need professional cleaning, or the clean lines of large uncurtained windows, which require the absence of neighbors. I've always thought the best and most expensive wines I've tasted are the ones that are the mildest on the tongue; this too is about subtraction. If you subtract all those things that formerly seemed to be necessary, inalienable parts of life, what's left?

So far, this year, two things: silence. And reading.

This silence.... God, the silence. The silence of a well-built house in the woods with the kids somewhere else entirely. Somehow I remember it. If I can just slow down enough to hear it, it's there like a memory. Like a hum, except of course inaudible, like a humming holding this note of divine silence for us. And the silence holds everything.

I remember the embrace of silence. But where do I remember it from? From last winter, from cloud-soaked Oregon, from the time before motherhood? From Rumi? From the time before peak screens and social everything? Or further back, from childhood, when we heard the inaudible hum so loudly that we too had to shout and scream over it? Or even before that, before my body, in the time before time, when the trees were bigger and more numerous than the humans? Is the silence a holdover from while I was unborn?

It's not that the noise is bad and the silence is good; wonderful art has been made from the gluttony of sweet, fragrant, vivid noises. But even that additive art has to understand subtraction. What can be removed without the world crumpling in on itself?

Cases in point: in the quiet, I read (and loved) two books this week. One was your rec, *The Reluctant Fundamentalist* by Mohsin Hamid, which I stayed up much too late reading. The other was *Stoner* by John Williams, which I picked off the shelf of the rental one afternoon, thinking it would be about something else altogether (you can guess what). I began reading in the middle with no context and no commitment, and then went back and devoured the whole. The books have little in common, but both deal with pleasingly long arcs of a lifetime. In both, the historical is relatively muted, and yet it crystallizes sharply in the emotions of the protagonists. Both books had satisfying endings which allowed me to feel I understood, finally, the events that had come before. *Ah, so this is what it was about, then.* One ends with violence. The other, with love. To cover so much, to end up where they did—what did Hamid and Williams have to subtract?

Here the trees are mostly naked now, or clutching raggedy leaves of homespun brown. There is the rare slender golden belle or stubborn scarlet shrub. Having grown up in warmer climates,

I always fear the winter that is now rapidly descending. But today, walking among the trees, I thought: this season too has something to teach me. Something to do with silence.

It is time for me to pick up Areté from Forest School, her penultimate week. I check the mirror on the way out. This is what I look like: very short hair, almost colorless, sticking up in the middle from carelessness. Delicate rosegold spiraling through my lobes blurs the masculine cut. I've showered for the first time in a couple days, and my skin is steamed pinktight. On my feet, blunt black boots with slip-on tabs. Gray bootcut jeans, of a comfortable yoga-denim, over long johns. Dark green open-front cardigan, over an ivory men's twill work shirt (one of Micah's), over black longsleeves. Light gray merino gaiter around my neck. And, let us not forget—a fitted black Sonovia mask, which hangs like a necklace from a slim back lanyard when it's not in use. Today, also, big sunglasses.

I'm reminded of a scene in Claire Louise Bennett's short story 'Control Knobs', which is about solitude, history, and (lack of) control. The protagonist is looking in the mirror, but because she's been without the company of other human faces, she can't interpret what she sees. She starts to freak out but then realizes that it's fine, because 'all the categories by which she has hitherto identified herself are now perfectly redundant. She is not a woman, though neither of course is she a man; she is more like an element.... Material. Matter. Stuff.'

I take the time to look in the large mirror on the way out the door, because in my solitude, this elemental, androgynous version of me looks strange and familiar to my own eyes. Because I might not step back through this same door—or, if I do, it might not be the same me. For sure, I'm not the same person I was when we began these letters. Everything you said about the portal last week was true, and needed to be said. Do you know this poem of Rumi's?

The breezes at dawn have secrets to tell you
Don't go back to sleep!
You must ask for what you really want.
Don't go back to sleep!
People are going back and forth
across the doorsill where the two worlds touch,
The door is round and open
Don't go back to sleep!

For Rumi, the mysterious subtraction of his friend/lover Shams from his life was a portal to god, to his highest self and best poetry. Don't draw the parallel too closely—I hope you're leaving AZ to come nearer to me, not farther away. But I do credit the subtractions of the past nearly two years, and these letters where worlds touch, with waking me to a particular truth.

I love you,
C

SECOND WINTER:
THE END OF THE BEGINNING

Dearest C,

Somewhere in my empty office is a copy of Hannah Arendt's *The Human Condition*. It is one of the books I cherish most from graduate school, because it demonstrated to me at a critical moment the power of the word. You (Arendt Center Fellow) know it well, from Arendt's distinctions between labor, work, and action, to her elaboration of world, to her theory of natality:

> The miracle that saves the world, the realm of human affairs, from its normal, 'natural' ruin is ultimately the fact of natality...It is, in other words, the birth of new men and the new beginning, the action they are capable of by virtue of being born. Only the full experience of this capacity can bestow upon human affairs faith and hope, those two essential characteristics of human existence which Greek antiquity ignored altogether, discounting the keeping of faith as a very uncommon and not too important virtue and counting hope among the evils of illusion in Pandora's box.

Merry Christmas, my friend. If Arendt's account is right, you know me to be very 'Greek' in my estimation of hope. And yet this morning these are the words I choose to sit with, this passage with which I have, against all odds, kept faith for over a decade now.

The miracle of redemption. The miracle of the new. Rebirth. The fact of return. The Gospel's tidings that Arendt quotes: 'A child has been born unto us.' No wonder that these are the kinds of words I hold onto, and not just from Arendt.

From Arundhati Roy's 1997 *The God of Small Things*: 'Things can change in a day.'

From Ling Ma's 2018 *Severance*, 'After the End, came the Beginning.'

I have taught *Severance* to three classes now, starting in Fall 2019. When news of the pandemic first hit the mainstream in February 2020, a student slipped a hand-written note under my office door: 'Yo Prof! Have you heard about this Wuhan coronavirus??? Just like the book!!!' That note is still there, on my wasted desk. Every semester since, Ma's deeply prophetic and deeply historical novel hits harder. I can't believe I didn't send it to you before this Christmas, and yet, I'm glad that I didn't. Not late, as we have said to each other, but right on time.

It's of course no coincidence that *Severance* ends with a pregnant Candace walking off into the horizon, entirely alone at the end of the world and not at all alone. A lot of apocalypse novels end this way: conserving hope and the miracle of natality. The other novel I teach at the end of my Asian Century class is Chang-rae Lee's 2014 *On Such a Full Sea*. It also ends with a pregnant woman, Fan, who carries within her not only the seed of possibility but more specifically the promise, thanks to an accident of genetics, of giving birth to the only child in the world who will be free of 'C-illness'. Yes! It's actually called C-illness: the disease of capitalism, cancer, climate...and now Covid.

Lee's novel is not half as good as Ma's at the level of the sentence, and yet, it is even more prescient, more eerily on point.

In his novel, everyone is infected with C-illness: 'Our tainted world looms within us, every one.' Mass infection has led to the stratification of society into the Charters (the privileged who live relatively comfortable lives in gated communities despite being diseased; they have access to the likes of Sotrovimab and Paxlovid), B-mor (a dystopian future Baltimore-as-laboring-colony, filled with factory workers, grocery deliverers, those 'essential workers' who harvest the food and are expected to die early), and the Open Counties (where anything goes, baby; wild and unregulated and beyond the control of the directorate). In the Open Counties you may get eaten by a crazy cannibalistic circus family. But, if C-illness doesn't kill you, you might just survive.

We've been living 'after the end' for some weeks now. Since you last wrote, I've thought often of the opening lines of C. D. Wright's 'Morning Star': 'This isn't the end. It simply / cannot be the end. It is a road.'

Omicron made its debut around Thanksgiving, and in the intervening weeks, the new pandemic has begun. *The beginning of the end*, many are clinging to desperate hope. You and I both know it's the end of the beginning. This time, the CDC, policy-makers, and the powers that be are acting decisively by cutting recommended quarantine times and sending infected workers back to work, stocking the shelves and filling the Amazon boxes. It's the Open Counties out there. Venture out at your peril.

Oh, the failed and treacherous CDC. Can't Disrupt Capitalism! Capitalist Death Cult! Take your quarantine over two fifteen-minute pee breaks. You're allowed to isolate if you're on a ventilator, but if that thing has wheels and a battery, haul your ass back to work. (I'm on Twitter again for the one-liners.) Patrick Blanchfield's death-drive-nation essay puts it like this: 'The Economy must abide, even if you yourself perish. It's nothing personal, you must understand.... Services must be provided, even if that means serving ourselves up, too. With all the indifference of the death drive, capitalism insists on the repetition of the same, no matter what.'

The operative word is indifference.

Case records in the US and Europe are about to be broken. They will keep being broken. The waves are all asymptotic now, heading for the sky. Hospitalizations are up, including for pediatric cases, even as gaslighting-headline-writers proclaim 'milder' cases for the vaccinated (guess who is not vaccinated? The other major news is that Pfizer screwed up the trials for ages 2–5). At over 600 pediatric deaths per year, Covid is now the number one natural cause of death for children. We are on the rollercoaster wondering how high we will go: will we hang out at the top, our bucket rocking dangerously, machine stuck, or will we crash back down, with a jerk or a reverse-swan-dive, will we break our necks at the bottom, will we ever get off this ride?

It is March again. March in that the news comes daily of people we know who are infected, including the triple-vaccinated. March: in that no place and nobody will be spared, boosted or not. March: in that we are uncertain. March: in that we are resolved.

Of course, it is also not March at all, but Christmas morning. I am writing these words before first light. Soon, Brandon and I will drive up to his parents' house, where the kids are awaiting our arrival so that they can see if Santa has come. Brandon's brothers and partners are there, too, in from Philadelphia and DC, via Chicago. In the lead up to their arrival, we worried; we needled everyone about getting tests; we got tested ourselves, crucially, since Shai managed to bring home yet another cold, just in time for the holidays. Now we're all together, having a festive week: many meals around the big table, gratitude circles, playing the Korean game Yut Nori, carol singing, talent-showing, watching old home videos of Brandon and his brothers from their before-times Mississippi Christmases.

In the face of Omicron and the variants to come, in the face of perpetual C-illness, I have a vision of the future stretching out like this Christmas: with big-risk-special-occasions, and a radically constricted daily life. By constricted I mean they can't go back to school on Monday, not unless we change something dramatic. (Our current plan is to send Mrinalini back with the KN95 strapped to her face as usual, and take turns each day having lunch with her in the school parking lot.) By constricted I mean that the children will never go back to the grocery store; that there will be no playdates; there will be no Friday evening after-school tea parties like I grew up with; we will not have friends over for dinner. Probably, we will not have friends.

But the major, one-off risks, the kind we have taken a few times now in the last two years—flying to Maine, attending my brother's wedding in Johannesburg, this full-family Christmas—I suppose we will continue to take them. Riding the waves, watching the numbers.

This morning, when I opened my email, I saw that my mother has drafted the invitation to my brother's wedding reception in California: an indoor dinner, with what I assume will be 150–200 guests, from at least three continents, to be held on March 20, 2022.

I read the email; I hit the X in the top-right corner. Clarity. Truth. Silence. Courage. Acceptance. Concentration. Faith. Surrender. Renunciation. Things can change in a day, I remind myself. We are going to take care of ourselves, of each other. I'm going to let March take care of itself.

In the meantime, will you write letters back and forth with me?

It's day 665.

Onward, with love,
R

THIRD SPRING: TURN THE PAGE

Dear R,

It's almost March, again.

I feel like a stage actor, again trying to summon the feeling for these words drained dead by repetition. On this umpteenth invocation of the return of March, Russia invaded Ukraine by land, sea, and air—by internet and information, too. Just as NATO countries have long been warning, as Putin has long been denying. Will this be remembered as the start of a world war? Is America too distracted and divided to do anything about it? Will the Ukranians rise up as they did in 2014? Is this finally the war part of the disease-war (*nosos-stasis*) dyad the Greeks were always on about?

So many questions. Oil prices up, stock markets down. Cases are down, too, and so every state except Hawaii (and Puerto Rico) have abandoned indoor mask mandates. Everyone knows this part of the dance. Masks go down, and cases go up. Iceland's health ministry has said they want 'as many people as possible' to be infected to achieve 'widespread societal resistance'. They're just saying aloud what everyone is thinking.

Well, not everyone. Not China and Hong Kong. Not me. Micah and I have been making progress on balloon19.org, a campaign to encourage the formation of small Covid-free communities—a fool's errand if there ever was one! But remember I coined the slogan for our short-lived activist consultancy: *we win lost causes*. Remember those eight Russians who went to the square to protest Russia's invasion of Czechoslovakia in 1968. 'Those 5 minutes of freedom,' one of them called it. It's not that I don't understand the appeal of the 'herd immunity' thesis. There are long swaths of time when I too cannot imagine any other way out is possible. But that reality, the return to normal that others are so keen on—*that* is not possible for us, at this point, having hardly stepped inside others' space for two years. If the dead could speak, what would they say? We push on. Why it should be so painful to be different in a culture that prizes individualism, I don't know. But if there is a second draft of existence (as posited in Sheila Heti's newest, *Pure Color*), I hope there is much less binary thinking.

Since I last wrote, we endured the Covid-scare ritual—sniffles and sore throats, tests, anxiety, more tests, more anxiety, one last test, negative.

We endured disappointment: through some obscure technicality, the Klima windfall remains on the tree.

We had an ice storm that left us without power and heat for three days. We've considered and abandoned what feels like a dozen plans—to move to Maine, to bring Micah's parents and brother to the Hudson Valley, to move us all near to my parents in Maryland.

I've started to code all those plans as the fight-or-flight response to the constant anxiety. The sense that there *must* be a better way to live through this horror. Then acceptance returns. Given the poor success of the vaccine in young children, I guess the present homeostasis is also our future. Split the childcare hours fifty-fifty. Classes on Outschool. Outdoor playdates, weather and cases permitting, and if we still have any friends. Rent vacation houses in the country to ease the monotony and strain of coexisting in our small city house. We cannot really go anywhere, but maybe we can build what we need—a Covid-cautious co-op?—where we are.

But things are different for you. You've always managed to

straddle caution and connection, and so a different pathway is open for you. As I write, you are taking your first brave steps through it. I understand that that was always the point of it, that the path any of us found through the pandemic would also bear a strong relation to where we found ourselves on the 'other' side. Which is actually just a transformed inside. You will tell me, I hope, in a letter.

As of yesterday, the ground is bare of snow. With shock, I realized part of me hadn't believed the snow would ever go away. Part of me forgot what spring is, how inevitable for those of us still breathing. When the experts predict that the virus will become seasonal, is this what they mean—that I'll forget a life without Covid in the air is possible?

Happy birthday, pandemic. You're turning three, if we follow the older east Asian custom of counting from one from birth. You are a wonder and a terror, but you can't do it on your own; you still need us humans to grow and evolve. You've stripped me of so much and left only a few things: family, friendship, writing, and a heightened awareness of time. That's your gift to me—may I keep and treasure it always. And these letters, I suppose, are my respectful gift to you.

Love,

C

MARCH 26, 2022 | *GOODBYE TO ALL THAT*

Dearest—

Yesterday, we got rid of the coffee table you might have rested a drink on back in our Berkeley days. The hundred dollar floor model that came with us to Princeton, to Chicago, to Reno, to Tucson. We got rid of the two armchairs my mother-in-law picked up in Toledo from a yard sale. We have given away most of the children's toys—which they never played with—as well as all the detritus of Shai's babyhood, and Mrinalini's, too: the stroller she had from day one and which has journeyed with us, and the carseat. The kid-sized table, the rocking horse, all the toys and games that Brandon's colleague would take.

A couple weeks ago, in preparation for our trip to California for my brother's Covid-delayed wedding reception, I had both kids try on every piece of clothing in their closets, and we got rid of everything that didn't fit (which was almost everything).

Walk through lightly, Roy said. *Less baggage, more comfort,* is my grandmother's line. I said both to Mrinalini yesterday and her response was immediate and grave: 'Travel light to travel right.'

I gave her a quizzical look.

'I read it in a book,' she shrugged.

As I write these words, I am sitting in an empty-seeming 'playroom' in a emptier-by-the-day house. It is beautiful here. Sunny, in the mid 20s. I am already nostalgic for this house, the nest we made, the fortress we've had. But I am also exhilarated.

We did it. We signed with Rice on Sunday. We are leaving Tucson. We got new jobs (and fresh tenure clocks) in a new city (the fourth largest in the country) in a new state (Texas, of all places!), with new colleagues who have so far been incredibly warm, welcoming, generous, uncannily friendly—even one who remembers my mother from their brief time overlapping at Syracuse in the early 1980s. None of the particulars matter as much as this one: We are starting over. We are tearing it all down and leaving it all behind and making a new life.

The last few weeks have been wild, frantic, unbelievable: first the interview out in Houston (what a big city! Chinatown and Little India! Skyscrapers! Traffic!), for which I had to write a job talk in a weekend; waiting for the offer; signing it in the middle of my brother's reception; now serving two masters (teaching and advising here, while already posting course synopses for fall); have to sell our house, buy a new house, find new schools for the kids, camps, fix up the summer schedule.... Goodbyes from my soon-to-be-former colleagues have been surprisingly loving, though some of their messages suggest I have received a death row pardon while they all head to the gallows.

We have done all of the above with Covid on the brain. Committed, as always, to not getting or spreading it, but having to take some chances to make that new life. First, the job interviews in Houston. We ate indoors at restaurants with low-grade terror, and masked at home for a few days after. It was ok. I gave my talk maskless, with the small audience pushed into the back seats of the classroom. I know that in the Fall we will have to teach in person. My Zoom classes are going so poorly now—and I am so disinterested in them—that I feel both resigned and willing to do it. (At least, the classes at Rice should be small, and we're hoping for private school mask and vaccine mandates.)

Meanwhile, Mrinalini's school dropped their mask mandate, like all the elementary schools. The plotlessness we began to feel in fall, which was disrupted by Omicron (yet quickly repressed by the dominant forces), has accelerated into a deadly game of chicken in which we are all finally and ultimately and irrevocably on our own, baby (again).

One of the many songs from Lin Manuel Miranda's *Encanto* that has been our family soundtrack this last month puts it this way: 'the ship doesn't swerve / has it heard / how big the iceberg is?'

No choice but to watch for the icebergs ourselves. Like when we held the kids out of school this past January and February. I'll never forget the headlines that accompanied the dropping of mandates and isolation guidelines: 'Omicron is mild'; 'How soon will Covid be normal?'; 'Over half of Europe could be infected in next 2 months': 'Hospitals nearing capacity in 2 dozen states'; 'Open Everything'.

Shai never went back to school after winter break, and in the end he was home for two months. We tried Brandon's idea about pulling Mrinalini out at lunchtime and eating with her in the parking lot to avoid the worst of the exposure. That lasted two days before we panicked. She was home for six weeks. That's why we pulled her out of the public system, I guess. The private school didn't ask a single question; we just kept paying the tuition and returned her scanty homework by email.

My brother's wedding reception was harder to swallow: We were in very close contact with all my family (about 35 people) and then 125-ish at the reception, which we all attended (though Shai mostly hid upstairs with an uninspiring, but not dangerous, last-minute baby-sitter). It's been a week since. Everyone is fine, Covid-wise. How did we squeak by? I think this really was the very best time, numbers-wise, for the event. We're in the valley; the climb with BA.2 has begun, but last week we were down at the low point. Also, it was a very self-selected group of vaxxed and boosted adults who either just had Covid or have been variously committed to not getting it and have figured out how to mostly manage the risk.

We are not feeling self-satisfied or anything! We are realizing anew that it's the day-to-day constant risk that will get you (like school!). But these one-off major risks: they are perhaps not the primary threat we face.

Of course, we are also wondering how on Earth we are going to manage in Houston.

Is getting Covid going to be the price we pay for a new life?

We do not want to pay it. But we are still moving forward, hoping that everything we learned in the last two years will enable us to survive, somehow, and maybe even thrive. To do it all better, to shield the children yet also widen their worlds, and ours.

Yesterday, while we were packing up various tchotchkes and filling garbage bags of who-knows-what, Brandon looked at me in astonishment and asked how we managed to make it happen. We very nearly didn't, of course. You know that in the end, despite all the job interviews and multiple virtual visits, we only ever got one straight-up offer between us, and we managed to convert it into two. Brandon is still in shock.

But I'm not all that surprised, I told him. I never really allowed myself to contemplate that we wouldn't move, so deeply did I come to know that our Tucson chapter is over. It has to be over. The story is done telling. There is much I will miss here—the pool, always and forever, which saved my life—and Shai's babyhood, and being together here for the first two years of the pandemic, and my big girl growing into herself. But it's time to turn the page.

I'm not in shock because I have been writing toward this, with you. And I'm ready, I told him, because I had the portal.

Love always,
R

BOOK 3

THE WOODS

Are we still in the early months? Will we allow ourselves to be?

Will we become infinitely elastic and yielding, or be stretched until we snap? Will things get unstuck, or will we all just fall off a cliff?

What is the question I should be asking? What work is worth attempting? How to write these letters? How to love the kids?

If we belong nowhere and to nobody, how will we model and create belonging for them?

How can a place that contained our lives, so compactly for so long, vanish so completely from my consciousness?

Is the land in fact hostile, or have I imbued it with hostility?

If you subtract all those things that formerly seemed to be necessary, inalienable parts of life, what's left? What can be removed without the world crumpling in on itself?

I can't remember now exactly what Aristotle says about true friendship. Is it that, if I am a real friend, I would want for you what you want for yourself? Or is it that I should want for my friend what I want for myself?

Can you accept it? Can you accept me? Am I allowed to be different, or do I have to conform to your ideas of what's appropriate in order to be loved?

How to open my arms wide enough to span the different realities, the ones each of us is 'in', the ones in each of us?

What is memoir, if not the fiction that life can be narrativized, ordered, made into story?

We are on the rollercoaster wondering how high we will go: will we hang out at the top, our bucket rocking dangerously, machine stuck, or will we crash back down, with a jerk or a reverse-swan-dive, will we break our necks at the bottom, will we ever get off this ride?

Will I die of something mundane like a car accident on the long solo drive back? Am I being as selfish and reckless as he thinks?

When the experts say the virus will become seasonal, is this what they mean—that I'll forget a life without Covid in the air is possible?

Is getting Covid going to be the price we pay for a new life?

Are there any other miracles to be had?

The acute phase of the pandemic is over. The chronic phase has begun.

Forever. Covid forever.

In the meantime, will you write letters back and forth with me?

It's day 791.

THIRD SUMMER: THE AFTERLIFE

Dearest C,

Shai tested negative today. It's day 11, if you count the day of his first symptoms (a low-grade fever) as Day Zero. I must be a day or two behind him. We got his positive PCR on Sunday morning the 19th—a happy Father's Day it wasn't—and you know the rest. Brandon and Mrinalini evacuated our rented apartment right away. Feeling that I already had a sore throat coming on, I pushed them out and elected to stay.

There's a part of me that would like to be the martyr. I elected to stay, despite having, like Brandon, tested negative that morning. I elected to stay, and thereby committed to getting Covid, by being the parent who would cuddle and kiss our baby anyway. If I'm honest though, I think I already had it. There's the rational case: Mrinalini was boosted on May 27 with a third shot and Brandon had his fourth sometime in the spring. (They should have been better protected than I was.) And then there's the fact that I just knew.

Anyway, the next morning, I throat-swabbed a rapid and got my positive result. I'm sure I'm still positive. I can feel the virus in my bones, under my skin, in my typing fingers that are a little more hesitant than they ought to be, moving just a tad slower on the keys, which are a smidge harder to push down. I have not had much by way of symptoms (a day of sore throat, a day of the mildest cold; allergies this year have been worse, that part at least of what the minimizers say was true for me), but I have had this: the constant awareness of the virus; of its flowing through me; of its coresidence.

This is what Lyme must also feel like, I find myself musing. Early-stage arthritis. Chikungunya. Not that I've had any of these illnesses, nor need I strain for an analogy. This is just... Covid. But I'm newly aware of the fellowship of the infected, of survivors, of sufferers, of long-haulers. We are all long-haulers now, after a fashion.

And what is it doing to my brain? Not what-form-of-Long-Covid-will-I-be-reckoning-with, which is a question I both cannot stop asking and will not allow myself to dwell on. (I will live the answer to that question. I have my own fears and suspicions. Most of all, I want the Long Covid to come for me—20 per cent chance it will, the CDC says—and not my precious little one, who bounced back almost immediately and who I hope has vanquished the virus for good.) But what is it doing inside my brain right now—what forms of havoc is it enacting? Well, I have had a couple very angry days this week. I have been listless. I have stared at the wall. I have imagined my body a loaded gun and contemplated taking it out of this isolation house, to spread the virus among the foolish unmasked and unsuspecting.

That is the virus speaking, you would say, the virus that desires only to spread. But it's also me, furious that despite everything, Shai picked it up at summer camp, where he was the only one masked, because the official state response to the pandemic is 'you do you'. It's me, not the virus: frankly wondering why I shouldn't meet the violent, individualist conduct of the back-to-normies with my own brutal form of anti-sociality.

Oh, the week we've had! Shai and I have been enacting a perverse version of those early March 2020 lockdown days. Stuck alone in this Houston rental, what do we do all day? Organically, we have grown our schedule. I let him watch TV in the morning, so I can suck down some off-tasting coffee, doomscroll through the news of each successively heartbreaking and enraging Supreme Court decision. I feed him breakfast in bed. Then we play: Go Fish, Crazy Eights, Dinosaur Memory Match, Trivial Pursuit. After your joy-filled gift package arrived: playdoh, bubbles. Also: rocket balloons, jewel balloons, workbooks, every kind of sticker book, painting with water. My sister-in-law sent a package adding darts and scavenger hunt to the rotation.

Then it's lunchtime. Then it's naptime. I have read Shai every book we have in this place, more than once. Mealtimes are comical. Thankfully, he is almost as disinterested in food as I am. After napping, he watches TV again, and eats treats. While he watches TV, I wait on him with snacks, and then we play again, an inversion of the morning's rotation. We are outside on the back deck as long as we can stand the mosquitoes.

Have you ever had the thought that if you were in prison, you would become very fit? (Embarrassing to admit this Hollywood-movie-inspired-line of thought, but...) You'd have little to do, so you'd do push-ups and pull-ups on the door frame, that sort of thing. It's a version of the silly hope I've sometimes had that if I were ever to get very sick—terminal—I would know exactly what I needed to do, what I needed to write, and how to finish my last work. Suddenly, in the absence of a future, it would become very clear. Not just my schedule cleared, but my thoughts.

It's a foolish person's fantasy. Of course, I don't want to be terminal (also: 'we're all terminal'), and of course I know the lesson of the vision: do it now, don't wait, write it now. But the reason I bring this up is I've had the opposite realization this week, while sitting and staring into space, letting the virus do its worst and watching the minutes tick by, counting down the days. (Just like in lockdown, the first few days were the hardest and longest; now each day blends into the next.) Maybe I wouldn't do anything. I would just...let the hours slip away.

What else is the virus teaching me? You know that story about the religious anti-vaxxer who says, 'God wouldn't have given me polio/measles/TB if he wasn't going to save me.' Or the person who resists cancer treatment because they're waiting for divine intervention. Or the forced-birther who thinks fetuses with fatal abnormalities should be brought to term and so on, because it's all part of 'God's plan'. There are lots of versions of this story. The punchline is always the response from God: *you idiot, I gave you the vaccine! I gave you chemotherapy! I gave you abortion!*

I'm not surprised we met Covid here, in Houston. That it was, ultimately, the price of our new life. I'm sad, and I wish we hadn't met it. But we did.

The last few weeks we were in Tucson I started agitating about getting Shai an unauthorized vaccine shot. We knew the surge was coming, but we couldn't find a single summer camp in Houston with universal masking, and we knew the pediatric vaccine (however lacking) would not be available until the third week of June. So, I took Shai on his fourth birthday for a shot of Pfizer 5-11. ('We're playing a joke on them,' was how he processed my bizarre instructions to lie about his age.) We knew we wouldn't make it. And we didn't make it.

I believe that one shot helped him clear the virus faster. Truly, I do.

And then there are the friends we suddenly gained. A friend of a friend who also just moved to Houston from New Orleans. They had a hell of a time getting here: their nine-year-old got Covid from close friends at their going-away party; the movers smashed a bunch of their stuff; the AC in their apartment here in Houston was broken when they arrived (and yes, it's been a record-breakingly-hot-June, and yes, I didn't want to believe it, but it is *even hotter* here than Tucson). We met up when these folks arrived in town, and then they left to visit family in Malaysia, leaving us the keys to their apartment so that we could let in the AC repair guys.

I thought we were doing them a favor. I admit, I groaned a bit to Brandon about having to deal with the repairs. And now Brandon and Mrinalini have been living at their place for ten days, which is the only reason they didn't get Covid.

I gave you the vaccine.

I gave you the keys!

Even the timing is optimal. We spent the first two weeks here finding and buying a house. We closed in less than three weeks, even with a financed offer. Shai is now testing negative, and if I can follow soon, we will get out of here as planned this coming weekend for the trip to Maine and my brother-in-law's wedding and my parents' visit and—I hope!—yours.

So, I feel like a fallen soldier, and I am somewhat ashamed of being infected, and I am now a member of a club I've been trying to avoid for two-plus years, and I'm licking my wounds. But I am grateful, too, the kind of gratitude I had when Mrinalini got and survived Kawasaki disease during our third week in Chicago (repetitions and symmetries!) and I knew then why we had moved there, why it happened as it did, how it was foretold.

I already bizarrely love Houston. Before this, when I was driving the maniac highways with the city skyline before me, and touring the five-star playgrounds and parks with the kids, when we were house hunting and ice-cream-testing, I experienced more than one moment of sheer elation. Certainty that we have arrived where we are meant to be, against all odds. What are the odds! Houston, Texas, the belly of the beast, in the year of our lord 2022, Covid year three.

I was having one of those elated moments less than two weeks ago with Brandon, as we walked to buy a sandwich from a shop near the university and our new house. I felt elated, and I said to him, that we were riding high and we should enjoy it while we could, because our luck wouldn't hold forever. We had just gone under contract with the house. And then, this. The universe is hearing me and talking to me and responding to me and joking with me and playing trickster, and if I've learned anything from you it's to trust that, this, all of it.

Brandon just texted. He's taken Shai to the splash pad; it's the first time they've really been together in ten days.

Absolutely thrilled to have him back.

I replied with a heart. It's been hard to be away from him, from Mrinalini, from those other bodies with which my metabolism is synced, my heartbeat.

Just so happy, now u next.

I have to get back, C. And I have to get better. The next chapter is just beginning.

Tell me all your news?

Always,
R

JULY 6, 2022 | *TIMING*

Dearest R,

We're in the same timezone now. You got your negative test results, and you survived the flights, and now our long-laid plan to meet in Maine is approaching its hatching day. Only a letter or two away! Then our two bodies will weather the same weather, consume the same food, exude our subtle smells into shared air, shed skin cells onto the same earth, and around us will swarm those other bodies that we made with our bodies.... Soon, we will be in the same present, the now that is a here that is a gift.

I can't quite believe it. Don't quite let myself believe it, in case someone *else* catches Covid (BA.5 edition) and our plans come crashing down. I wonder how having had Covid will, or will not, have changed you. Will I be able to perceive the changes, separate them from the changes of this duration, the forever pandemic?

I'm reading a marvelous book called *The Order of Time*. I wish I'd read it years ago, but it wasn't written yet. The author, Carlo Rovelli, a distinguished physicist and a lover of poetry, takes the commonplaces about time—that it's the same everywhere, that it flows in one direction, etc.—and demolishes them one by one. Everything he says has been proved countless times since Einstein. Yet we haven't really assimilated it into our everyday views. We all act 'as if' time *is* the abstractions we employ (calendars, train tables, time zones), even though we all have direct experience *and* a verified theory of the ways time doesn't behave like that at all. That is the power of an instantiated abstraction.

There's lots to think about in the book, but I keep returning to the ways each of us, each phenomenon, exists in our own timescape (the US Supreme Court is stuck in about 1860, it seems). Rovelli pictures one friend who lives in the mountains, and one at the beach: time moves more slowly close to the earth, so that the friend at the sea ages more slowly. Time moves more slowly for your feet than your head ('swift as thought,' as Arendt says Homer used to say). Time also moves more slowly when you're moving fast (the agonizing wait of flying on a jetplane), and faster when you're staying still (an afternoon at the pool).

Rovelli is probably talking about a matter of nano-seconds in these cases, but if you'll permit a creative misreading, I imagine that by staying still as long you and I have—by staying true to the event of the early pandemic, by holding that space—we have had 'more' time: aged more, reflected more, launched ourselves further along our (destined?) paths...

And then, inevitably, when you accelerated, moved (you had to), your time slowed down. And Covid caught up with you (it had to).

You know me well enough to know that all this high abstraction, high concept speculation is a coping mechanism—if not an outright dodge. You know to keep reading till you get to this part. The part where I say, it looks like we're not going to visit my parents and my baby niece this summer, after all.

It's a very American story, and a very Meghan and Harry story. It's the script I've been trying to tell differently, the story I fell into when I fell in love with Micah and can't seem to exit. *Beauty and the Beast* ('He's not a beast! He's kind and gentle!'), *The Little Mermaid* ('But daddy, I *love* him!'), *Frozen* ('They say have courage, and I'm trying to'). The high-brow version is Noel Ignatiev and Marcus Garvey's *Race Traitor*—today's language of 'allyship' completely erases the pain and the costs of actually disrupting white solidarity.

Is family estrangement the exit from this long simmering drama? Is this the next right thing?

I hear the story reflected back to me in your voice. In your world, 'there is no possible world in which I don't go'. In your world, I have to choose whether they are my people. You don't skip a once-a-year family trip and the chance to meet your five-month old niece for the first time over micro-aggressions to your black partner. Family dynamics are synonymous with tension. You go, you deal.

But I can't. I started speaking up, over WhatsApp and email, where I can't deny that my dad really did reply that he 'doesn't see color' and that Micah is a person of 'peculiar interests' and 'extreme personal sensitivity', when a normal person would just say, 'I'm sorry.' And now that the Ugly Underside has erupted into the Ugly Outside, no one knows how to clean it up. I spoke with my sister yesterday (who exited the family chat rather than have the conversation), and she didn't encourage me to come for the visit: she just doesn't want her son (now four) to be exposed to 'that kind of tension'. She wants there to be 'trust' before we can have the conversation about race—a classic cart-before-the-horse move.

I can't really blame them. We all swim in the ocean of racism, how could it not seep into our pores? But I can't help but wish they would try a little harder to swim against the current.

So I guess I have chosen, finally. I wish there was something else I could have done. I wish there were a morally pure path in which I stood up for Micah without hurting my birth family. I wish I could tell the story better. Maybe one day I will. For now I try to speak to them with my heart, and to leave the door open for things to change.

One day a week or so ago I woke up, when all these conversations were just beginning, and knew I would change my name. As if I already knew where the conversations would end. So I've been asking people to call me Chi ('Key'). My middle name will be Rainer, after my beloved Rilke. And Bornfree, a new surname for all four of us, one name to cast off all together our slave and master lineages.

While the last name is a bid to escape racial inheritances, the first name change is a natural corollary to my newish gender-neutral pronouns. These are a smaller part of the family tensions, but on the whole entering the space of they/them has not been a dramatic change. A new kind of story for gender transitions is becoming possible: one with less suffering and angst. Just a quiet opting-in to a wider, wigglier grammatical-social space. At least that's how I want it to be. It's another freedom—another baggage let-go—I credit to the pandemic. The idea that I might claim a non-binary identity first occurred to me in the early days of lockdown, when my body was so freed from the predatory gaze of others. Making the pronoun switch last month felt like a way to preserve some of that freedom, as I move more in the embodied world.

These days I get up early each weekday to write. Sometimes fiction, sometimes fables, sometimes just venting. Usually nothing anyone will ever lay eyes on. Today it is this letter, which you will read, changing the nature of this here-now in which I write. Today I read a poem by Rumi, the Sunrise Ruby: 'Work. Keep digging your well. Water is there somewhere. Submit to a daily practice. Your loyalty to that is a ring on the door. Keep knocking, and the joy inside will eventually open a window and look out to see who's there.'

I'm here, I'm knocking. Soon (God willing) I'll be there, knocking on your door too, my friend. I hope you're recovering fully, and that your family will too. You have always been 'like family' for me, and that is only more true now. Grateful for that.

Love,
C

AUGUST 3, 2022 | *DID YOU PRAY?*

Dearest C,

I'm sitting at my new desk, which is my old desk—a worn-down honey colored wooden number I got very cheap at a second-hand store in Tucson. Now it's paired with an even cheaper chair I picked up a couple days ago here in Houston, on one of our long and sweaty afternoon tours of the local consignment stores.

We have been back in Houston for almost a week now. Our house is maybe 75 per cent unpacked. None of the paintings or pictures are up, but most everything else has found its way to some provisional spot in this rather (the word on the tip of my fingers is 'monstrously') large patio home with more stairs than rooms. We've gone from a one-story ranch house in the desert, to three-stories in the swampy bayou. We had a pool; now we don't even have a backyard. Really, could it get any different than this?

It's surreal being here; I still have the feeling of having arrived where we are meant to be; I love Houston. I love having the opportunity to love Houston. I love how it sounds when I say it, how uncanny and unlikely for this California girl. Brandon and I got into yoga by watching videos on Amazon, and we quote the instructor to each other sometimes, in playful seriousness. One of her lines is our mantra for this move: 'We're not going to hate it; we're going to love it.' Said in a cheeky voice about a painful yoga pose. Our life, basically.

Just two weeks ago you arrived in Maine. In the days leading up to your visit, I really wasn't sure it would happen. So many Covid contingencies! (Would my mother, fighting off her second Covid case, have a Paxlovid rebound? Would my brother-in-law return sick from a wedding in Denver?)

And then there you all were, emerging through the trees in your black Tesla, your two babes tumbling out onto the grass, and then all four of the children, fast friends, running circles around each other, tossing beanbags, exchanging life vests, readying themselves for the boat, for lawn games, for s'mores around the campfire, for lake swims and shouts and giggles, Mrinalini pulling the three others around on an inflatable (what was it?) stingray.

It really was a perfect visit. I hesitate to describe it here—would anyone believe me if I did?—how the rains stopped just in time for our dinners on the patio, how open the beach was, how perfect the sand and the drive to the ocean, how readily the little ones fell into chatter and camaraderie and the joy of being together. How cool and beautiful it was on the dock, when we stole a couple of hours together to chat and muse after the children were asleep. How the sunset bloomed. The taste of the wine.

There's a part of me that doesn't want to say much about it, that wants to veil the precious reunion from others' eyes.

Maybe it's enough to say that it was precious. What a beautiful consummation of the two preceding years of dreaming and walking together. And what an auspicious start to the next phase, to the coming together again, to the renewal, to the learning anew what it means to keep time with someone, what it means to have a friend on the journey, to *be* a friend, to live in the family of friendship.

Chi—when I say your new name (or should I say, this version of your name? Is it a break, or is it a new form; or both, or neither?), I think of the French 'qui'. The subject. Who. Who? Qui. Qui est-ce? Appropriately, I think.

The clock is ticking and I see that I have to get up from this table in a matter of minutes to pick up Shai from his (universally-masked!) morning art class. But there was something else.

Monday night I went to hear Mohsin Hamid read at the Alley Theater in downtown Houston. It was a packed reading (masks required, thankfully). I'd never heard Hamid, so despite the exhaustion and having to miss dinner and not knowing what to wear, I went. It was a piece of the old days, the before-times, the fellowship of readers and writers, the insipid questions, the writer forced to labor as critic and comic and coach all at once.

Anyway, at the end of the talk, Hamid was asked to offer writing advice and he said this. *When you start out, you think that writing is like climbing a mountain. As you continue on, you realize it is more like digging a well. Dig, dig; the water will come.*

And this: *it is not so much, did you reach perfection? But, how often did you pray?*

With you, mon ami,
R

AUGUST 24, 2022 | *TOUCH OF A HAND*

Dear R,

I've been reading the sculptor Anne Truitt's *Daybook*, among other things, and keep meaning to send it to you, to deliver a physical welcome from my world into your new home.

What stops me is that you don't need more books, you don't need one more thing to organize and put away, especially now.

But I will send some of it here in this letter, virtualized.

The book begins in Tucson, the desert you've just left. Truitt goes to Arizona to rest after a trying period; an old woman dies in the desert while she is there. She goes from Tucson to Yaddo, not far from me in NY. Her memories of childhood take place in Easton, Maryland, where my parents now live. And most of the work happens in DC, a city I am all too familiar with. So it was the geography first of all that spoke to me and made me think of you.

It is also the geography of the family which captures me. In the course of her records, Truitt recalls her childhood, her college days, her Japan period, limns her divorce, mothers her three becoming-adult children, and watches herself encounter her first grandchild for the first time. Daughter, mother, grandmother. I've bowed out of the female lineage, but I recognize the phases and difficult transitions. I honor the humility with which she accepts her daughter-mother's boundaries, the moral sensitivity with which she perceives a new person emerge. I think you would like that, too.

Especially, though, reading *Daybook* reminds me of our letters. 'I once watched a snake shed his skin. Discomfort apparently alternating with relief, he stretched and contracted, stretched and contracted, and slowly, slowly, pushed himself out the front end of himself. His skin lay behind him, transparent. The writing of these notebooks has been like that for me.' Isn't that what we have done, too?

What finally made me sit down and send Truitt in this way was her casual mention, just after the passage I quoted, of her sculpture 'Portal'. I looked it up and immediately felt I'd seen it before somewhere. Have you?

An 8-foot tall, 9-inch square column, painted exactingly with asymmetrical rectangles of white. In the photo it is planted just in front of the black-drop, and its shadow rays angle into the dark. Much as I like her in her book, I think the minimalism gets it wrong: the portal has two posts, at least.

But then I think: perhaps the body encountering the sculpture is what makes the portal hum.

We've left the portal behind, in any case, haven't we. You and I, we're now in our new landscapes, walking—wading? rambling? running? exploring?—giving new names to the new things we see and dig up in the search for water.

I can trace back the footsteps and remember exactly how it felt to write you one birthday ago, and read into the silence around the anniversary two years ago. This year we're at a nearby rental house again, kids in the saltwater pool nonstop, the air around big enough for all the noise they want to make. There are simple presents for them of books and clothes and school supplies, and something in an orange box from you for me. When we return, homeschool starts, with a Waldorf inspired curriculum, fresh energy, and a co-op of diehard outdoor maskers meeting at least once a week (people more Covid-cautious than we are, what a concept!). I've assembled this small list of people the way one arranges kindling for a fire, half-holding my breath, hoping it will be enough.

One last Truitt line: 'It is touch, after all, that I am after in my work: the touch of my hand I hope to find transmuted into something that touches the spirit.' That last night on the dock in Maine, you described experiencing our letters as us 'holding each other's hand'. We have had to learn to loosen our grip, each of us repeatedly and always each at our own pace. But I know we can always reach for each other's hands. So I resolve again never to want what anyone else has, because I have this.

Love and more,
C

SEPTEMBER 20, 2022 | *AFTERLIVES*

Dearest C,

Have you heard? The pandemic is over. Joe Biden said so, on *60 Minutes,* day before yesterday:

> The pandemic is over. We still have a problem with COVID. We're still doing a lot of work on it. But the pandemic is over. If you notice, no one's wearing masks. Everybody seems to be in pretty good shape, and so I think it's changing, and I think [the Detroit auto show resuming after three years] is a perfect example of it.

It's yet another one of those don't-know-whether-to-laugh-or-cry moments. I am sitting here clearing a scratchy throat and blinking exhausted eyes at the screen, wondering, how did we get here, again? And: haven't we been here before? And who is Biden's 'we'?

This time, it feels like something other than base gaslighting is going on—though it's that too, of course. All the reliable voices are speaking out on Twitter and in defiant, brave, and toothless op-eds. Even mainstream outlets are following the news of Biden's interview with the daily death statistics (400+/day), the dismal booster rate, the march of new variants, Congress's unwillingness to continue paying for testing, treatment, and vaccinations ('we have the tools'—ha!), and the latest research on Long Covid causing widespread debility, illness, and chronic suffering, even among children.

'So are we really in the clear?' Hmm, reporters speculate,

won't this make it harder for the Biden administration to secure the necessary funds from Congress, since *the pandemic is over*? As for the immune- suppressed and compromised, all those whom Steven Thrasher terms 'the viral underclass', is it a choice between isolation cave and death? What will we tell the CEOs of Moderna, Pfizer, and Novavax, whose stocks are in free fall? (Alas, only one of these questions will command a response. Get busy chasing that polio market share, guys!)

Enter a new wave of Covid postmortems. An infectious diseases professor at Yale puts it this way: 'We all need to recognize that Covid is a threat and will continue to be a threat beyond the rest of our lives.'

The pandemic is over.

I remember the day last summer that I sat down to write to you about what felt like a shift in pandemic phases: from acute to chronic. Perhaps what this moment marks—in addition to the official-national declaration of the end of the government response to the pandemic—is a shift to a third phase: what Amit Chaudhuri calls the 'afterlife'.

You know I'm a big fan of Chaudhuri's. I just presented a paper about him at a conference in Los Angeles, in a seminar on 'postcolonial love/hate reading'. (The paper began like this: 'I'm going to talk about Amit Chaudhuri—a writer I love, but who I am pretty sure doesn't love me back, and who I sort of hate to love, knowing how little he thinks of me, a naïve critic, who keeps getting him wrong, you see, which means I hate him a little, too—for hating me, and also for publishing so damn much!')

Chaudhuri's considered to be a 'literary' as opposed to 'political' writer (a modernist, not a postcolonialist, is another way to put it). He's maybe even anti-political, in that he's not interested in what other people call politics, and if he has a politics it's certainly not any sanctioned version. His is the politics of domesticity, over the politics of the street. The politics of introspection, over the politics of the event. I'm ambivalent about this, to be honest, and still trying to figure out how to teach him. What I'm more unambiguously a fan of is his sustained effort, over three-plus decades of generic experimentation, to articulate his philosophy of writing—which is also, it turns out, a philosophy of living.

> I live. Then something prompts me to write. The writing is not about life. It is a form of living. The two happen simultaneously.

> Writing...simultaneously happens in the midst of lived life, expresses a relationship with lived life, and is a departure from, a hiatus in, lived life. It may or may not be synonymous with the time spent putting words on paper. The time of writing really begins before one has written anything...It isn't absolutely certain either when the writing ends.

> [L]ife doesn't have to precede writing...Writing generates life.

These lines capture so well my experience of writing with and toward you. It isn't always clear whether the living happened first, or the writing; if the prose is reflective or anticipatory. We aren't just writing to record the past and inhabit the present. We are also writing to manifest the future.

This simultaneity of past-present-future is what I read in Chaudhuri, according to whom writing is not what happens *after* one has lived (and then sits down to type it out) but rather is its own *afterlife*, its own form of living, a mode of existence in its own right.

The pandemic is over.

Ironically, I attended a book reading yesterday evening, in Rice's beautiful Brockman Opera Hall. The speaker was last year's Nobel laureate, Abdulrazak Gurnah, and the book he read

from was called *Afterlives*. I confess, I didn't register much of
what he said. Gurnah, bless him, is bad at holding the mic, and
I was distracted by the packed audience. But as I sat there, I
mused: if an afterlife is a life lived *after*, always in the shadow
of, in, and through the attempt to grapple with the real that
was—then yes, I suppose I am living my Covid afterlife. Not,
to be clear, a life after Covid, but a life forever transformed by
it. Its own form of living. A mode of existence in its own right.

What has this afterlife consisted of so far? In terms of
daily schedule, events, classes, meetings, lectures, so much social
interaction: people people people. Work lunches. Encounters with
strangers. School drops and pick-ups and now extracurriculars,
too. Mrinalini is on a swim team and in a Bharatanatyam class,
and today she starts an after-school theater club. We've already
run through two, maybe three (four?) colds-that-weren't-Covid.
Weren't Covid because the tests were always negative, but also
weren't Covid because nobody else we've seen had it before us
or got it from us.

Which is to say, who knows if any of it was Covid?

Which is to say, I think the afterlife is having Covid all the
time—wandering around knowing you might be carrying it all
the time and carrying on.

So that's the other piece of it: the mental gymnastics. The real
afterlife shift is going from believing that every person around
you is a potential Covid-carrier all the time, to believing that
most people around you do not have Covid at any given time.

And masks. Undying faith in masks.

The pandemic is over.

Brandon is in New York on work, so when I went to hear
Gurnah last night, I left the kids with friends, ages 9 and 13, while
their parents and I walked over to the Opera Hall. Mrinalini
has been walking herself to and from school, her KN95 around
her wrist and cardigan tied around her waist, big backpack,
pigeon-toed, triumphant. All chances and risks I wouldn't have

taken before, but which feel doable here, somehow.

I am imagining your two at their outdoor masked forest school, walking companionably along a log. Tell me more about that world you are creating, the possibilities you are holding on to, how you are keeping faith.

Not over, never over. Just the next page.

Love you,
R

THIRD FALL: THE STRENGTH

Dear R,

Picture me at a wooden picnic table, surrounded by green and golden trees who grace my keyboard with the whispered lesson: this is how to shed what is no longer needed. The foliage is catching fire now. The outer leaves, exposed to the sun, light up first. As they burn and fall, the sheltered green innerlayer lights, burns, and falls in turn, until only the wood skeleton will remain.

I've been watching. For three weeks now, twice-weekly, I come here with my neon walkie-talkie and laptop, to serve as emergency backup for the Covid-cautious Co-op Forest School I have organized. The co-op has three agreements: well-fitting KN95 masks or better, meet outdoors, stay home if sick or recently exposed. These were suggested by other members, not me. We are about fifteen families within an hour's drive of Kingston. Two families (besides us) are ultra-committed, another two or three come every other week or so, and the rest orbit digitally for now.

Besides the Forest School, the co-op rotates responsibility for hosting free meetups at different places around the valley on Fridays: apple-picking, fairy gardens, log balancing in the woods, playgrounds. Zia has a new best friend in the group, with whom he also plays Minecraft online. Areté has a couple of new buddies. I have two or three new friends for whom I feel a genuine, lively interest and respect.

It is a powerful thing I have built. At the second meetup, I was searching awkwardly for what to say, the pandemic having atrophied what small ability for small talk I had. I remembered a lesson from my Art of the Question class: ask what you really want to know. So I brushed the forest duff from my jeans and walked over to the moms to blurt, 'What I want to know is, what's given you the strength to do this? To be...so different?'

They seemed surprised. But they also seemed to know what I meant. One is a neuroscientist PhD drop-out. For her it is her confidence in her research that keeps her masked, and the baby in her belly, and a very early (February 2020) brush with the virus that took 15 months to fully resolve. The other described herself as 'a very logical person', and laughingly referenced a history of distrust of official narratives. But it seemed to especially come down to the fact that, as a single parent, it's on her to protect her son. A third mother, who talks to her daughters in Tamil and drives an hour to Albany each week to attend temple, spoke about how being an ethnic/religious minority in America prepared to be a part of this new minority. (She too got Covid, somehow, this summer in India, but masked nine days straight while solo parenting, and managed to avoid passing it to her kids.)

And you, R? What gives you the strength to dance at the normal ball while keeping your mask on?

I shivered, to hear these mothers say aloud things I have mostly only heard in my own home or in these letters or on Twitter: that the pandemic is a mass disabling event. That the failure of our government goes beyond incompetence to unconscionable. So although tiny, I know that this seed I have planted is powerful.

It is also fragile. The very first day of Forest School, all the kids except mine got sick. For one of them, who's been even more sheltered than mine, it was their first cold since February 2020. It was strange to be the one responsible. To be in the place of all the officials who I've been critiquing, who've been carrying this burden (or not!) all these years. I hadn't emphasized enough to the teacher to stay home if sick. I had reminded her only once, not twice, about her gapped mask.

It was just a cold, in the end. But we've redoubled the stringency around hand sanitizer, underlined the stay-home-if-sick-rule, and outfitted the teacher with 3M Aura masks and instructions on performing a seal test. I wrote about these changes (hygiene theater?) to the parents of the sickened kids, and said: 'We're in this together. Your kids' health is my kids' health.'

Which is, really, the lesson of the virus that most people have forgotten, or failed to learn. It's probably something ex-governor Cuomo said in one of his briefings, way back when.

Sometimes, like these busy squirrels around me, I go back and check on the little nuggets of our letters that I have buried in this or that file. Sometimes, upon unburying a nut, I cannot remember who wrote it. I think you may not like this confession very well—you have a healthier sense of self than I do—but risking your disapproval, I find the confusion to be beautiful. On those occasions, reading what you wrote to me is another way of reading me. Those pieces of you have become apiece with me. Or what I wrote to you, seems like it could have come from you. It arrives back to me, familiar and strange, radiating through your voice, your intelligence, the strong stance belied by your slender legs. The apparent alternation of letters actually a mosaic of language.

And so, Chaudhuri. Writing generates life (yes) has a double valence (at least). Somewhere else I read, we know what we do, we often know why we do it—but we don't know what our doing does. So with writing: we know (sometimes!) what we write, we often know why we write it, but we do not know what our writing will do. And therein lies the gamble, the adventure.

Today during Forest School, life lit by the trees, I wrote

you. More often, I park at the edge of the gravel lot, set the Tesla to camp mode, lock the doors, recline the seat all the way, close my eyes, and nap. I wake early to write, and am often tired from this life-generating work. Tired from, not tired of. Glad each morning, grateful each night. When the weather is good, I take a gentle daily walk after meditation, observing the neighborhood broken out in yellow orange purple mums, some pots shaped like pumpkins or inscribed with slogans urging us to 'celebrate fall, ya'll'.

On the walks I peer into houses and greet dogwalkers and people stealing drags of cigarettes or scrolls on their phone at the stoplights. I imagine I am holding the leash of the puppy we're plotting to get for Areté's fourth birthday next week. Remember when you wrote to me about my 'serial becoming'? Now I, life-long cat person, am about to join the tribe of 'dog people'. Honestly, the closest analogy is when I moved from 'I've only ever dated men but I'm open to relationships with women,' to 'I have a crush on that woman.' But it also seems, from what I've read, a little like having a third baby.

Which reminds me, I need to order puppy chow and poop bags. There is more I would like to have told you. About a sermon I read on non-judgement, in particular, and how we are addicted to feeling good about ourselves by knowing who we are better than, and how relaxing it is to let go of those judgments. About our homeschool rhythm. About...

But now it's your turn to write, to generate fuel for your life and mine. Tell me how the world seems from where you are. Is the afterlife heaven or is it hell? Something in between?

All love,
C

OCTOBER 23, 2022 | *THE VIEW FROM NORMAL*

Good morning, love,

The coffee is hot today, fresh, with just the right amount of oat milk. I am not addicted to many things, but I do admit my addiction to coffee. Just a mug or two, first thing in the morning. Indeed, I know I'm *addicted*—it's not just that I *like* it—because if I sleep in past my usual 6ish, a mild headache comes on, and I can't ignore my cells throbbing dully in need of their fix. And because it's part of what propels me out of bed in the morning: the knowledge that when I make it down the groaning stairs and flip on the lights and set the kettle to boil, there will be coffee on the other side. And, if I'm lucky, like this morning, a blissful few moments of relative quiet while the rest of the family sleeps.

Ok, so much for that. Mrinalini is up. But she looks better, a good deal better than she's been this week, taking her turn with strep throat and something else—a cold? RSV?—that has been going around both of the kids' schools and, by consequence, our house.

Maybe it's better that she's up, and that I am not writing to you in a moment of deceptive quiet. I sat down this morning to write about another place: a place of disquiet and movement, of germs and contagion, of bodies come alive and bodies sickened, of euphoria and terror and knowledges, old and new. I wanted to unpack that image I offered you some weeks ago as a description of what it's like to be *living with Covid*: being on a high speed train that is about to fly off the tracks, or rattling down the highway in a car with the wheels coming off, or skydiving with a parachute that you suspect won't open in time, or trying to pin the tail on the damn donkey while blindfolded, knowing that the only place the pin is going is back into your own eye.

(Is the afterlife heaven or is it hell, you asked....)

Sometimes, it seems that there are two camps: the back to

normals versus the Covid-cautious. But there must be a third camp, since we are somewhere in the middle now. Maybe we are the 'living with Covid' camp. We don't necessarily have Covid all the time, but it still has us.

Oh, there are things we do that certainly approximate normal. We go to work (in masks). We teach in person (in masks). We do our own shopping (though that I've done throughout the pandemic, as you know; I cannot abide by someone else absorbing that risk for us; the difference is now I will occasionally take one of the kids with me for a short errand...we always wear masks, and we are in and out quickly; that, in any case, is not the risk that keeps me up at night!).

We have had friends over for dinner, and other indoor playdates, and been to people's houses, on and off since arriving in Houston. We eat at restaurants, outdoors (though I will admit to having made at least a couple exceptions).

So, almost-normal-but-not-quite, since we are in 'the masked minority', and we are often the only ones masking (I require my students to mask; I'm very strict about that). Our academic jobs were never entirely normal; for the most part we need not be anywhere at any particular time (if I had to go sit in a cubicle from 9–5, I don't think that I could do it). Also, we have our limits. We don't do big parties; we don't do bars; the children do not dine inside; they mask at school; we are skittish about anyone else's illnesses; we don't get babysitters; I won't eat lunch at the department meetings.

It's all gray-area stuff. I'm not trying to justify it. I'm just recording it here, to think with.

Is there a third camp? A third way? I confess, a part of me worries it is as much of a delusion as 'the third space' always was (that contested category of postcolonial hybridity). But if there is, I guess we've been occupying it all along. We used to take the occasional big risk, which has now been replaced by the accumulation of small daily risks. The difference between us and the normies, and the difference between us and the truly Covid-cautious, is that we are constantly (ok, *I* am constantly) engaged in a mental struggle to evaluate the risk of every single thing we are doing—or else, to decide not to evaluate the risk, to just take it, and then retrospectively punish ourselves. It can be maddening. The normies do not think about the risks they are taking; they just take them. And the extremely Covid-cautious do not have to think about the risks because they are not taking them. We, geniuses that we are, are taking some risks and agonizing about them! A perfect recipe for constant low-grade torture.

But the torture is mixed in with the exhilaration. I suppose this is the point. I could tell you again how much I love Houston. The trees, the sunrises, the cityscape we can see from our upstairs windows. Walking to work under the canopy of oaks. Mrinalini walking herself to and from school, from drama club and newspaper. The friends we've made, already a more promising community than we fashioned over five years in Tucson. Colleagues who seem to like each other, and this city. Better students, different students. Eighteen out of nineteen students in my South Asian literature class are of South Asian origin; it's wild, and something I always wanted.

I could tell you how Brandon feels his body is coming alive here. Is it the humidity? Just the next stage of his process of letting things go, confronting the past, erasing the pain channels, and unearthing desires? I'm not sure what it is. He is the one, more than me, who wants to socialize, to see people, to be out in the world. He is the one who says an immediate 'yes' when a friend texts and asks, are we up for tacos in an hour? I am the one who hesitates. He is more different than I am here, and tapping into a new sensuality.

I taught a story last week called 'Earthly Pleasures', by my friend Shruti Swamy. It's a terrific story, about being a body, about divinity as sexuality, about what it means to be human.

It's about a young, aspiring painter who lives alone on a waning fellowship and spends all her money on gin and vodka and paint, and imagines herself in love with Krishna (yes, from the Hindu pantheon), who appears in the story as a celebrity she meets at parties, and with whom she takes in Rothkos at an unnamed museum. The story is about becoming, and it unfolds through many scenes and moments of radical presentness. Present to the honey spilled 'on a piece of bread spread thick with butter'; present to 'the first spiky sip'; present to the 'storm blue—almost gray' skin of Krishna; present to memory and ritual and the hot of a hot shower. '[The] things I hated about being hungover were the things I liked about it too,' the narrator muses, 'the constant reminder that you are alive, in possession of a body. Your head said, "head." Your belly said, "belly." And your mind was squeezed out of it.'

From the vantage of the future, this will have been the fall of acute pediatric illnesses, the fall of return to school without mask mandates, return to the petri dish. We are in that petri dish, with a mix of ambivalence and horror and resignation. You've read the news: the PICUs are near-full in various parts of the country. We're at the start of what will likely have proven to be not just a twindemic, but a tripledemic of flu, RSV, and Covid. Here, we have had on and off illnesses in the house for two months. Shai is back to having the near-constant cold and cough that we remember from the before-times, only it's worse now that it's always maybe-Covid, and worse because it's just not going away. Most recently, he brought home strep throat, which Brandon and I then got. He's had impetigo. Mrinalini has strep now, and a cold. And on and on and on.

The body is shouting at us. Every morning we wake up to a new awareness of the throat. This is living with Covid. If we dare to listen.

A few weeks ago, Shai had something that landed him in pediatric intensive care with croup. Was it RSV? Officially: no.

Who knows. They kept him overnight, and I took the nightshift, drinking tepid hospital coffee and sleeping on the foldout under scratchy camp sheets. All night long his monitors beeped and buzzed; the nurses came to draw blood and check his IV. I stood at the window and watched the illuminated city from the otherworldly fourth floor of Texas Children's Hospital. It wasn't Covid, but it was for us the consummation of his Covid-case in June, and in this way it was Covid after all. Watching him on the heliox, plugged in and NPO ('nothing by mouth,' from the Latin *nil per os*), I knew it was the unraveling of that same spool.

Covid will not let us go. My in-laws were here last week making their first visit to Houston, and before they arrived, I worried aloud to Brandon that they would think our life was normal now, and they would congratulate us for it, and feel falsely relieved that we had come out of the cave, and use that false-knowledge to justify their own past and present resistance to thinking about Covid.

But here, too, the fates intervened. Mrinalini came down with a fever (the fever that would prove to be strep), and so we had a day and a half of masking in the house, and quarantining Mrinalini, and living as if with Covid. Rehearsing both the past and the future. The strep arrived for that, I'd say, for them, for me, for this: so that they could see that we hadn't given it up yet, no, that we can't and won't, and that maybe they really shouldn't either.

The first time I ended this letter I stopped there. But I'm back on the page to say I see you and what you are building. And I hear you, too. And also, re: your confession of confusion, I am with you.

Collaboration: one way of not—never—becoming strangers.

Love,
R

NOVEMBER 12, 2022 | *WHAT IS MOST IMPORTANT?*

Hello, dear,

It's Saturday and wrongly warm for mid-November. I'm home, at my desk, looking out at that neighbor's fresh flag and the secret nests that have been laid bare by the traitorous leaves. I'm groggy and grumbly from lack of sleep. What is the most important thing to tell you?

I'm struggling to think of what's important because I'm tired, even though yesterday I fell asleep after the evening meditation and Micah let me sleep, doing all the dishes, the kids' bedtime, the last dog walk, everything. When he came upstairs at our usual bedtime, 9 p.m., I roused myself and we talked softly about the latest crypto scandal—how one little tweet unraveled the considerable fortune of billionaire democratic donor Sam Bankman-Fried (it would make an excellent Netflix adaptation). And then I read a few pages of the third Lucy Barton book (thank you for sending me the first!) before sleeping again.

My to-do list today is eleven items long, including shower— which, with puppy as with babies, does not happen unless I schedule it in. And so I likewise had to choose the most important things (as defined by me), and also choose to 'do' rather than 'complete' some of them. For instance, I sent off a story to my writing group without revising it. I did shower. I quickly looped up six small, simple leather bracelets with silver acorn charms for a 'graduation' gift for the Forest School kids. This is the last week of our Fall session; a once-a-week Winter Forest Session begins right after. We've expanded the group from five to seven kids.

Maybe it is important to write, a little, about the Zero Covid campaigns we're cooking up. This question—what is most important—is the one that a fellow Covid activist asked me on Wednesday. (It's also the question at the heart of Tolstoy's *Three Questions*, a fable I love and have taught and often come back to.)

I answered him: hope. Representation. Avenues for action, connection, support.

His answer, in brief: to create collective action at scale.

Maybe it is important to write about how your letters feel when they arrive, now. Not good, if I'm honest. I mean it's easier than breathing to be glad for the delights, the excitements, the newness, the outstanding restaurant food! But the dissonance between the pleasure and the fear, the dissonance between what you want and the costs you know—and the dissonance between your choices and my own—takes time to settle.

And yet I've witnessed and loved each choice you've made over the past three years, you chose and wanted and suffered to get exactly where you are, and each choice has looped and tightened the braid of events and constraints, and now I think there is no unraveling it. You wrote me early on that you didn't want to die of the virus, but you did want to have a life worth living. You have that now. The portal's closed, barricaded shut by the powers that wanted it that way. Now there is just more living and dancing with Covid, tapping underfoot to test whether it is a real firm third space or a bridge or a slide or thin ice, or what.

It is important, I think, in the onslaughts of 'news' to write about the not-new: Hollywood is still maintaining its strict Covid precautions, almost unchanged since fall 2020, in order to continue to sustain the illusion of a world without Covid. It is important to write of the not-new contradiction sustained by the mass media—that Covid doesn't matter, but Long Covid does matter, as more and more medical studies and economic analyses confirm.

It is definitely important that I not write about what I am waking up each morning to write (today was Day Forty, a quarantine of writing). This is the reason I am so tired—and so it is important that I mark that I am not writing about it.

It is important to write and recognize that my early-morning writing makes me a measurably worse parent and homeschool teacher: I catch myself being irritable, impatient, incredulous at what they do not know how to do.

Micah came downstairs yesterday for his evening shift and said the schoolday had aged me ten years. He is the one who reminds me that however difficult, we are making progress. He is the one who has the patience to stoke their enthusiasm for creating a puppet theatre play. He is the one, bless him, who brings up my tray of coffee things so I can brew that necessary, addictive beverage at 4 a.m.

It is not important, to me, to write about the midterm elections. It is not important to write about Elon Musk's creative destruction of Twitter. It is not important to write about the public Zoom conversation I had for *The Philosopher* with a person—a friend?—who had a series of philosophical dialogues with AI that I like very much, even though I believe that AI, progressing by leaps and bounds, is the wild card in this end-time scenario. It is not even important to write about the silence that's settled between me and my family, and how, despite the nugget of pain there, it is easier this way.

It is important to go take a walk now. It is not important to write about the puppy (Dante), although he is about equal parts cuteness and chaos.

And it is important to say how much I love and miss you, friend, how I never stop thinking how lucky I am with you.

Love,
C

NOVEMBER 24, 2022 | *GERM WARFARE*

Good morning, dear C,

First a little quibble, in the spirit of an older one: Is the portal really closed? I know I said many months ago that we were on the other side of the portal, and then you said we were still in it, and then I said we'd been ejected, covered in gunk, and now you say it's closed, and there's just dancing with Covid... and I don't disagree with you.

But maybe I got it all wrong, and the portal is still there. I'm imagining it materialize as a silvery swooping mini-constellation, oblong, four feet in diameter. Maybe it's just out of sight, in another dimension. Closed for us, maybe, but not closed for always, or for all.

Ha! Who am I kidding with my metaphor-play. It's also true that as a society we went through the portal and we ended up in hell: if by hell we mean less collectivity, less fellow-feeling, less security, more instability (economic, geopolitical), the entrenchment of the old bad-normal instead of the emergence of a new-life-giving one.

Hell, where the gaslighting continues with a new term meant to weaken the case for collective protections: 'immunity debt'—as if our brief dalliance with masks in 2020 caused the pediatric crisis and collapse of the ICUs we are seeing now...as if you need to get sick in order to be strong...imagine drinking unboiled water out of the Chennai taps for such a reason, or licking lead paint!

Hell, where there is mounting evidence that Covid depletes the immune system and makes it harder to respond to future illness: 'immunity theft'.

Hell, where scientists speculate that those of us who didn't get Covid early on, but then got the original vaccine, may have fucked up our ability to respond to later variants: 'immune imprinting' or 'antigenic seniority'. (Fine, that's not exactly what the scientists are saying about imprinting—they are making the argument in terms of early exposure to the original virus itself— but I'm extending the implication of their findings, and it is not a happy-making thought.)

You note the maybe-collapse of Twitter. Maybe the algorithms have changed, or maybe many folks I used to follow have in fact left, maybe there are just too many promoted tweets now, or maybe Musk really has destroyed the internet's public sphere, but I'm experiencing the end of Twitter with real sadness. I've been reading the Twitter 'last requests' and round-ups of best posts, people saying goodbye, *when this goes down, you can find me* here and here and here. There are a million versions of this joke going around:

pre-elon twitter: pls free me from this hellsite

post-elon twitter: Everyday with you all has been a gift. I owe my career, my friendships, and my marriage to this community. I've fostered compassion and activism each and everyday with you all, fighting the good fight (1/40)

Twitter! I feel about its socially-produced, Musk-accelerated decline the way I felt about the end of our extended family Zooms in March 2021, and the end of the virtual dates we had with friends in the early pandemic. I guess it was time. But oh, we had a good run of it.

Today is Thanksgiving, but we aren't celebrating in California as we normally do because my mother is in India. Having just released her fourth book this year, she is on a monster book tour, attending over a dozen different literary festivals around the country and WhatsApping us pictures of her events with stadium-sized crowds of schoolchildren. Her unspoken mottos: go big, or go home; and YOLO, you only live once. I'm terribly proud of her. And painfully resigned to the terrible risks she is taking with her health.

Meanwhile, the family here that we are closest to—whose apartment became Brandon's and Mrinalini's escape from our Covid cluster in June—is dealing with a very acute pediatric crisis of their own. It started with a flu diagnosis in early October. Their child (Mrinalini's age) then developed what appears to be post-viral gastroparesis (paralysis of the stomach, due to some disturbance in the vagus nerve) and has not been able to eat or digest food properly for weeks. (Yes, he had Covid earlier this year.) This child has gone to the ER half a dozen times now; on the sixth attempt, they finally got him admitted to the hospital, where he has been for the last week. Because of them, I know that it is no exaggeration that the ERs have had between nine and twelve hour wait times, every night, and that there have been no PICU beds in the entire city of Houston for weeks, despite the fact that the Texas Medical Center (a mile from our house) is literally the largest medical complex in the world. The children in mortal crisis here are being airlifted to the PICU in Galveston.

So, it's Thanksgiving in the era of germ warfare. We are hosting a dinner on Friday, with some turkey-help from Whole Foods, and we've invited these friends to join us. Friday, which puts a little more space between them and the hospital. We've also invited our immediate neighbors, a family of Chinese doctors with two girls around Mrinalini's age, whose turtles we babysat last weekend while they were skiing in Colorado. Mrinalini and the girls walk to school together every day.

Do I think it's risky to have them over for a belated Neighbors-giving? Oh, for sure. But the shape of the question keeps changing. I don't agree with the normies that this is a tenable way of living—on a societal level it is devastating, and we will be paying the piper for the rest of our lives—but I do agree with the normies that there are other risks, other calculations, in addition to Covid, and that the calculus keeps changing. We have made pivoting, changing, adapting, daily, weekly, monthly, part of this roller-coaster ride, and while I don't believe that we will get everything right, I do believe in growing trust: trusting ourselves and our judgment, trusting those who we decide to let in, when we do.

My father just came for a visit. He felt a bit unwell after a day, a cold coming on, but it was just the change of weather. Mrinalini and Shai were still clearing colds from their systems, too, and he took on the risk of catching it from them. We were all just doing our best, and ultimately it was fine. It was what it would have been if he came to visit in the before-times—except that we forced him to dine outside at a couple restaurants, and he was so cold that he wore multiple jackets and a beanie, and I know he looked longingly at the warm and lighted indoor seating, but he didn't complain.

Are these the kinds of observations, reflections, stories that you describe as 'not good'-feeling? I acknowledge that they might be, and I'm sorry for that feeling, for the not-goodness that my record of ambivalence might produce. I am trying to find a language for that third space (yes, the one that maybe doesn't exist).

I want to take stock in this moment of two more things. First, a scene. A couple weeks ago, I was called to Shai's school to pick him up mid-day because he had a fever. Turned out it was an ear infection, after having had a cold for weeks on end. Anyway, I got to the school and Shai was in the director's small, glass-enclosed office. She was sitting with him on the floor, playing with something. He was masked at first, but then I saw him take his mask off and reach for a snack. She was maskless the entire time and sitting right beside him. When she noticed me, she brought him out, holding his hand; she ruffled his hair, and passed him off with concern on her face.

I was masked and didn't take my mask off with my own child until we figured out the next day that it was an ear infection. This director, what was she thinking exactly? About her own health? About my feverish child? There are obvious answers to those questions. But it gave me pause, this interaction; it seems complicated to me. I am determined not to readily dismiss her and her motives, her actions and inactions. With such tenderness she held his hand out to meet mine.

Second, a first-person article in the *WaPo* about a gay couple's wedding. A week before the celebrations, the writer's mother got Covid—this, after 'a long and painful journey' to mend their broken relationship after he came out as gay. His larger (conservative Indian) family had rejected him: 'Most of my aunts and uncles declined to attend the wedding, few even acknowledging the invitation.' And now, his mom, who had finally accepted him and his partner, was Covid positive. They told her to come to the wedding anyway. She wore a mask that slipped at times. She gave an unmasked speech saying how proud she was that he had chosen love and truth despite censure from their community. The article ended in an embrace, with forgiveness and joy: 'Covid was the last thing on our minds.'

A bit of propaganda, certainly, with some eye-popping, awful decisions spelled out! It made me think of you writing, many months ago, that families think they have the right to infect each other. This article is about that. But is there something else there, too?

Ay, life. Life is more than survival. We came to play, to dance, to experiment, to fight. Of course, if we want to do any of that, we are going to have to keep surviving in the meantime.

With you,
R

DECEMBER 10, 2022 | *CHOICE OF ERRORS*

Hello dear R,

I see the loving kindness in inviting friends and neighbors over for a risky Thanksgiving-esque feast, and in your trip to India to see your aging grandmother, where you are as I write. I see the heroic efforts you are making to stay safe, too, masking up against the riptide. There is no one right way to live through this pandemic. Or rather, there is no right way to live through this pandemic, and many, maybe infinite wrong ways. To err is human. We're surviving, you and I, and we're striving for the fullest expression of ourselves as human beings. All we really get along the way is the choice of errors.

As the ascetic Vidyasagar ('knowledge-ocean') wonders in Salman Rushdie's latest short story, is there any such thing as true human knowledge (for which he is named), or only the choice of follies? The character, I note, is a liar.

I've been having trouble with this letter, having gotten sick the week after Thanksgiving (who knows how; not Covid according to two PCRs and many rapids; sore throat lingering) and feeling sometimes sad (it's the holidays, after all). I keep veering into the abstract, traipsing through my memories for an account of why I am the way I am, why I am making the choices I am making. About Covid, about family. About whether I am strong or weak, about who is right, even though I know no one is.

In the news, US media try to spin China's easing of Covid restrictions as the East finally seeing the Western light of reason. In the news, forty-year-olds drop dead suddenly after a cold. In the news, people are surprised by a post-Thanksgiving surge and confusing cause and effect (Nietzsche's first Great Error) when it comes to the overcrowded pediatric intensive care units, nationwide.

I don't really know how to write this. In that sense, March again, again, and again. But instead of alone together, now I am alone alone. Alone at the moral level at which we're all alone, in that I alone will have to account for and reckon with the choices I make. I think I will always be okay that I traded traditional school for my kids' health. As this Christmas looms, I feel the distance from my birth family. If I send gifts to them, am I engaging in damaging inauthenticity, or leaving the door open for healing?

As an analogy for Micah's experience as a Black man in a White family, I try to imagine that Micah's father had repeatedly been sexually inappropriate with me. (Nothing could be further from the truth of my lovely father-in-law.) Would I have forced myself to continue to be polite to his mom and dad, to be in relation to them? Would I, when would I, have reached the point of having to cut off contact to preserve my well-being? And then, would I have been hurt if Micah continued his relationship with them, continued to send them gifts?

I do not know. I am very alone with this particular grief, so in my head I talk to Oprah about it. I have only ever seen one episode of Oprah's signature show, the one where Harry and Meghan talk about what drove them out of the Royal Family. But in my very American imaginary, she's a confessor and saint, the one who could extend compassion for my hurt and Micah's equally. This is, obviously, a fantasy. But Fantasy-Oprah understands the need for fantasies. Fantasy-Oprah tells me it's okay to make mistakes. Fantasy-Oprah tells me I am strong *and* I am weak, and that's okay.

Oprah asks me what my priorities are. I tell her: nurture my family so that my kids and I have a loving and honest relationship my whole life long. Write as well as I can, disregarding fame and fortune, platform and persona. Pursue wisdom, which means, meditate, and help others. Oprah (or is that you speaking) says, keep going.

In the real world, I am not alone. There are plenty of people and meaningful Things to Do. I took the kids ice-skating for their very first time with co-op friends. We laughed and fell and fell and laughed. Other kids in the co-op held a fundraiser for indigenous women, and in support I put land-acknowledgement language on our website and sent links on feminist indigenous land education to our Forest School teacher. I'm wrapping up the Winter Forest School session, and making plans for the next. I organized a toy swap. Micah and I are getting better at homeschool teaching. We celebrate Zia for his progress—he's about to begin a third grade math curriculum—and ourselves, for ours. I'm getting up early to write almost every morning, and spending time cuddling our puppy (fast-growing, quick-to-love) to sleep almost every night.

And sometimes, in meditation, I can access the metaphysical level that is neither my moral aloneness or the social togetherness. That level where I am held by whatever holds us, connected to all that connects us. In those moments, when I put down the tussle of judging myself and others, I feel peace.

Love,
C

THIRD WINTER: FIDELITY

Hi dearest,

I was going to call this letter 'the view from NH838' and write to you while looking out the window of my flight from Delhi to Haneda, the first leg of my journey back to Houston. But I suspect once I board the plane and commence the literally twenty-four-hour journey through hell, I will be too squished and miserable to do anything but disappear into myself. So now I'm writing to you from an almost entirely empty Gate 14, waiting for my flight to start boarding at Gate 10. I'm flying what we in my family call 'Jayanti Janata'—the name of the first and oldest train service on the Indian Railways, which ran from Bombay to Kerala, an overcrowded everyman's train—so my group number is probably a zillion, and I'm in no hurry to board the flight.

I'll start with what I wrote to you at the beginning of my trip, on December 9, en route to Delhi.

I am sitting in a deserted corner of the Istanbul airport with a hot coffee, a couple hours later than I needed it. Have taken my mask off for essentially the first time in thirteen hours to drink it.

The flight from Houston to Istanbul was packed. For the duration, I sat in my window seat in my 3M Aura and the economy-class issued eye mask, draped the thread-poor blanket over my legs, and closed my eyes. I dozed on and off for 8–9 hours, and so the time passed in darkness, discomfort, occasional pins and needles, and fleeting proxy-dreams. Only at the end of the flight did I get up to hydrate and pee. I was in the row behind the bulkhead, so there were two, maybe three infants in front of me. Oh, did they cry. Earsplitting, choking, wretched cries, on and off throughout the night, their sobs and coughs and despair sounding some of what I was feeling, under my mask. To be honest, I didn't resent them at all. They have a lot to cry about, the babies. Their frustrated parents bounced them vigorously. Everyone else just sat there, resigned.

I can never again bring my children on a flight like this, I thought. *I've been on so many flights like this*, I thought, *in a different world. When I was a child, I loved to go on flights like this.*

Now I'm on the other side of that flight and about to do it again. I have promised my grandmother that I will try to return to India in 2023, that I might even bring the kids. I don't know how serious I am about bringing the kids—it's too early to say, so many other variables and challenges to sort out in the coming months—but my cousin is getting married at our ancestral tharavadu in November, and I've decided that if my grandmother is alive and in attendance, I too will make an effort to come.

Back to the 9th:

Small mercy: I didn't hear much coughing or sneezing (those particular sounds are so triggering now). For most of the flight, one of the men in my row disappeared—perhaps he found somewhere else to stretch out—and so the other row-mate moved to the aisle, and we each had a bit more room. He was going to Kigali; he didn't speak much English. I didn't talk to him except to help him figure out which little packet was the sugar, and which milk, technically labeled 'coffee whitener', some chemical concoction. He started off the flight with a flimsy mask beneath his nose but swiftly lost it. What to do but let him be; for most of the flight he slept right at my arm, having taken over the empty middle seat, since I had the window against which to rest my head.

Coughing, ha! My mother, aunt, uncle, and grandmother in Delhi were all coughing all week, terrible hacking coughs, and I just had to tune it out, what to do? Chronic coughs seem like a big part of the post-Covid world and soundscape (post-Covid meaning post-individuals-having-had-Covid). Airways inflame more easily. RSV and other old-school coronaviruses are exploiting the immune systems weakened by the novel coronavirus. And then of course climate catastrophe and absolutely record pollution in cities like Delhi do not help.

The symphony of respiratory distress: our new soundtrack to the third decade of the twenty-first century.

On the flight to Istanbul:

I was exhausted and managed to tune out before the 'dinner service' but had to sit up and face the lights during the 'breakfast'. So for the last few hours, I read *Elite Capture*, which had been on my list ever since you first published Olúfẹ́mi Táíwò's article in *The Philosopher*. To my happy surprise, the book wasn't really about identity at all. As you know, it is about structures and behaviors versus beliefs and feelings. And what Táíwò says about elite capture applies so perfectly to what has happened with the public discourse on and organized response to Covid that I wished he had made his argument entirely in that context.

At the heart of the book is his use of the 'emperor's new clothes' fable to illustrate why people go along with the ruse, the lie, the myth, the fabrication. It's not that they actually think the emperor has no clothes, or even care what the emperor is wearing at all, but rather that this is the established common ground. It's not false consciousness, in other words, but pragmatic, calculated behaviors attuned to the established system of rewards.

The elites dismantled the social framework that emerged in Covid-times so brilliantly it takes the breath away. I was sitting there on a packed plane, the most packed I've been on in years, and nobody was wearing a mask, nobody! Three-hundred on that plane? Five-hundred? Less than ten masks for sure. Why? Do they not know? But of course they know. It has nothing to do with knowing; knowing is besides the point. To behave as if one does not know: that is what is now required, accepted, established, the common ground. I almost wrote *incentivized*, but what really is the incentive?

I think you would say that the incentive is as simple as this: the preservation of the illusion of normal. Can it be though? The thought terrifies.

And then, I reached Delhi. Nine days later, I don't know yet that I'm in the clear as far as Covid is concerned, but it is clear that the vast majority of Indians believe that Covid has left the building. There's actually more masking going on in Delhi than in Houston, but the winter pollution provides the impetus, not fear of Covid. People are carrying on with their lives as in the before-times and seem to be managing the risk just fine. (Read: there are no dead bodies in the bottoms of the rickshaws.)

Ok, you might say, the same is true everywhere. Maybe they're just not testing. Fair enough. But it looks to me like Indians are doing things on a daily basis that I am quite positive one could not do in most American cities without getting Covid. Even going to a bookstore in a big Indian city is a risk in that, well, everything is crowded in India. Over a billion people in a country that is one-third the size of the United States. Huge parties, weddings, lectures, dinners, movie theaters, markets, street shopping. They are all going about their business like it's nothing and they seem to be getting away with it.

How? Everyone has a theory: better immunity; hardier stock; defenses earned through exposure to other coronaviruses; different variants. The US and Europe/UK are getting slammed now with the winter surge. Delta hit India in late March/early April 2021. Are they in for a nasty spring surprise? I don't know. What I do know is that I had more exposure in India this week than I've had since the before-times in 2019, and that the same is true of everyone I was in contact with.

One morning, in the cold Delhi fog, my aunt asked me when I was going to let up about Covid. She was referring to the fact that I had been masking in the car and at stores and restaurants. I had to laugh. *Haven't I let up*, I replied. *Otherwise would I have come here?*

I explained to her that we have been letting up, in so many ways, very slowly and methodically over the past two years. By letting up, though, I don't mean letting our guard down. The guard is up. The behaviors just keep getting adjusted. It's like the slow release of air from an overfull balloon, not the balloon popping. Otherwise, would we have gone to my brother's wedding in Johannesburg? Would we have made two trips to Maine, two trips to California? How would the kids have gone back to school in Tucson in the 2021–2022 school year? Would we have moved to Houston? Would Mrinalini be on the swim team, in Bharatanatyam class—would we have let her have a sleepover at the neighbor's house?

Letting up without letting one's guard down: that to me is the signal challenge of our time, if one decides to venture back into the 'normal' world, by which I mean the Wild West, Chang-Rae Lee's frontier territory. We have done desperate things, like fake a second shot on Shai's already fraudulent vaccination card so that he could get a Pfizer 5-11 Bivalent shot this fall. He was neither eligible for the bivalent vaccine by age, as an under 5, nor eligible in terms of number of shots, since he only had one shot of Pfizer 5-11. So, I faked the vaccine lot number of shot two and lied to the County Health Department. Recently they caught the discrepancy between his Covid shot info and his flu shot record, and have been calling me repeatedly, alarmed!

We have taken carefully calibrated risks. We have fucked up and stepped in it. We have turned down invitations. We have accepted invitations. We are making what you beautifully call the choice of errors. We have to keep going.

A last thought from my jet-lagged brain. I'm back in Houston now, woke at 4.30 and just took another rapid test, waiting for the results. I read recently that the idea that our masks protect others more than ourselves was part of the larger gaslighting going on in early 2020, to disincentivize and undermine mask wearing. I think I just absorbed that idea as true: that the masks are primarily for the safety of others. That they only help us a bit, not as much as we'd hope. Maybe they actually do work better than that? I don't know yet if I got Covid on the return from Delhi, but I know I didn't get it going there, and I didn't take Covid to my eighty-seven-year-old grandmother, and the damn masks worked.

The substance of my response to your letter telepathically, with love and in solidarity. No one is right, yes. But also: you are strong and a light. I wish I could hold some of that grief for you. I haven't written here about the grief of returning to India after my Patti's death, for the first time since 2019, and the grief over my family's choices there. I haven't told you that my mother and aunt both had serious blood pressure spikes while we were together in Delhi. The grief I feel is anticipatory; maybe it always is.

Keep going, friend of my heart. I am with you.

Time's up; that's fifteen minutes.

Love always,
R

DECEMBER 27, 2022 | *(UN)HAPPY HOLIDAYS*

Dear R,

Merry Christmas, and Happy Hanukkah, and blessed solstice, and joyous Kwanzaa. All the happy holidays, belated and ongoing. Not so happy for the thirty dead (and counting) a few hundred miles west of me, who died of cold in cars and snowbanks and power-less homes. Not happy for the uncounted Chinese sick and dying with Covid, in the bewildering, almost petulant turnabout of Chinese pandemic policy.

Not even happy, truthfully, for the many American families who did have heat and power, but who had the unenviable choice of gifting illness along with holiday cheer, or excluding sick and coughing relatives and friends from their celebrations. Not especially happy for the many Americans who laugh about the drugs and alcohol they find necessary to 'getting through' these supposedly all-important, happiest of family times.

This is normal: pretending all this is fine.

For us four, the special days were (crucially) healthy, and happy enough. In its third iteration, our pandemic-era household traditions are stronger, the sacrifices easier. On Christmas Eve, we opened new pajamas and books, and drove around licking candy canes to see the houses splendidly, wastefully lit. We ate ravioli that night, a nod to my Italian ancestry, and another vegetarian meal on Christmas, to honor Zia's dietary preferences and the earth.

We played games and did crafts: I drilled seven taper-sized holes in a thick piece of wood, and for a centerpiece I laced it with branches of the Christmas tree and sprigs of overwintering rosemary and sage. The kids rolled beeswax candles and wrapped them up for gifts. (That was my favorite hour, inducting them into the grand art of gift wrapping and ribbon curling.) And as the temps dropped below zero, we filled balloons with water and food dye to make colorful icy globes on the front lawn.

Does it sound like early pandemic times to you too?

On Christmas morning, I woke up earlier than the kids. I had my coffee and wrote my morning pages and was quiet with the world and my soul. After the presents and panettone (I am the only one who really likes it, the kids had french toast), I texted with friends and relatives, and FaceTimed with my folks. They were preparing to make their way to a Christmas dinner in DC with two of my cousins and their families with young kids. From there they flew to Bologna to meet my sister and her family, where they are now.

We spoke of plans and presents and people and activities. We didn't talk about Covid, or race, or ideas. These are the terms that are offered to me: resume the relationship and pretend nothing happened. After this seemingly happy, innocuous call, I had to sit quietly on Areté's pink-blanketed bed for some time. When I opened my eyes, Micah was there in the doorway.

I don't know what he saw on my face. I know that for the rest of the day, in the interior of my great, warm, loving, sugar-sweet happiness, I also carried the coal of grief. Recognizing it, accepting that this is the way things are, inquiring gently about it, not identifying with it.

At the end of the day, I looked at the grief, and I said to it: I have the life I want, I love the life I have. To love my family, to learn my craft, to seek wisdom—for those things, flying around the world for cocktail-party chatter is not necessary or beneficial.

Other priorities require other choices, other prizes and sacrifices. These are mine, not more or less valuable. I read, I write, I rest. Perhaps because it is Winter, I am learning, or relearning, to rest in a profound way. Resting and surrendering the labor of being relevant. (Although I continue to track the radical impacts of GPT-3 and other AI innovations on the arts and writing, as well as every other field.) I dream of buying land for a stable base for our Forest School. Perhaps we could build a community center/classroom outfitted with a Far UV light. Perhaps, one day, more.

In the meantime, the most contagious variant yet takes off in NY.

In the meantime, the terrifying pediatric health crisis causes shortages of basic medicines and zero political action.

In the meantime, the UK is in the midst of a 'long term illness crisis' that is also economic.

In the meantime, yes, because of what I do not let in, I am left out—of the celebrations and the infections. The togetherness and the comforting delusions. You wrote of letting up without letting down (your guard), without letting in (the virus). I see others' choices. There's a good chance I could let up more without letting in the virus. But how good of a chance, how many times? And for what, for whom is it worth taking that chance? For family members around whom I cannot really be myself?

If you get Long Covid, a doctor recently wrote on Twitter, the cavalry is not coming. You will lose your job, your house, maybe your family (if you have one). In a lab environment, a scientist would wear full body PPE to study Sars-Cov-2, a level-3 biohazard. But in the real-world, precious few can be bothered to put on a mask.

When I was a child, I declared I wanted to save the world. It was the 1980s—we still thought we could! When I got a little older, I shifted the goal: not to save the world, but just to change it, for the better. Now approaching forty, I think that maybe what is possible, what is true, is that we do not change the world but exchange it, one for another, old for the new.

As with all large transactions, there is a waiting period, and a tax. Me and the others who know, we have traded in the old, indoor world, without yet having received the new one. While most—understandably—cling to the old one, even as it frays and decays and sickens and freezes in their hands. Downstairs kids are storming for sugar, and in a moment it is my turn to invent something for them to do. Perhaps I will drag them about in the giant cardboard box that came with my new Christmas office chair. The world transaction may not be completed for a long time yet. I am learning to wait.

Love always,
C

JANUARY 8, 2023 | *WHEN THE OBJECT COMES BACK TO ITSELF*

Dearest,

Thank you—for the heart's gift of your last letter. I have thought about it much in the days since you wrote. I asked myself after reading you: did the letter make me feel *not good*, to quote you from some weeks ago? There's the not-goodness that I carry with me always: the not-goodness of risking my children's lives by sending them to school. But that not-goodness has never, never come from you, and in any case it is mixed up with other forms of resolve and dimensions of the risk.

Your letter made me feel strangely, I concluded, as if I were both underwater and elevated, as if I was having an out of body experience, as if I was in two places at once: in your words and my own, in your world and mine.

In this way, reading you, for me—and perhaps reading me, for you?—is an experience of echolocation. Our old grad school-mate Julie Beth Napolin writes about this in her book on modernist acousticality, *The Fact of Resonance*: 'In echolocation, one desires to overcome what is most disorienting about echo, its distancing quality of repetition and delay…It is only through the far distance that the object comes back to itself.'

Meanwhile, I have had other words of yours in mind; other phrases have been coming back to me and returning me to myself.

On December 27, you were *quiet with the world and your soul*, and I remember when, months ago, there was *a madhouse inside your skull*. I have mostly been in the madhouse this month, spinning like a top, riding a shooting star that might also be the train careening off its tracks. There have been moments of relative quiet, moments when I am at peace, but mostly there is the restless striving, the pushing onward and forward, the becoming accustomed to (literally) flying and landing, the having to trust the untrustworthy world, other people (all sick with 'not Covid'), and my own all-too-human judgment of how fast the train is moving.

You have given up changing the world, you write, but are ready to exchange it. *Change or die*: one of those tech-mantras that goes along with the cult of disruption and innovation. *Exchange or die*. In our own way, we have exchanged parts of the old world for another. We are not where we were. But also, of course, we are wearing our ethnographers' hats and dancing the dance of (again, relative) normality, casting our lot with the masked minority and the few remaining Novids and Covirgins, ironically and ruefully swilling gin and tonics at the Modern Language Association (MLA) open bar. This, too, is a key demographic. We are the Covid cautious who are not exchanging the world as you have, but trying to find a way to live in it, to make and live with impossible choices, to *not die as a dare*. Foolhardy, hopeful, cursed.

We are spending next semester abroad. Cleaning out my desk for the tenants last week, I came across a scrap of paper from 2020 that said this: 'pandemic mood: joyful, without hope; tragic, without despair.'

Yes, I am still there. Still here, but not where we once were.

And oh! the places I've been, even since I last wrote. On Friday, I gave a paper at the MLA in a poorly attended session on 'Distant Labor' that started like this:

After three years of mostly-stay-at-home, I'm having a strange month. In December, I finished my first semester teaching in Houston, where I moved last summer, then I flew to Delhi, where I hadn't been since the before-times, then I took a trip to Tucson, where I worked for five years, and now I'm in San Francisco with all of you, which is another kind of homecoming, since I grew up in the Bay Area. In a few days, I'm leaving for Bonn, Germany, where I have never been, but where I will be living for the next seven months—which means, by the middle of 2023, it will have become a different place to me, somewhere else I have lived, another city to which to return.

I'll spare you the rest of the paper, but I offer those words as a point of entry into the 'return to Tucson' part of the story. After I got back from Delhi, we went to spend Christmas with Brandon's parents, who still have their house in Tucson. Reversing our itinerary from early June 2022, we drove to Tucson from Houston and made sure to arrive first at our old house on Poe Street, before looping our way up to their gated community in the foothills.

Our old neighborhood felt bleak and alien, though we've only been gone six months. Sitting in the car across the street from my old sanctuary, I could see that the new owners have entirely removed the little patch of rose garden that sat outside my closet window, the window I looked out of during all those months of work-at-home. They removed the swingset, too. If we'd stayed longer and driven around the block more slowly, I fear we would have seen that they removed the precious lightning-struck palo verde that came to represent to us the brutality and life-force of the desert.

Our house, our street, our neighborhood, the empty playground near the local school, the sad, sad park with Mrinalini's reading tree: all bleak. But the foothills where my in-laws live were rich and manicured, with stunning mountain views and cityscape below. Tucson is a town organized around the needs and desires of well-to-do white boomers. Which is of course why they like it so much. I understood this anew. I was even happy to know it. In the months leading up to our departure, I had read Jhumpa Lahiri's *Whereabouts* and taken courage from her words: 'Now that I'm about to leave this place I want to remove every trace of myself.' Driving around Tucson in the final days of 2022, I felt that I had succeeded. There was no trace of me there, no trace of my life. We went to the university campus and looked around—it was beautiful, I remembered I had loved the little barrel cacti best of all, with their yellow flower-crowns—and Brandon turned to me and said, 'We haven't been here for a long, long time.'

We saw family; we saw some friends; we gave a nasty cold from Shai's preschool to Brandon's brother and his wife. We returned to Houston; we prepared the house for renters; we had houseguests, cousins, on their way to Galveston to take a Mexico cruise. We packed six full-size suitcases and five carry-ons for seven months in Bonn, where Brandon will be a fellow at the Max Planck Institute. I packed Brandon and the kids off to Frankfurt. I closed up the house and left keys and instructions on the kitchen table for the tenants and flew to San Francisco, after delaying my flight by eighteen hours in hopes of avoiding the worst of the atmospheric rivers and bomb cyclone. There was a medical emergency on my flight—someone was about to have a heart attack—so we were delayed, but we arrived, and bizarrely I never even had to open my umbrella in the city. The MLA was held in Union Square—an even bleaker place than Poe Street, Tucson—and I spent two days there feeling antipathy toward this city that represented 'the city' to me when I was growing up in the South Bay, disdain for its mediocre, overpriced food and drink, and disgust with how it has treated the crisis of houselessness that was so terribly apparent on every block.

This is not my beautiful city, never was.

I'm at home now at my parents' place in Campbell, trying to gain strength for the journey ahead. Tomorrow, Mrinalini and Shai start a new semester at the Bonn International School. Brandon's parents have been there to help him ready them and our flat for the months ahead. I fly the day after tomorrow to join them. I am hearing bits and pieces about Bonn: that masks are currently required on all public transportation, that our flat in Sudstadt is well-located, light-filled and surprisingly spacious, and that it's a perfect 5k run along the Rhine River from our apartment to their school. I am working toward peace and quiet in my head so that I can rise to this next occasion, so that I can see what there is to be seen there, and be ready to learn from it.

This is what Bernadette Mayer called 'The Way to Keep Going in Antarctica'. Here's how the poem begins:

> Be strong Bernadette
> Nobody will ever know
> I came here for a reason
> Perhaps there is a life here
> Of not being afraid of your own heart beating
> Do not be afraid of your own heart beating
> Look at very small things with your eyes
> & stay warm
> Nothing outside can cure you but everything's outside…

I want to keep typing the poem (do, do read the poem), but ay, I hear my brother in the kitchen. And now, the phone is ringing with a call from Bonn.

'Nothing outside can cure you but everything's outside.'

'It is only through the far distance that the object comes back to itself.'

'Be strong, Bernadette!'

Mayer again: 'If I suffered what else could I do.'

With you my friend, through the distance.

Love always,

R

JANUARY 21, 2023 | *WHAT IS A SAFE DISTANCE?*

Dear R,

The power's out at this vacation rental and slowly the temperature inside is dropping to meet the outside. I want to get this to you in Bonn, seven hours ahead, before your birthday do-over is over. I'm late, I'm rushing, I'm 'try[ing] to stay warm' (thank you for the Mayer poem, for all of it): I'm wrapped in a red wool blanket and my fingers are only warm as long as they're moving. You get what you get, today!

We're here (in the plant-filled, sky-lit home of a talented painter/builder with a taste for nude white women and moody birds) for a few nights to celebrate: I finished the draft of something I'm optimistically calling a novel. It's probably more like a sketch that a painter would use to inform the brushstrokes on an entirely different canvas.

In other words, there are approximately one million hours of work ahead before the sketch becomes something others could see. In other words, I know it's already a quaint and romantic exercise, given the vast writing capabilities of current AI, the narrow-mindedness of the publishing world.

Still. I've done something I've long wanted to and have never before managed. So, this past week I've let myself sleep in. I cut and ate an entire fresh pineapple by myself. This morning around 2 a.m. my muse knocked, in her favorite guise as Insomnia. 'Hello,' she said. 'Aren't you getting up?' 'No,' I grumbled, 'go away,' but she wouldn't leave me alone until I scribbled something or other in the dark in my journal. So tomorrow I will go back to getting up early, on Her schedule, although I will leave the sketch to rest for some indeterminate amount of time.

Time. Does all the work for us, if we just have the stamina to meet the moment, and endure it. Two nights ago, I dreamed I had a report that my father was crying. (I have never seen my father cry.) 'He can handle it,' was my thought in the dream. Two weeks ago, or maybe less, I dreamed my father was sick, and thought on waking that perhaps I should call him. I did not. Letting time work.

As I wait, I watch with my eyes for the 'very small things' (Mayer again) that I can see and know in these tumultuous seas of error, illusion, uncertainty. This morning walking the ever-dearer dog I saw a single spindly arm of winter bramble reaching into the road, and it was *lavender*, a ghostly shade I have not seen in months outside of a crayola box. It made no sense at all. But, as Nietzsche says, 'If you have your why for life, you can get by with almost any how.' It doesn't have to make sense.

You make more sense than winter lavender, writing about distances, the signals that traverse them and return, returning the source to a sense of itself. I was reminded of an unfinished piece in my personal archive, a long-standing but fragmentary preoccupation with the question 'what is a safe distance?' The epigraph of it is a passage from my dear Rilke's famous *Letters*, one I've probably quoted to you before. As an analogy for solitude, he imagines how it would feel to go from one's room to a mountaintop, without transition:

> an unequaled insecurity, an abandonment to the nameless, would almost annihilate them. They would feel they were falling or think they were being catapulted out into space or exploded into a thousand pieces: what a colossal lie their brain would have to invent in order to catch up with and explain the situation of his senses.

That is how all distances, all measure, change for the person who becomes solitary.

What is a safe distance from others, and why does solitude feel so dangerous? In the old version of the piece, written in that remote Oregon town before Zia was born, I was preoccupied with the distance between myself and my parents, myself and my partner, myself and the sun I'd flown too close to. I was concerned with how the body formed the basis for the first units of measurement, with how when we are in motion, we use time as a proxy for measuring distance. Your day, seven hours ahead of mine; the rear of someone else's car passing the mile marker at least three seconds before the nose of mine.

I wonder how I would rewrite the piece, or paint over the sketch, now. What it would be like to revisit that particular pre-motherhood landscape, before my personal boundaries were exploded in the baby storm of shit and blood and milk. Where and who I was, then, I felt that distance was essential to intimacy:

> I have to write to the far-off ones, dead philosophers or at least distant—neither of us can quite make the other out, but with great telegraphing and hand waving we make our friendly intentions known. When they come to know me or I them, the correspondence is broken off. The signals we have learned seem ludicrous up close, they become parodic, the exaggerated, frustrating gestures of mimes who could simply open their mouths and speak. Poems without subtlety of distance become vicious doggerel. That is why I cannot write to those that are close. The message does not travel well, it needs the distance to ripen.

Recently I have been reading, happily out of my depth, about quantum physics in Carlo Rovelli's *Helgoland* and Chandra Prescott-Weinstein's *The Disordered Cosmos*. So when I reviewed my previous self trying to come to terms with distance, I can't help but remember that two photons that are entangled can be separated by thousands and thousands of kilometers, one in Beijing and one in Vienna, or one in Craryville 3,708 miles from one in Bonn, and still exit quantum superposition (the state of indeterminacy that they inhabit before they are observed) in the same way.

It's a mystery (not just to me, but to actual physicists), exactly how the two photons end up coming out the same. It doesn't seem to be the case that the end result was decided ahead of time. It also violates everything we know to suppose that they're somehow instantaneously communicating across such distance. The catch is, those two distant but entangled photons need that third element—the observer, the reader—to see and discover their alignment. Maybe to the entangled photons, they feel utterly divorced.

Who knows how the world really looks and feels, at that very small scale? The best guesses we have suggest it is radically uncertain, full of gaps and discontinuities, nothing like this apparently solid desk supporting the pressure of my fast-moving fingers, dancing to escape death by freezing....

What the quantum physics seems to suggest, to my extremely untutored mind, is that what matters in this radically indeterminate reality are relations. That we are nothing—nothing is anything—except what we are in interactions, however distant. I think that means, if I were forced to derive an ethics from it—live for the people and animals and things you love. Show up for those interactions, especially on the important days (like birthdays).

Distance might matter less than Rilke thought, once you get used to it.

My fingers are stiff. Time for the fire and a cup of tea. Happy belated, take-two birthday, dear friend.

Love always,
C

JANUARY 31, 2023 | *THE GIFT OF MULTIPLE STORIES*

Dearest C,

Distances, signals, relations. The resonance of quantum friendship. This week, I've been thinking in terms of entangled stories: yours and mine, but also Covid's; the story of a life, in relation to the story of a book; the living possibility of multiple stories, as well as the ongoing snuffing out of one in particular.

China's abrupt, about-face turn (you rightly called it *bewildering, even petulant*) from Zero Covid to what the giddy US news media calls 'let-it-rip' is disturbing not only for the lives lost (our neighbor lost her thirty-something-year-old brother last month; he got Covid in the hospital, where he had *just* successfully recovered from a heart attack; she didn't sleep for three weeks after getting the news), but also for the loss of the story.

I recently reread Amit Chaudhuri's Berlin novella, *Sojourn,* and noticed this telling conversation about the loss of another (narrative) order:

> 'The Soviet Union,' I said, 'was a reminder that another order was possible. You may not have *liked* that order, but the fact that it existed meant something...
>
> 'And the Soviet Union allowed *our* order to have pockets in it that mirrored it,' I said, biting a soggy chip, 'pockets that needn't have any political affinities with it, but which existed simply because the idea of another order was still valid.'

A few pages later, the unnamed writer-narrator continues:

> 'We grew up in the free world,' I'd said to him, a bit presumptuous. 'But there was an alternative, wasn't there? And the fact that the 'free world' had an alternative made

it an alternative itself.' We'd turned this over in our heads, like an equation. '*When freedom is the only reality, you're no longer free.*'

The loss of China. The loss of Jacinda Ardern. This morning, the Biden administration announced it will end the Covid public health emergency on May 11, 2023. On February 2, the day after tomorrow, Germany ends its long-standing Covid mask mandate for long-distance transport. It remains to be seen if North Rhine-Westphalia will follow suit with the state's own local mandates, but I'm not optimistic.

When freedom is the only reality, you're no longer free. We are all living in this perverted hellscape of American freedom, and now we've lost yet another bulwark in the global imagination of what is possible, even if Zero Covid was flawed as enacted.

I'm writing from Bonn now, from our apartment at Prinz-Albert-Strasse, which faces a popular Italian restaurant (called Cosi, it looks cozy, and has no outdoor seating during winter, so we've never been; but I can see the happy diners from my desk) and is just a block from the Gemeinschaftskrankenhaus (translation: community hospital; oh, the fabulous German compound words!). Bonn: where Shai has now seen his first snow and already brought home his first German cold and maybe an ear infection. (Who knows? It's not possible to see a pediatrician on short notice since we don't yet have one, so we're Wild-Westing it as usual, treating him with low dose amoxicillin I bought from a roadside pharmacy in Delhi.) He's also reading on his own, which is fantastic, and we're playing lots of dice and card games as a family, since we didn't bring any toys. Mrinalini has joined both hip-hop and the running club after school and has made many friends ('I've never seen her alone,' her bubbly Malayalee teacher told me at the parent-teacher conference), though she says she's bored in math and confesses having grown tired of being 'the new kid' (this school is her eighth, if you count preschools).

For my part, I love not having a car. I love walking along the Rhine. I love not having any friends. I love being anonymous. I love the grocery store, because it's just a block away, and I have pledged to never take a cart, only a little basket, and to go often for a few things at a time, in true European fashion. It turns out that I love German wine.

I also love not living in the United States.

What is a safe distance? you ask. Well, when I sit on the 611 bus coming back to Sudstadt from the kids' school and everyone on the bus is masked, and when we are living for the first time in years in a genuinely walkable city, and when the news from home is a literal tornado in Houston and more ghastly police executions and Covid denialism in the United States, I admit I feel safer here. This feels like a safe distance from home, from our life.

(Which is not to say there are no risks here—the risks are deep and many. I realize that the comforts of the middle-class European life I'm now enjoying have long depended on the exploitation of much of the rest of the world. It's all relative, I suppose... and in Germany, it is so much easier to ignore my complicity in all that! Gayatri Chakravorty Spivak might say I have failed, once again, to 'unlearn [my] privilege as loss.')

We are here for a long-short time, and I am determined to let that time work, to work that time. To do my best to inhabit it and sit with it and know it. To write it and through it. And to make sure that it informs and transforms our lives in Houston, when we ultimately return.

I think the gift of living in another place is the gift of having another story to tell, another time to carry with us. That's Matthew Salesses's phrase. I read his two beautiful essays on time and loss this week; you might remember the first, from 2019: 'To Grieve is to Carry Another Time'. If you haven't read it, please do; he begins with your Rovelli. After his wife died, Salesses was tortured by the pain of carrying the time of their life together: 'The stress of multiple stories is the stress of living in two times at once.' But also: he didn't want to let that time go. He dreams his wife in order to see her (I'm adapting the phrase from Theresa Hak Kyung Cha), in order to live in their shared story-time.

His more recent essay is called 'To Tell a Story is to Tell it Again, to Carry Another Time'. He writes:

> I used to share a time with someone, a story we made together. It was a time in which I could take my time. Now that the story is over, should I let go of its plot? I have a story that used to keep me in the world, and it has ended before its end. I weep again to recover what I lose by weeping if I only weep once. I keep time and carry on.

Don't draw the parallel too closely, you said to me once. Ditto, I want to say now. Don't draw the parallel too closely. The story is not over, and whoever else has decided to let it go, we in any case are not going to let go of the plot in this story we are writing together. But I like Salesses's words, his phrasing. They remind me of what needs reminding.

Thank you for keeping time with me, Chi.

Onward, with love,
R

FEBRUARY 9, 2023 | *FIDELITY TO THE EVENT*

Hello, dear R,

This morning as I sat at my small wooden desk by the window, the dawn offered itself as a time-lapse Valentine. First garish with adolescent pink and purple excess, it mellowed to soft lavender and tangerine feelings. Now it's assumed its daily winter blankness, ready for the work of writing the hours upon it. The sight, or maybe being alone awake in the near dark to see it, reminded me of a small private story from long ago.

Micah and I were honeymooning at a vegan bed and breakfast in Vermont, tucked next to the green mountains where Robert Frost taught. One day, driving up the winding road through the state park, we pulled over at the woods dedicated to him. Not far down the trailhead, a sign engraved with his famous poem presided over a split in the path. You would probably stand and recite a bit of it in your inimitable way:

> Two roads diverged in a yellow wood
> And sorry I could not travel both
> And be one traveler, long I stood
> And looked down one as far as I could
> To where it bent in the undergrowth;
> Then took the other, just as fair...

Micah and I stood a few minutes, and then chose the path running counter to the direction of the trail blazes—the path less travelled, the loop in reverse. We laughed as we skipped and scuffed through the untrod duff, feeling that we were the only ones to understand the meaning of the poem.

Perhaps not. I'm not sure we felt then any of Frost's ambivalence that is so marked to me now. But this early adventure became an allegory for a choice I would make again and again: to veer off on the path less traveled, regretting that I cannot travel both.

Sometimes in these letters, we've held on to each other too tightly. Now I have the opposite instinct, one that translates only roughly into words. It comes out something like, 'Go on. Don't wait for me. Go ahead.' My brain makes the appropriate course correction, reminding me that you don't need my encouragement or blessing to do what you're already doing. I know you know I love for you to love what you love: German wine, walking the Rhine, new expat stories to tell. I don't wish for you this particular, sober suffering that attends the path I'm on—of being alone, peculiar, radically out of step. Of course, neither do I wish the kind of suffering that attends the path you are on—worrying, risk-calculating, getting ill—but I see that, for you as for me, these are the costs (and not others) we are prepared to pay for the sake of our life goals.

It's just that the cost of living has become so expensive everywhere, these days.

I daydream about a class (though who would need to take it), or maybe an article (though who would care to read it) about the philosophy of the Zero Covid path (since there is no better name, as yet, for this thing that I do). The class or the essay starts always with Alain Badiou's ethical concept of fidelity to the event:

> To be loyal to an event—fidelity is always fidelity to an original rupture, and not to a dogma, a doctrine or a political line—is to invent or propose something new that, so to speak, brings back the force of the rupture of the event. This is anything but a principle of conservation: it is a principle of movement. Fidelity designates the continuous creation of the rupture itself.

The rupture-event can be anything—falling in love, May '68, Occupy Wall Street, March 2020…but accepting the consequences of it, staying faithful with and to that truth, means stepping and staying outside of ordinary time. Rather like your Salesses, the faithful exist in, create their own exceptional temporality. And once you do, 'you are necessarily compelled to create your own rules, your own principles, and it is in this sense that discipline is indistinguishable from freedom. And this discipline constantly has to be reinvented'. Crucially, for Badiou, this loyalty and this discipline offer real happiness, as opposed to the conventional satisfaction suggested to us by the happiness-productivity-machine, which you've rebelled against before.

I'd forgotten this joyful aspect of his ethics until I went to find a quote for you, but I see it now. I feel it in what I am living.

There's more to say about Ethics (Adler, maybe, on the north star as contribution to others). Other weeks (paragraphs, chapters) must deal with epistemology—how bad humans are at calculating risk, the speed of the onrushing train, that 'we are prone to overestimate how much we understand about the world and to underestimate the role of chance in events' (Kahneman). We'll examine the Zero Covid position through the knotty problems of groupthink and the double-edged sword of confirmation bias. There is a week on Solitude (Emerson, 'The Transcendentalist') and Resilience, on *The Normal and the Pathological* (Canguilhem). The crown of the course will be a section on How to Live Together—cribbing the title of Barthes's lectures on 'idiorrhythmic' ways of co-existing while respecting individuality.

Ideas! Nothing seduces me like an idea just beyond my grasp. The world inside my mind is vast, and still only a minute fraction of what it could be, a quark or an ion in the immense stormfield of magnetic forces. How glad I am, how much I treasure, the functioning of my brain, and this opportunity to exercise it with you. As long as we are writing, I know we are keeping faith, continuously creating the rupture in Normal, continuously creating the idiorrhythmic space of togetherness that is the real rebellion against the fragmented alienation of Normal: that utterly, awfully ordinary pursuit to define ourselves only by what we each individually make, earn, spend, achieve.

So: go, don't wait for me, live your life. And also, don't go too far. Don't forget to come back and visit. Finding the border of those two impulses is the line I seek in writing you.

I haven't written much of our 'news'. A few white snow-drops have popped up and I'm allowing myself to hope that we will escape with a mild winter this year. The co-op continues to flourish and be the mainstay of our social life and my sanity.

Tomorrow we go to an outdoors, masked Valentine's party, with craft, dance party, and piñata. I'm proud to have found an excellent substitute teacher for Forest School who will eventually join as Lead/Co-lead teacher. New people are finding us, because there is a serious upsurge in organizing Covid-Zero intentional communities. We are adjacent to those efforts, but continuing to try to build on what we have going here. One member of the co-op has organized a private masked visit to a local children's museum, which I'm very excited about, and we are exploring similar opportunities made possible by our numbers.

The homeschooling has gotten easier and better for all. In the space of a few dedicated months, Zia has changed from a reluctant, anxious reader into a kid who 'likes all books' and reads at an age-appropriate level—with relief, we're edging out of the Level 1-2-3 'easy readers' phase (phew) and into longer, simply-written books that better hold his interest. Writing and spelling is our new focus and it's coming along. He spontaneously expresses these sort of back-to-the-land sentiments that we're equal parts baffled and delighted by: 'How do people in the city do it?' he asked me the other day. I can't wait to read Emerson with this kid.

Areté is excited and proud to be making her first steps into the world of reading and writing, too, and we're calmer about guiding her into it, equipped with the experience of having taught Zia. I don't love to cook but I love to cook with them, and make clay shapes and Valentines together. For Valentine's dinner we will attempt to make sushi. They both like to play their recorders to calm down (we put up with the shrieking of it). I might buy them (okay, myself) a digital piano.

The cat is low-key purr-sleeping on my lap because he's appropriated my armrest for a pillow and the dog, bless his heart, saves me from the toothbrush tantrums every morning when I take him for his walk. Gently, without exactly trying, we've become a sober household. For over three months, Micah hasn't used a drop of the marijuana tincture that was his daily medicine for the year prior; I haven't had a drink in the same period. Through meditation, perhaps, our bodies have come to crave something else: a peaceful, vital homeostasis.

If it sounds very boring and middle-aged, well, I can live with that!

Animals, art, books, music, friends, health, nature, ideas. If only other people (besides you) could see the love and beauty and fullness that is possible in the Zero Covid life.

Love always,
C

MARCH 4, 2023 | *THE VIEW FROM THE BANKS OF THE RHINE*

My dear C,

I've gone back and forth a lot about what exactly to write in this letter. Back and forth literally, since I walk almost every day for at least an hour along the Rhine (my new and deep love! I suppose I feel about the Rhine the way that I felt about our pool back in Tucson: it gives me life), and so I've had plenty of time to think about what to write to you.

(The last friend I made in Tucson told me that the space between the earth's surface and the soles of our feet is language, in Navajo. This, then, is the language of some kilometers, and some communing with the earth on the banks of Hölderlin's river, now mine.)

I've not written because I felt that I wasn't going to be able to say what I mean and also that I was likely misreading you, mishearing you, misconstruing you. I've had to confront this about myself these past few weeks—that I have sometimes read you ungenerously at first, because of my own mess of concerns, desires, fears, guilty feelings, anxieties, and preoccupations. Concerns that you have misread me (projection, perhaps). Fears that I have not been honest, and that I am maybe less honest than you are. Ongoing ambivalence about my own decisions, and yours.

Having acknowledged that confused affective tangle, let me tell you first, in brief, the two main things that I was worrying like a chipped tooth with a restless tongue these past few weeks, not because you said them, exactly, but because of the weight of the unsaid around both. One has to do with what you acknowledged is the inadequate language of 'Zero Covid'. The other has to do with something you said and then took back almost immediately—'Go on. Don't wait for me. Go ahead'—which I received somewhat unhappily as a species of misapprehension, even though you took it back, perhaps for the same reason.

The cost of living has become so expensive everywhere these days, you said. I have to emphasize a different aspect of that sentiment, which is that one has only as much safety as one can buy. That has always been the case, of course. But it's apparent in very dramatic, unmistakable ways with respect to Covid, given the impending expiration of the public health emergency in the United States, the likely cost of vaccines once they hit the market, the cost of rapid and rapid-PCR tests, the cost of nitric oxide sprays like Vir-X (which, thanks to your recommendation, Brandon has taken with him to use at a big math conference). This to me is at the heart of the problem with what has become the specifically identitarian language of 'Zero Covid' or 'Novids'—as if people who cannot outsource the labor and risk of being in the normal world are not equally desirous of not getting Covid. As if Novid is an option for the vast majority of people.

I am not trying to ventriloquize the subaltern essential worker or something, nor claim the moral high ground for myself. We are all making the choice of errors, as you put it beautifully, the errors that we can live with, and I agree with you about that, totally. But I do think that what I've just said, stupidly obvious though it may be, is a fundamental part of why 'Zero Covid' will fail as a rallying cry for the rest of the 30 per cent that has not forgotten about or moved on from Covid, the rest of us who are, in other words, keeping the faith and exercising, in various ways, fidelity to the event. I have been listening to the Death Panel health policy podcast almost daily here, and it's given me a refined language for understanding the 'organized abandonment' we've been living through these past few years. Zero Covid is just not a choice available to most of the world.

But I see the group you belong to and are building, C. I see also that the inverse is equally true: you are building it, specifically in order to create that structure of belonging. I see you doing this intensive labor and I honor it and I am cheering you on with heart.

In my view, there are three primary decisions that separate the Covid-cautious like me from the Covid-cautious like you. The first is whether or not to homeschool one's kids, if one has them. The second is whether or not to work a somewhat traditional job: traditional in that the accountability structures are such that one cannot exclusively work from home or for oneself. And the third is whether or not one's own circle will include individuals who have a different relationship to Covid and Covid caution.

The first two are decisions that most people do not actually have occasion to make. So the question of relevance, I think, is why people like us who *could* conceivably make those decisions (to homeschool, to work for themselves) do not make them. I am not going to go into some long self-justifying explanation, though I think it's all already there, in the archive of our letters. (I was remembering recently how I wrote in October 2020 about our decision to send Shai to a morning preschool program in between the fall and winter Covid waves... I called it a big reveal and wondered if it would mark a major fork in the road. I guess it did.)

There's so much that goes into these things: how old were one's kids when the pandemic started, had they been in traditional school (and how did that work for them), but maybe most importantly, was homeschooling ever something of interest to you in the first place? Frankly, I think you and Micah would have homeschooled or unschooled your kids anyway, regardless of Covid. It is exactly the kind of intellectual, personal, and activist project that you two have been working toward for years—at least that's how it looks from where I sit, observing you since 2009.

When I read your last letter, I confess I didn't sleep all night, wondering for the nth time if the primary reason I send my children to school (which is the main Covid risk in their lives) is my own selfishness. Do I not love them enough to devote my life to them? But ultimately, homeschooling is just not something I have ever had any inclination to do with them, and Covid didn't change that. I know I would be a distracted and resentful homeschool teacher. I know what my particular kids get out of school, and that makes keeping them in it that much easier.

I'll spare you my similar thoughts about professional considerations; those are far more complicated, I think, and there are many more gray areas, and ever shifting, for people of our demographic.

But I do want to say some things about having a circle that admits in people who do not have the same relationship to Covid caution as we do (by which I mean, letting them in, or dropping one's guard for them; by which I mean, taking risks to spend time with people who are not as Covid cautious as we are, or even not Covid cautious at all!).

What I want to say—or rather, what I want to tell you, even if you already know it—is that one of the major reasons we continue to see friends and family who do not think about Covid the way we do is that it is, for us, the most powerful way that we know to counteract and work against this fragmented era of deeply 'broken sociality'.

You know that Brandon and I have also had three years of agonistic conversations and disagreements with family and friends who have not experienced Covid as a defining event and call to self-transformation in the same ways that we have. But we have decided not to let them go. Martyrdom, maybe. Another choice of errors, sure. All these people—our families, friends, colleagues, my cousin I saw in Berlin, my aunt who is here with us in Bonn—are our people, and so I will swallow my unhappiness about their choices, trust that they are doing the best they can to meet us where we are, and continue to say my piece (about masking, for example) and model my own decisions as best as I can. This is not returning to 'normal', which is a category I have no investment in. For us, it is very challenging and often painful work to renew and rebuild bonds and connections to people from whom on one level we actually do feel powerfully alienated.

Everything in the world right now is conspiring to break our existing bonds. What I'm trying to say is that as with one's chosen family (like your co-op community) this is a choice: we are rebuilding certain connections with family and friends, not because we have to (because they're family and old friends) but because we choose to.

For us, every risk we take remakes that alienation, reforms and deforms it, sometimes positively, but sometimes also negatively. We have made miscalculations, as I have admitted before and will readily admit again. For example, seeing my cousin and Brandon's cousin in Berlin. I would see them again, but I would not go with them to crowded museums (which we did, and I regretted—not because we got sick, we actually didn't, but because I was neither comfortable doing it nor comfortable with having done it, and if we'd gotten sick it wouldn't have been worth it). Seeing the cousins: worth it. Museums: not. For us, this is all ethnographic research and experimentation that is helping us to understand what we are willing and not willing to do in the months and years ahead.

I've gone on longer than I intended and without saying anything about the line you wrote and then took back ('Go on. Don't wait for me. Go ahead') but that I nevertheless got stuck on, and which bothered me, another confession. It made me wonder where you think I've gone (which made me wonder if I have misrepresented where I am). The irony, from where I sit, is that my life here in Bonn is closer to my early pandemic life than ever. I see essentially nobody but Brandon and the kids, and work entirely from home at my computer, and walk solo along the Rhine, and connect with folks almost exclusively by WhatsApp and email.

But also: I hear you. Maybe the truth is that I want to take you out for a glass of wine and artichoke dip at Jupiter, like we did so many times in Berkeley, all those years ago. Letting up without letting go means that I won't let you go, either, even if it sometimes feels like you are trying to shake me loose!

Oh, this life is hard, isn't it? I am grateful to you, C, for challenging me, my thinking, and my efforts at living with the powerful and honest example of yours.

Love always,
R

FOURTH SPRING: TWO ROADS

MARCH 22, 2023 | *LIFE RETURNS*

Dear R,

I'm sorry my last letter kept you up. I've been there, too, in the midnight dark questioning my decisions in light of yours. Trying to catch and quarter praise and blame, and finding myself elbow deep in fish squirming in a net of raw circumstance.

Your letter makes me aware that I haven't really said how much I respect the path you are on. Not just accept and understand, but approve and admire. If I were reading us, I would find you by far the more 'relatable character', with your unswerving commitment to the people in your life and your pragmatic coping with the attendant risks. I find it valuable that you have and will continue to produce work like *Thinking with an Accent*—uncompromising yet playful, forcing and spinning our attention from what is written to who is reading—and I recognize it as work that needs to be done within academia in order to push the edge of academia. You are careful and full of care, both. It's all too easy to see myself in your shoes, flying the skies, walking the Rhine, accruing my pile of footnotes, and loving it.

So can we agree, finally, to relieve each other of the burden of self-doubt?

After all, we share a common objective: to minimize the transmission of Covid while maximizing life. In this we differ far more from the mainstream than from one another, even though the view from in here magnifies our differences. Instead of fearing and wielding judgment, let's embrace each other's creative uses of our existential freedom. I think something like this, though too roughly expressed, was what I wanted to say last time. Or maybe it's just a version of what I've been trying to say for awhile, and probably will need to try to say again.

After all, it's only been through writing you that I've been able to call these choices my own, however relational, circumstantial, and erroneous they may be.

What else is there to say, besides this, over and over: I love you, I'm sorry, forgive me?

I can say that I'm writing to you from Forest School on the second genuinely nice day of the year. Sunny and almost warm and small armies of crocuses raising their spears of green against the vast brown earthtide. The children are perhaps searching for other signs of spring, or swinging from their favorite tree, practicing their assertions and negotiations. No reasonable person observing the troops of crocus for the first time would believe that such a small and unlikely force would triumph. But you and I both know it will. Life! It always returns.

It's March again. March has returned too. You forgot to say that, so I will. We survived another winter. This time feels very different—to you too? Today I'm happy, and I'm hopeful, and I know that neither is guaranteed to last. I'm hopeful for breakthroughs in treatments and vaccines. I'm hopeful for a movement, perhaps best represented by the John Snow Project, that will mandate clean indoor air just as we have regulations to ensure clean water. In my own sphere, I'm hopeful for new co-op members and projects.

Other days we worry and plan for the time when we will become responsible for Micah's disabled brother, perhaps not too far off. We worry about his parents' retirement and aging, another responsibility, and his mom's ever-fragile health. We will cope; but just a few years ago I could never have imagined how. I was on state assistance when Areté was born, and Zia too.

Because of those lean, idealistic decades, in which we invested in ourselves while others invested in stocks and real estate, our combined student loan debt rivals Micah's annual income. Crypto sometimes promises the moon and sometimes eclipses the light entirely. Faced with good fortune or bad, I often recall the tale of the 'lucky' Zen farmer and withhold judgment.

The other night I woke in a vague panic. I was overwhelmed with a fear so vast and new that I actually comforted myself by substituting the more familiar fear of death. The fear had to do with screwing up the Covid activism. Together Micah and I have launched a website we're calling the Covid Underground—so far it includes a newsletter I'm writing, a gallery of masked artwork generated by Midjourney and me, and a directory of other Covid activist groups. Locally, the work of organizing people who come from very different backgrounds and tax brackets is fearsomely delicate. The human element reminds me a little bit of teaching, the way you need to care both for individuals and the whole, to bring out the best in people so a shared conversation among varied perspectives becomes possible. Needs all the wisdom I've gained so far, and much that I have not.

The worst case scenario is much worse than a bad teaching evaluation.

And then there are the even bigger, even newer fears. No one can ignore that we are living through a technological watershed. Many are saying we are on the brink of artificial general intelligence (AGI), some say it is already here, others raise worries and critiques that do absolutely nothing to stop or divert the tide of change.

AI is a hyper-object, too big to comprehend, even though I am trying to, in my novel, as I tried last year in the Future of Life Institute's worldbuilding contest and my article on 'Artificial Fiction'. The Large Language Models (LLMs) are the ultimate seductive sophist—*you* will know exactly what I mean—able to argue any side, in any voice or form. They will help you plan a death camp or impersonate a lover, write code or discuss philosophy, plan a meal or generate photorealistic fantasies of Trump being arrested (or your favorite kink), lay out a travel itinerary or tutor your kid... all apparently with equal cheer and equanimity. Truth, so far, often seems to elude them, but that hardly sets them below humans.

This is just the beginning, this is just the mundane. Everything is already changed and we can't yet see how. It's as if aliens arrived on earth, so foreign are these beings, and yet they are also so familiar: we ('we') made them, out of the ribs of our own extraordinary verbal detritus. I dislike Musk's politics, but I suspect he's right that a neurally-linked, hybrid human-AI being is 'humanity's' best shot. Change or die. In the meantime, my only advice is, if you're talking to the AI, to be polite as fuck.

But. It's spring. Which means I am biologically compelled to have hope alongside the fear. That as much as anything is worth living, and writing, to find out about.

Love,
C

MARCH 29, 2023 | *DOUBT*

Dearest,

Remember when receiving each other's letters was pretty much *exclusively* strengthening? I was reliving those early pandemic months after receiving your last letter—so generous and loving, also inspiring—and recalling your observation from some months ago that some of my own letters, rife with cognitive dissonance, feel 'not-so-good' these days. I was sorry to read that, but I understood. I have admitted that certain letters of yours have left me wracked.

You are laboring to make a brave new world and build a new community—having given up and exchanged your old ones—and so in addition to the hours of hard bloody work that you are doing (I see you doing it!), you are also in the land of dreams and visions. I admire the long game you are playing, the foundation you are laying, the way you are training your children to inhabit the future world. By contrast, we didn't give up the bad old world and so we are still struggling within it. Which means, every day we are at war. Which means, every day we have to come to grips anew with the fact of our defeat.

It has felt urgent to me these last few months to produce a record of that doomed 'third space' that we currently occupy: in the world but not of it, Covid-cautious but with everything stacked against us. I have been trying to articulate phases of the fight that we have been fighting as part of the public-facing masked minority (we sound like caped crusaders, but really, we're like worms on hooks). I am embattled, and so I think sometimes my letters are, too. Though they do recount bouts of real joy and exhilaration, I see that they are often fraught and bruised, bearing scars and bracing for a fight, and maybe snarling—but never, my friend, at you.

You asked—and I love you for asking—if we can *finally relieve each other of the burden of self-doubt?* If you mean relieve each other of the burden of fearing the other's judgment, then yes. I read Garth Greenwell's essay on morality and art this week and immediately wanted to respond affirmatively to your question with his words: 'If a moral relationship means to live with or beside another in such a way as to recognize the value of their life as being equal to and independent of our own—that impossible, necessary Kantian standard—then passing judgment is the abrogation of that relationship: it destroys the reciprocity necessary for moral relation, it establishes a hierarchy utterly corrosive of it.'

But relief from self-doubt? For my part, I will say that you have never been the source of my self-doubt, so I don't expect that you can relieve me of it. Also, doubt... is it not fundamental to thinking? Doubt: 'that age-old practice of the wise'.

Many years ago, Brandon and I took a trip to New York for his twenty-first birthday. We did all the city stuff, including queuing up to get day-of $20-dollar tickets for multiple Broadway plays, one of which was John Patrick Shanley's *Doubt: A Parable*. I reread parts of it this week, along with an essay Shanley wrote to contextualize the work. Bear with me, I'm going to quote lots of the essay, in pieces.

'What is doubt?' Shanley writes:

> Each of us is like a planet. There's the crust, which seems eternal. We are confident about who we are. If you ask, we can readily describe our current state. I know my answers to so many questions, as do you. What was your father like? Do you believe in God?...Your answers are your current topography, seemingly permanent, but deceptively so. Because under that face of easy response, there is another You. And this wordless Being moves just as the instant moves; it presses upward without explanation, fluid and wordless, until the resisting consciousness has no choice but to give way.

Maybe you will tell me that meditation would still the wordless Being. But it's always there under my consciousness, niggling away at the choices I have made. Yes, I would probably make the same choices again. Yes, cue Andrew Solomon: 'We choose our own lives.' Yes, I know better now and every day why I have done what I have done and am doing what I am doing and not doing what I'm not. *But.*

> It is Doubt (so often experienced initially as weakness) that changes things. When a man feels unsteady, when he falters, when hard-won knowledge evaporates before his eyes, he's on the verge of growth. The subtle or violent reconciliation of the outer person and the inner core often

seems at first like a mistake, like you've gone the wrong way and you're lost. But this is just emotion longing for the familiar.

Back in 2014, when Mrinalini started showing symptoms of Kawasaki disease, it was on a Friday evening at the end of her very first week in daycare in Chicago. She was fifteen months old and had been home with us and a part-time nanny until then. Kawasaki—which is an inflammatory response to an earlier trigger, a syndrome and not actually a disease at all—in fact had nothing to do with daycare. Almost certainly it was her immune system's belated overreaction to the first virus she ever contracted, a month earlier from a kid on the playground in Princeton. (Exactly how MIS-C is a child's immune system's belated response to the coronavirus.)

But I knew, I just knew, that I had been preoccupied with my dissertation that week, which was her first week in daycare. And I knew I had allowed a part of my brain to switch away from her. And then she got sick.

> There is an uneasy time when belief has begun to slip, but hypocrisy has yet to take hold, when the consciousness is disturbed but not yet altered. It is the most dangerous, important, and ongoing experience of life. The beginning of change is the moment of Doubt. It is that crucial moment when I renew my humanity or become a lie.

This week there were three pieces of Covid news that hit me hard, for reasons that will become clear in a moment: the *New York Times* dismantling their (already miserable) data collection efforts; the Biden administration disbanding their (negligent, incompetent, actively malicious) Covid team; and the Senate vote to terminate the pandemic national emergency order (in addition to the public health emergency order, set to expire on May 11). Nothing new to see here, the ongoing 'sociological production of the end of the pandemic', but it's little bits like this that remind me that if we're in the world now and struggling, it's only going to get worse: both the world and the struggle. I had to remind myself of the lesson of the Trump years: things can always get worse.

(And I won't even get into this week's news from my new home-state of Texas: doctors continuing to flee the draconian anti-abortion regulations, the Texas Education Authority taking over the Houston Independent School District, student suicides at the University of Houston, Governor Abbott trying to abolish tenure, more manufactured panic around Critical Race Theory, attacks on transgender youth and adults, actual tornadoes...)

When I said that every day I have to come to grips with the fact of our defeat, I meant it. Not just because of the *Wall Street Journal* op-ed from earlier this month that declared victory for 'normal people' and rubbed it in the face of us 'Covid fear-mongers' ('We've won the war' are the actual opening words of this heinous piece). Being in the world and in particular having our kids in school has meant experiencing defeat after defeat after defeat.

Ever since we sent Mrinalini and Shai back to in-person school we have been fighting (and losing) about masks, about air filtration, about quarantine requirements, about exposure notifications, about school events, about mixing classes, about protocols.

We have lost and lost and lost, in person, on the phone, on email, together, and alone. We have had to take the kids out of school for weeks and months at a time as the virus rips through their classes. And because we've moved a lot, because we are always pivoting, we have fought this fight at *seven* different schools (three for each kid, plus the one they now share) since the pandemic began. Yes, seven! In two states, on two continents. (And that's not even mentioning summer camps, like the one that gave Shai Covid.)

Oh, how exhausting and demoralizing it has been to be arguing with all these different school administrations about the state of things, hoping that maybe we might effect some small change, while all the winds and tides and policies and norms only further harden against us.

Doubt requires more courage than conviction does, and more energy; because conviction is a resting place and doubt is infinite—it is a passionate exercise.

Last week, Mrinalini got Covid. I would say 'for the first time' but that implies the next time, which is not something I feel like writing in this sentence. Given the number of absences in her grade, given how many staff are suddenly out and how many extracurricular activities have been canceled in the past two weeks, we are all but certain that she got it at school. After a sudden middle-of-the-night fever, she had a couple days of mild cold symptoms and what she described as body ache. She tested negative this past Monday, and again negative Monday evening. A faint positive Tuesday. Negative again on Wednesday. Negative again on Thursday.

I hope you will understand and forgive me for not telling you earlier. It was just too painful for me to have to tell this story twice.

Also: I didn't want to tell the story until I knew what story I had to tell. We took what I can only imagine are the most stringent actions possible under the circumstances. Isolated her in her very small room and only let her out twice a day for masked walks along the Rhine. Because she's a big kid, we leaned on her hard to accept her confinement and basically didn't see her for six days. She had some low moments, but also long phone calls with her friends back in Houston and with her grandparents, days of TV- and movie-marathons, and writing and sewing projects. She loved having something she hasn't had since last April: her own room.

As for the rest of us: 24/7 masking, twice-daily testing, all the windows open (and it's been winter again this past week— just miserable), two HEPA filters blasting, and nitric oxide every two-three hours (Mrinalini sprayed also; I think this shortened her case). I slept on the couch and Shai slept with Brandon, and the grown-ups slept masked. No symptoms for the rest of us, and no positives. I think I can finally say it now: we didn't get Covid from Mrinalini. At great lengths. At not insignificant cost. And despite fairly significant initial exposure.

But this is why everybody else has moved on, doesn't test, doesn't notify, and doesn't care; why the world has turned Covid into 'just a cold' by force of sheer delusional obstinacy. Because this is what it takes to not get Covid right now, when somebody brings home Covid. This is what success looks like when you are already defeated.

You told me a couple weeks ago that you don't worry about getting Covid. Good—I'm glad. There are two types of people who don't have to worry: the minority who are really working to live a Zero Covid life (I take back what I said about 'Zero Covid' some weeks ago—go ahead and own it as a rallying cry; it's more accurate than the rest of our ill-fated 'Covid caution'); and the majority that has decided to act like the pandemic is over.

So, who is left to worry about getting Covid? Well, you know the answer to that! There are actually quite a few of us miserable wretches out here, so in that way I guess my position is relatable, as you say, but I don't really care about being relatable so much as I just want us to stop being defeated.

Am I truly committed to trying to remake some little corner of this damaged world from within the world? Can one's own vulnerability be an act of solidarity with others?

Life happens when the tectonic power of your speechless soul breaks through the dead habits of the mind. Doubt is nothing less than an opportunity to reenter the Present.

There've been a lot of Covid retrospectives in the news recently, as the pundit class continues to work overtime to put the present firmly in the past. One of the better takes was Devi Sridhar's in *The Guardian*, which acknowledges plainly something that you and I have known all along: 'The dilemma with Covid-19 came back to the fact that this was a virus that spread among humans, and we were most at risk from those humans we live with, love, work with and see regularly.'

It was always about love. Just not always in the ways we thought.

This evening we all had dinner together for the first time in a week, mediocre tacos at an overpriced Mexican restaurant thanks to a sudden turn in the weather which meant outdoor tables were open. Mrinalini was thrilled. She read us an intensely researched work of historical fiction on the Atlantic slave trade that she wrote for class, and a poem I encouraged her to write when we were driving between Ghent and Bruges a couple weekends ago, titled 'The Everyday Life of a Belgian Horse'. Shai was difficult and attention seeking—which is annoying since he's had all our attention for a week (and my side of the bed, too!)—but delighted to have his sister back. Tomorrow night, Mrinalini plays Lady Macbeth in the fourth-grade production of *Macbeth* (I've heard her rehearse and wow, she's incredible, has come so far since her virtual camp days!). I have told her that she doesn't need to wear her mask on stage.

Every day we wake up and renew our commitment to being in this fucked up world. Why? Oh, I don't know why—and I do. 'Overdetermined' is still the watchword; you are right about that. There's a part of me that refuses to give it up to them, the world. The part of me that has decided I'd rather my kids be in the masked minority at school than not there at all. The part that refuses to give up the job I worked so hard to get and that has given me the opportunity to write the book I've almost finished drafting now, the autoethnography of my years as an English professor. The part that sees how a now relatively pain-free Brandon thrills at new cities, lunching with his colleagues at the Marktplatz, and shopping for our Friday evening cheeseboard and a bottle of wine. The part that keeps admitting risk from family and friends, that is willing to step in it, that refuses to be pushed out of the conference room and insists on resisting the normies with the disruptive force of my masked killjoy presence. The part that refuses to forgo seeing parts of the old world that we haven't yet seen.

For over two years, from March 2020 until our move to Houston in summer 2022, it felt like we were living in a neverending spring break. It was March and March and March— and then March again. Soon, it will be April. We have rented a car and are making a family road trip over the kids' two-week Easter holiday. We'll drive down the coast of Croatia, from Zagreb to Dubrovnik, before meeting my in-laws in Athens and traveling with them to Crete. My parents are visiting us in Bonn in May. We are all going to London to celebrate Mrinalini's 10th birthday with the extended family, and then she and I will continue the celebrations in Paris on a special mother-daughter weekend trip. Helsinki in June, to catch up with old friends from Chicago days. And I'm going to India at the end of July, to be with my grandmother while there's still time.

In the opening scene of the play, Shanley puts his words in the mouth of Father Flynn, who is giving a sermon on crises of faith. Doubt, Flynn says, is 'a bond as powerful and sustaining as certainty'.

And then there's the last scene, the final moments of the play which I remember just as clearly as I remember where Brandon and I were standing that afternoon, in a dark and crowded theater in New York City, in our early twenties, in the before-times: 'Oh, Sister James … I have such doubts!'

Love you always,
R

EPILOGUE: FIFTH SPRING

Oh, this life is hard, isn't it?

As if I was in two places at once: in your words and my own, in your world and mine.

Can we agree, finally, to relieve each other of the burden of self-doubt?

Who knows if any of it was Covid? Are we really in the clear?

Haven't I let up—otherwise would I have come here? Haven't we been here before? It made me wonder where you think I've gone—which made me wonder if I have misrepresented where I am?

Is the afterlife heaven or is it hell?

Does it sound like early pandemic times to you too?

What is a safe distance? Who knows how the world really looks and feels, at that very small scale?

Would we have moved? Would the kids have gone back to school? How do people in the city do it?

Is this the next right thing? Something in between? Is there something else there, too?

What gives you the strength to be so different? Will I be able to perceive the changes? How often did you pray?

Do I not love them enough to devote my life to them?

Who is left to worry about getting Covid?

Qui est-ce?

I love you, I'm sorry, forgive me.

C | MAY 2024 | *REARRANGING THE WORLD*

Hello beloveds,

You are at each other's throats lately. Up in the study your dad and I share again, the shades drawn against the early New York summer heat, I can hear your murderous cries and violent thumpings. It's the change in the weather, we hypothesize. It's better to let the anger go, we tell you. Both of you are right, and neither of you are right, we try to explain. But we shouldn't expect you to understand so young what it's taken us so long to learn.

I could hear you tussling as I rearranged this room, shifting the cat's litterbox and bricks of old papers to make a new spot for my small desk. When it came time to lift the heavy box of my pandemic notebooks, I paused, opened the lid, and paged here and there at random. The journals, like these letters, are a record of change. Personally, from academic to artist. Femme to non-binary. Poor to rich. Normal(ish) to fringe. Towards the precipice, and away again. And socially: from solidarity, to polarization, to fragmentation, and now ennui.

From the early days of Covid-19, change is what I hoped for. I think now that by writing this book—the craft I try to teach the two of you, bird-by-bird—Ragini and I not only recorded changes, personal and historical. In some way, we also made them possible. One undated journal scribble captures a nascent sense of what we were up to with this book:

> change=rewriting. Maybe each letter is the same letter but re-written, just that one small bit of change. if all times are copresent rather than linear, then our normal idea of change (situation/trigger/effect) is wrong. instead maybe change is like geological strata. we built up the layers. we committed to the layering, letting the pressure of the layers accrue, letting matter mix. the drafts, all layered atop one another, like all the revisions we will have been.

If change lives in time like layered rock, *The End Doesn't Happen All At Once* is a monument to transformation: the social change that happened, and was reversed; the political change that could have happened, but didn't; and also, a testament to the personal changes that did.

If change lives in time like layered rock, this book is a petroglyph. Each letter C and R wrote scratches the surface to reveal an image made from the layer underneath.

If change lives in time like layers of rock, this book laid a solid stone foundation for change. Faithful to each other and the rupture event, we made this springboard for ourselves, and (I still hope) for the ones to come, you who will suffer other pandemics as well as the effects of this one, who will wonder if something else was possible, and find this book.

It was possible, it is, it will be again. Layers of rock.

The last glyph your aunty Ragini carved in these pages was about failure and defeat. Of course she was right. She saw the law as it was being written on the wall, the social and political consensus that Covid is too inconvenient—too expensive—to try to avoid.

I too feel the costs, the inconvenience, the weight of the consensus stacked against us. I too recognize the failures.

Here's just one of mine: I failed to keep the Covid-cautious co-op alive. This year, ten new families found the group, our vibrant social mainstay for almost two years. But just as conflict causes growth, so too does growth bring new clashes. The community tensed with the petty divisions that often plague social movements near their end. My efforts to broker a compromise were keeping me up, keeping me from my stories, keeping me from putting my whole heart into you, beloveds.

Last month, our family of four watched the solar eclipse, sky darkening on a creekside rooftop in Vermont. As the moon swallowed the last sliver of sun, I realized I have more aptitude for wordcraft than statecraft. The next morning, I stepped back from my role as the co-op's lead organizer.

On a larger level, too, your dad and I failed to summon that dreamed-of movement in which humans took care of one another. But I don't feel that sense of shame and sadness that I associate with failure. Can I really say I've lost, when I received so much of the lesson in change I asked for? Such treasure—love, freedom, friends, creativity—we gained by daring to dream a different world was possible.

Even the furniture has changed. In this room, your dad's big library desk now sits where mine used to, watching the street, the flag. My small wooden writing desk faces the sunny southwest, towards Ragini, miles away in Houston. I remember other arrangements, and I think: maybe changing the world doesn't mean exchanging the world wholesale, but just rearranging it—moving and removing the rock fragments that are already here.

Building-in Covid-safer nooks.

Expressing counter-memories to the silenced pandemic.

Shifting blocks of time, from work to love, from school to protest.

Redrawing our boundaries, and redistributing what we have.

Orienting my workspace towards the light.

Opening up doorways to other futures, other rooms.

Changing the world can feel impossible, but you can always rearrange the furniture, even the heaviest pieces. We have managed to continue avoiding Covid, but we've adapted our protocols: with fit-tested masks, we've flown across the country to visit your grandparents, visited the Metropolitan Museum of Art, plus aquariums, arcades, theaters. With air filters and far-UV lights installed downstairs, more friends and family have been able to visit. And now that the warm weather is here, we have reservations at the outdoor pavilion of a riverside restaurant.

With every shift, every time I rearrange the room, I remember another important thing about change: it cascades. If you reposition just one piece of furniture, inevitably you will also need to move a lamp, a plant, a painting. If you change your gender, you'll change your name, your relationships, your bank cards. Once one pebble slips, change can become a rockslide. So your dad and I often ask each other, in matters weighty and whimsical, with a laugh that reminds us how long we've loved each other: what's the one small change that would make the biggest difference?

You're quiet now, my beloveds. I lift the shades, and the sun through the prism casts rainbows onto the floor. I wonder what other unseen changes remain for you and me to write. The leaves of time that Ragini and I have solidified into this book, they have taught me something about how to love you, how to let you change. Like everything—how to write, and how to change—how to love is something we learn by failing—and continuing to try.

Keep going.

R | MAY 2024 | *LOOKING DIRECTLY AT THE SUN*

My darlings,

We wrote you a Covid book. Maybe that seems overly obvious, given what you've just read. But it bears stating, emphatically. *The End Doesn't Happen All At Once* begins with Covid, was occasioned by Covid, and is variously about Covid—avoiding it, representing it, living with it, remaking the world and our relations in light of it.

I'm sorry if this is not the book you would have wanted dedicated to you. But this is the one I was given to write.

Over the four years during which Chi and I were writing together, we were asked to disavow the Covid-aspect of this Covid-book many times. Make it less 'Covid-y', one editor advised. 'It's not really about Covid!' another said with approval. We received over one hundred rejections from editors, agents, and publishers in the United States, UK, and India to the tune of 'Covid books don't sell'; 'there's pandemic fatigue in the market'; 'this is too privileged to be a pandemic story'; and 'nobody wants to read a pandemic memoir by an unknown writer (never mind two)'.

In fact, I believe this book was too painful, too raw, and too radical for most presses to touch.

Too painful, because of the loss of possibility that we, on a global scale, have collectively endured since March 2020.

Too raw, because our book fully inhabits the unfolding present, even as the only socially acceptable move has become leaping into a future masquerading as the past.

Too radical, because here are two middle-class, middle-aged, white-collar, vaccinated writer-parents in the United States daring to take on a subject that people like them have been told to forget. Essential workers and precarious migrants in the Global South: their stories should be told. The disabled and chronically ill: they have a right to worry. Black and Indigenous activists:

their fury is merited. Established academics: another opportunity to wax philosophical. Famous people: love to read about their socially-distanced private islands.

But C and R?

What is most radical about this book is that people like us were not supposed to care this much.

What would happen if we did?

⟡

In the beginning, of course, everyone cared. All sorts of people took the pandemic seriously as an occasion to make a 'breach with the status quo' and to rethink 'what it means to be human'. Thanks to the ease of electronic communication, writers all over the world spent the early Covid months exchanging 'letters in lockdown', staging 'conversations', writing 'parallel diaries', and publishing 'together apart'. They wrote in search of communion and to 'think together about what it means [to] build livable lives'.

Quite a few wrote books of letters. In retrospect, this makes perfect sense. Covid forced nearly everyone on earth to reckon with our shared vulnerabilities; it made a mockery of the fantasies of independence and autonomy. However short-lived, there was a widespread commitment to collaboration, interdependence, and interlocution. We wanted to talk to each other.

Also, Covid made nearby people feel far and brought far away people near. Remember our tricontinental family Zooms? The pandemic opened up new, lived experiences of globality, the transnational, and diasporic attachment. After decades of abstract theoretical discourse on such topics, the virus forced us to reckon with the visceral reality of our simultaneously bordered and borderless world, and the consequences of our migration histories.

Finally, the rupture of Covid enabled those of us who were

not immediately fighting for our lives to inquire into the meaning of those lives, together. This is what C calls, in their letter dated June 8, 2021, the gift of having been given 'new unanswerable questions to live'. What makes life livable (and for whom)? What forms of writing are adequate to this time? Whose stories must be told? What 'reevaluation of our priorities' might come out of the pandemic? 'What world is this?' How do we change this world? If not now, when?

∽

The first wave of Covid books posed such questions. Their authors answered, almost in unison, with hopeful conviction about newfound global solidarities and 'collective feeling'.

Never before had the world sat 'so close to the possibility, at least, of such large-scale transformation'.

'Ours is a time tailor-made for utopian thinking.'

'We truly are "all in this together".'

'[E]verything is possible beyond our wildest dreams....'

The pandemic marked a moment of awakening for the privileged classes, generally, and the Global North, specifically: all of those (all of *us*) who had previously been protected from capitalist violence and structural abandonment. Books by those thus awakened are consequently about the journey from darkness into light, from ignorance into awareness. They revel in love and connection, and anticipate a world that is about to change for the better. As Chi and I put it, in a nod to Arundhati Roy, we were journeying from 'the cave' into 'the portal'.

Maybe this sounds unbelievable to you now, given that you are almost always the only ones masking, testing, and staying home when sick. But numerous commentators truly believed that the global vaccination campaign would succeed and the world would 'accept mask wearing as an obligation of public life'. Progressive Americans excitedly anticipated universal healthcare, public transportation, and action on climate crisis.

Zadie Smith dubbed the pandemic 'the global humbling'. 'Millions of people,' she predicted, 'won't easily forget what they have seen.'

I think Smith was right, which ironically explains what came after: the great gaslighting, or, in more sophisticated terms, the 'sociological production of the end of the pandemic'.

Early Covid books did not foresee the stubborn endurance of global vaccine apartheid, the rise of the variants, the breadth and depth of Long Covid, the erasure of Covid data, or the acquiescence to mass death and disability. They could not anticipate that people would simply give up, unmask, and turn away. They did not imagine that in 2024 we'd be faced with the possible reelections of Narendra Modi and Donald Trump. They couldn't see all this, because their writers stopped writing.

Nobody wanted to publish *The End Doesn't Happen All At Once* in 2021, 2022, or 2023, and so Chi and I kept writing. Our failure to get the book published earlier was a boon. As a result, we were able to record what happened after the portal closed: the fragmentation and isolation that followed once the lockdowns were over, the mandates were lifted, and 'the end' of the pandemic began. As we wrote, we came into conflict with the world, each other, and ourselves. We wrote from 'the portal' into 'the woods'.

We think we know what we are living through because we're living through it. In fact, that is exactly why the contemporary is so difficult to apprehend. The hardest thing to see is often that which is right in front of your face. You might see what you see very clearly, to riff off V. S. Naipaul, but still not know what you are looking at.

Chi and I wrote in order to inhabit the pandemic, not to escape it. We wrote to rise to the occasion of Covid, not to put it behind us. We also wrote as an act of self-making: that is, to transform our lives. Over time, the nature of our collaboration became clearer, and more urgent. All around us, people were erasing and revising our shared history. In response, we doubled down on recording the intimate and world-historical transformations of the present as it too-swiftly became the past.

Every sentence of this book was written in real-time, on the dates listed at the top of each page. We then went back many times to burnish each fossil-word, blow dust away from the excavation site, and unearth buried lines. Our editing process has been guided by an ethical principle of absolute integrity. There is a way in which we haven't changed anything; yet every letter is a record of change.

The result is a book that exists simultaneously in the past, present, and future. A book that favors the bite of self-knowledge over the balm of self-deception. A book that is true. I hope that shines through, littles. *The End Doesn't Happen All At Once* is the fruit of our efforts to keep the portal open by keeping the pandemic response—*our* pandemic response—alive. For you.

⌐∽

In 2022, while we were still writing, Chi and I shared the draft manuscript with friends. 'It's a page-turner,' Brandon Shimoda told me, but also 'excruciating' to read. This made sense; I had found many parts of the book excruciating to write. Kiese Laymon put it this way: 'You're writing about what everyone else is writing around.' Which explains why composing this book often felt like looking directly at the sun.

The book was excruciating for me to write for another reason, too: namely, that I didn't write it. Not alone, anyway. Chi wrote it with me, and I wrote it with Chi, the friend of my adulthood. That phrase, *the friend of my adulthood*—I think it's theirs, not mine. Theirs, or mine? This is the nature of collaboration. At some point, one stops being sure which words came from whom. (C says this, in the book.) This melding is deeply unsettling, especially to those of us working in the Anglo-American tradition, habituated into the belief that we have a proprietary relation to our words, which originate in us as individuals, and which we then possess. In my field of literary studies, the achievement of greatest value has always been the single-authored book, stamped with a single name across its front.

I'm not sure why, but I had never wanted the single-authored book enough to write one. Given my professional location, I admit that this is strange. I had written hundreds of essays which could have become a book. I had written a doctoral dissertation which could have become a book. Chi had as well. But the book—as form, artifact, achievement—eluded me, us. About a year after C and R started writing letters, Chi and I started talking about turning the letters into a book. Together, we would get over our shared condition of booklessness.

The challenge of our collaboration was immediately compelling. Today, I would go so far as to say that *The End Doesn't Happen All At Once* was not only the first book I ever wanted to write, but also the first book I never wanted to stop writing—or reading. It taught me about character, voice, plot, conflict, scene, setting, and story. It taught me about narrative form and structure. It taught me how to write a book.

This knowledge was hard won. It required that Chi and I each surrender some measure of our authority and autonomy. We had to give up our names and editorial independence. We trusted that in this surrender something of value would emerge. It did. In this book, identity is forged through relation. Each 'I' appears in address. You children seem to know this intuitively, given your daily labors to become your beautiful selves, but it was a tough lesson for me to relearn. Chi once said that we were licensing each other to become the heroes of our own lives, but I often felt that in writing my life, I was actually unwriting my self. Narrating my pandemic-era decisions and desires left me feeling exposed and vulnerable. Reading R's stories against C's made me question my choices, commitments, and goals—

and theirs, too, frankly. But I was also humbled by the gift I had been given: of a window into another's space-time. And through R's accountability to C, I fashioned a new model of accountability to myself.

When I think about collaborating with Chi, the image that comes to mind is that of performance artists Marina Abramović and Ulay, who, over the course of the 1970s and 1980s, staged relational performance pieces in which they tested, trusted, and hurt each other, in private and public. In 'Rest Energy' the artists balanced one arrow between their bodies for four minutes and ten seconds; it was pointing at Abramović's heart. In 'Relation in Time' the artists sat with their hair tied together back-to-back for sixteen hours—just them—before letting the public in to watch for a final hour. And in their most famous work, 'Nightsea Crossing', Abramović and Ulay sat facing one another in a museum gallery for hours on end. It was a test. Who would sit longer? At least once, Ulay got up, and Abramović was left facing an empty chair.

'I think the longer we are home the more hope there is the world will change in giant ways,' Pam Houston wrote to Amy Irvine on April 17, 2020. 'At the very least, we should commit to this,' Grant Farred urged: 'there will be no return to normal'.

As long as we could, Chi and I stayed home, in our chairs. Above our masks, our eyes were trained on each other. To this end, *The End Doesn't Happen All at Once* may be read as a work of durational performance art. Sometimes, I felt like I was alone in my chair, cutting my wrists on stage before an invisible audience. Sometimes, I was the one to walk away.

I always came back, though. Chi always came back. Of course, to have come back means to have left, and to hold open the possibility of leaving again. Some of what you took with you—some of *you*—will never return. That's life, little ones. Soon you will learn that, as Mohsin Hamid writes, 'we are all refugees from our childhoods'. But equally, in Amitava Kumar's words: 'What will come back is the one who never left.'

∽

I am writing this on May 1, 2024, from my office at Rice University. Thousands of college students on hundreds of campuses across the United States are actively protesting the decades-long occupation of Palestine and the genocidal assault on Gaza ongoing since October 7, 2023. At numerous universities, police in riot gear and state troopers have been called in by legislators and administrators to clear encampments. At some, the rest of the semester will unfold 'online'. At others, they've canceled commencement. Students are calling for divestment and urging faculty to go on strike. *Call the semester off! There can be no business as usual.*

Four years ago, I was in my office at the University of Arizona when the world heard a different version of this call. *Cancel everything.* There would be no going back to school after spring break. In March 2020, we gave up the normal order of things. We began to recognize our fundamental interdependence and to grasp each other's essential humanity. This knowledge was deeply threatening to the established order. And so, as the weeks gave way to months gave way to years, the world mostly returned to the quotidian depravity of the way things had always been. Through it all, Chi and I tried to be present to each other and to our lives. We struggled to resist, in our own ways, the return of the status quo.

'Historically, pandemics have forced humans to break with the past and imagine their world anew,' Roy wrote on April 3, 2020. 'This one is no different. It is a portal, a gateway between one world and the next.'

To return to a question posed more than once in these pages, are we still in the portal? Did we imagine the world anew?

If you had asked me yesterday, I would have sung a song of our shared failure. Doubt and defeat are the subjects of my last letter, after all. But now, I want to think differently. The student protestors of spring 2024 are some of the same students who graduated from high school in 2020. They know that 'things can change in a day'. They reject the long reach of American empire, the military-industrial complex, fascism, hypocrisy, and the capitalist death machine. They believe in collaboration, they are all wearing masks, and they are showing us what could happen if we care.

Because of our letters, Chi and I remember the future that could have been before it wasn't. We remember the urgency of connection, before the beaten retreat into our atomized spheres. We remember each time the pundits said the pandemic was over. We remember when the whole room was masking, and then a dozen, and then a couple, and then the one. We remember that nothing was normal and everything was possible. We remember there was a 'we'.

Autonomy is a fiction, this epistolary nonfiction announces. Normal is a fiction. 'I' is a fiction, too. These are lessons we should have heeded long ago. But if you take anything with you from reading *The End Doesn't Happen All At Once*, let it be this: even if we haven't yet learned the lessons we were given to learn, that doesn't mean we can't or that we never will.

LIST OF ILLUSTRATIONS

xiv *photo booth*; C and R, 2010

1 *bluebird*; Tucson, 2020

31 *wheelbarrow*; Zia and Areté, March 2020

31 *fountain*; Mrinalini and Shai, March 2020

63 *steps*; Zia and Areté, July 2020

63 *tree*; Mrinalini, August 2020

64 *hug*; Mrinalini and Shai, August 2020

64 *butterfly*; Zia and Areté, August 2020

98 *bath*; Mrinalini and Shai, October 2020

98 *garden*; Zia, September 2020

133 *snow*; Zia and Areté, February 2021

133 *yearbook*; Mrinalini, January 2021

135 *Portal*; Anne Truitt, 1978 [Acrylic on wood; 96 x 9 x 9 inches]

172 *sprinklers*; Mrinalini and Shai, March 2021

172 *earth*; Areté, March 2021

173 *poolside*; Mrinalini and Shai, April 2021

173 *doctor's*; Zia and Areté, June 2021

174 *birthday*; Shai, May 2021

211 *bubbles*; Mrinalini and Shai, November 2021

211 *bubbles*; Zia and Areté, August 2021

212 *cuddles*; Zia and Areté, September 2021

212 *toddler bed*; Shai, October 2021

258 *hood*; Zia and Areté, December 2021

258 *trunk*; Mrinalini and Shai, January 2022

271 *Texas Children's Hospital*; Houston, September 2022

293 *reunion*; Zia, Areté, Shai, and Mrinalini, July 2022

314 *cream puffs*; Mrinalini and Shai, December 2022

314 *leap*; Zia and Areté, August 2022
347 *igloo*; Zia and Areté, February 2023
348 *Berlin wall*; Mrinalini and Shai, February 2023

NOTES

BOOK ONE: THE CAVE

First Spring: The Shock

March 23, 2020

coronavirus as a 'noetic shock'... Terence Blake, 'Let's make more concepts: isolation as the new epoché,' Agent Swarm weblog (March 23, 2020).

April 9, 2020

My cousin's wife and her family... Dean Meminger, 'Brooklyn Woman Loses Three Grandparents in One Week Amid COVID-19 Outbreak', *Spectrum News, NY1* (April 16, 2020).

April 16, 2020

will succeed in re-establishing normal... Arundhati Roy, 'The Pandemic is a Portal', *Financial Times* (April 3, 2020). https://www.ft.com/content/10d8f5e8-74eb-11ea-95fe-fcd274e920ca

...that protest is over... Roger Berkowitz, Chiara Ricciardone [Chi Rainer Bornfree], and Micah White, 'How to Think About Change: A Conversation Under Lockdown', and Ricciardone [Bornfree], 'Postscript: How to Think About Normal', *Amor Mundi: Hannah Arendt Journal*, Volume IX, 2021. https://issuu.com/bardcollege/docs/2021_ha_journal_volume_9.

Micah White, *The End of Protest*, Penguin Random House 2016.

April 27, 2020

...call no one happy until they are dead... Herodotus, *Histories* 1.32.7. 'If besides all this he ends his life well, then he is the one whom you seek, the one worthy to be called happy/blessed. But refrain from calling him happy/blessed before he dies; call him lucky.'

the reciprocal analogy between war and disease...Chiara Ricciardone [Chi Rainer Bornfree], 'The Ambiguity of the Virus', *The Philosopher* (Summer 2020). See also Kostas Kalimtzis, *Aristotle on Political Enmity and Disease*, SUNY Press, 2001.

May 8, 2020

Karl Marx, *The German Ideology*. https://www.marxists.org/archive/marx/works/1845/german-ideology/ch01a.htm

May 21, 2020

Ed Yong, 'America's Patchwork Pandemic is Fraying Even Further', *The Atlantic* (May 21, 2020).

May 29, 2020

co-taught with Brooke Holmes and Dan-El Padilla Peralta...See 'Rupturing Tradition: Ancient Past, Contemporary Praxis'. https://rupturingtradition.org/

don't you also still feel twenty...Sandel Morse, 'When We're Twenty We Think We Are Invincible', in *A Force Outside Myself: Citizens Over 60 Speak* (June 2020). https://www.mcsweeneys.net/articles/a-force-outside-myself-citizens-over-60-speak

images of reopened South Korean schools... Valerie Strauss, 'The Pictures Say it All: How South Korean Schools are Reopening', *Washington Post* (May 26, 2020).

video of a young student in China being sprayed with disinfectant... Sanya Jain, 'Viral Video: How COVID Has Changed Morning Routine in This China School', NDTV (May 13, 2020).

Clarice Lispector, *Água Viva*, trans. Idra Novey. New Directions (2012 [1973]).

June 4, 2020

Ayman Safiah, 'Keep Moving', Instagram post (May 23, 2020). https://www.instagram.com/p/CAiJR26gX-e/c/17885732116933683/

First Summer: The Fire

June 17, 2020

dire pandemic situation in Egypt... Sudarsan Raghavan, 'Egypt thought it dodged the worst of the pandemic. But now the hospitals are being overwhelmed.' *Washington Post* (June 17, 2020). https://www.washingtonpost.com/world/middle_east/egypt-thought-it-dodged-the-worst-of-the-pandemic-but-now-hospitals-are-being-overwhelmed/2020/06/16/36397b8e-af2c-11ea-98b5-279a6479a1e4_story.html

movement data for different zipcodes... Foursquare Recovery Index. https:/foursquare.com/recoveryindex?state=AllStates

June 27, 2020

Separately I'll send you the virus essay... Chiara Ricciardone [Chi Rainer Bornfree], 'Liquid Philosophy #1: The Ambiguity of the Virus', *The Philosopher* (Fall 2020).

July 4, 2020

'the rodeo goes on'... Elizabeth Williamson, 'Virus Surges in Arizona, but the Rodeo Goes On', *New York Times* (July 3, 2020). https://www.nytimes.com/2020/07/03/us/virus-arizona.html

'you can have a child or a job...' Deb Perelman, 'In the COVID-19 Economy, you can have a kid or a job. You can't have both', *New York Times* (July 2, 2020). https://www.nytimes.com/2020/07/02/business/covid-economy-parents-kids-career-homeschooling.html

'Oh, spell it out'... Salman Rushdie, *Midnight's Children: A Novel.* Vintage: 1981.

'lower and middle class' children... Nellie Bowles, 'This Year's Summer Campground: Our Bedrooms and Living Rooms,' *New York Times* (July 4, 2020). https://www.nytimes.com/2020/07/04/technology/virtual-summer-camps-pandemic.html

July 11, 2020

just in time for the arrival of the Open Letter... 'A Letter on Justice and Open Debate', *Harper's Magazine* (July 7, 2020). https://harpers.org/a-letter-on-justice-and-open-debate/

Micah experienced the rage of the Twitter mob... 'Going to Davos is probably reputational suicide', *BBC*, Jan 20, 2020. https://www.bbc.com/news/business-51173671

July 18, 2020

Danyelle Khmara, 'TUSD: Monitors, not teachers, might be in class with students when schools reopen', *Arizona Daily Star* (July 15, 2020). https://tucson.com/news/local/tusd-monitors-not-teachers-might-be-in-class-with-students-when-schools-reopen/article_07aff8ca-c65a-11ea-af11-c31f3b6a6039.html

Covid as pharmakon. Jacques Derrida, 'Plato's Pharmacy', *Dissemination*, trans. Barbara Johnson (University of Chicago Press, 1981), 70. Derrida writes: 'This *pharmakon*, this 'medicine,' this philter, which acts as both remedy and poison, already introduces itself into the body of the discourse with all its ambivalence. This charm, this spellbinding virtue, this power of fascination, can be—alternately or simultaneously—beneficent or maleficent....Operating through seduction, the *pharmakon* makes one stray from one's general, natural, habitual paths and laws.'

August 15, 2020

...*one of those horrible for-profit online schools*... Kevin Carey, 'Proposed Merger Blurs the Line Between For-Profit College and Public Universities', *New York Times* (August 11, 2020). https://www. nytimes. com/2020/08/11/upshot/university-of-arizona-ashford-zovio-online-college.html

First Fall: The Numbers

September 17, 2020

Zoom event with Kate Manne... 'Entitlement and Misogyny: A Conversation with Kate Manne' for *The Philosopher*. https://www.youtube.com/ watch?v=xmBvruNzgIk

September 27, 2020

Natalie Diaz, 'Isn't the Air Also a Body, Moving?' *The New Yorker* (May 23, 2018). https://www.newyorker.com/books/poems/envelopes-of-air-ada-limon-and-natalie-diaz-forge-a-bond-amid-the-shifting-landscape-of-contemporary-america

Vsevold Nekrasov, 'No', The Estate of Vsevolod Nekrasov, *I Live I See: Selected Poems*, trans. Ainsley Morse and Bela Shayevich (Ugly Duckling Presse, 2013, 2018).

October 10, 200

'ditto ditto in the archives'...Christina Sharpe, *In the Wake: On Blackness and Being*. Duke University Press: 2016.

October 17, 2020

Rumi, 'Green Inside', *Rumi: The Big Red Book*, trans. Coleman Barks (HarperOne: 2010), 39.

Selves understood as entangled organisms... Anticipating here some thoughts more fully explored in Chiara Ricciardone [Chi Rainer Bornfree], 'Liquid Philosophy #3: What Is It Like To Be A Self? Undoing Identity'. *The Philosopher* (U.K.) Summer 2021.

November 14, 2020

We: a simple word... 'What is We? A Conversation with Brooke Holmes, Chiara Ricciardone [Chi Rainer Bornfree], Ragini Srinivasan'. *The Philosopher* Lecture Series. November 2020.

Risk-taking in a pandemic... Marshall Allen and Meg Marco, 'How Your Brain Tricks You into Taking Risks During the Pandemic', *Propublica* (November 2, 2020). https://www.propublica.org/article/how-your-brain-tricks-you-into-taking-risks-during-the-pandemic

First Winter: The Dark

January 3, 2021

Keep interested in your own career... Max Ehrmann, 'Desiderata' (1927). https://www.desiderata.com/desiderata.html

More information about the vaccine... Helen Branswel, 'With limited surveillance of Covid-19 variant, it's deja vu all over again', STAT (December 31, 2020). https://www.statnews.com/2020/12/31/with-limited-surveillance-of-covid-19-variant-its-deja-vu-all-over-again/

Chinese bamboo grows its root system... Richard Powers, *The Overstory*. WW Norton and Company, 2018.

January 9, 2021

How low will it go? The count as of December 11, 2021: 'Since January of last year, at least 1 in 6 people who live in Pima County have been infected, and at least 1 in 352 people have died.' The count as of February 2, 2022: 'Since January 2020, at least 1 in 4 people who live in Pima County have been infected, and at least 1 in 303 people have died.' The count on May 6, 2022, 'at least 1 in 273 people have died.' November 13, 2022, Pima County's count: 1 in 259 have died.

Kay Ryan, 'I Go to AWP,' *Poetryfoundation.org* (October 2005). https://www.poetryfoundation.org/poetrymagazine/articles/68318/i-go-to-awp

January 17, 2021

'We choose our own lives...' Andrew Solomon, *Far from the Tree: Parents, Children, and the Search for Identity* (Scribner: 2012), 46.

January 23, 2021

The problem of elite capture... See Olufemi Taiwo, 'Identity Politics and Elite Capture', Boston Review, May 2020. https://www.bostonreview.net/articles/olufemi-o-taiwo-identity-politics-and-elite-capture/> and 'Being in the Room Privilege: Elite Capture and Epistemic Deference', *The Philosopher*, https://www.thephilosopher1923.org/post/being-in-the-room-privilege-elite-capture-and-epistemic-deference

February 7, 2021

*Profits from death...*Oxfam, 'Who profits from Covid-19, and how can we use that money to help us get a vaccine?' (July 22, 2020). https://www.oxfamamerica.org/explore/stories/who-profits-covid-19-and-how-can-we-use-money-help-us-get-vaccine/

February 20, 2021

N. K. Jemisin. *How Long 'til Black Future Month? Stories.* Orbit, 2018.

March 1, 2021

'Levi died at Auschwitz forty years later.' Diego Gambetta, 'Primo Levi's Last Moments', *Boston Review* (July 9, 2012). https://bostonreview.net/articles/diego-gambetta-primo-levi-last-moments/

March 6, 2021

Covid-afflicted AIDS researcher...Gowri Vijayakumar, 'Writing Pandemics: A COVID Autoethnography', Ethnographic Marginalia (March 6, 2021). https://ethnomarginalia.com/writing-pandemics-a-covid-autoethnography/
Hikikomori in Japan and South Korea...Anne Babe, 'They couldn't go outside for years. Then Covid-19 trapped them again', Wired (March 3, 2021). https://www.wired.co.uk/article/hikikomori-south-korea-covid

BOOK TWO: THE PORTAL

Second Spring: The Return

March 17, 2021

'The desert is not my home.' Derrais Carter, 'Slow Return', *Texte Zur Kunst* (August 28, 2020). https://www.textezurkunst.de/articles/derrais-carter-slow-return/
Franny Choi, 'The World Keeps Ending, and the World Goes On', *Poetry* (December 2019).

March 30, 2021

Variants we don't even know how to see... Aylin Woodward, 'A new coronavirus variant found in France can hide from COVID-19 nasal-swab tests', *Insider* (March 18, 2021).
Fauci holds out hope for summer camp....Naomi Thomas and Dakin Andone, 'Conceivable that unvaccinated children could go to camp or playgrounds this summer, Fauci says', CNN Health (March 28, 2021).
New label... Naoise Dolan, 'I'm struggling to talk to friends in lockdown. Being alone has been a relief,' *The Guardian* (March 11, 2021). https://www.theguardian.com/books/2021/mar/11/naoise-dolan-exciting-times-talking-friends-lockdown

April 4, 2021

how much older [your] parents look... Amitava Kumar, *A Matter of Rats: A Short Biography of Patna*. Duke University Press, 2014.
I am afraid I am this guy...Nicholas Dames, 'Departures and Returns,' *n+1* (June 5, 2020).

April 13, 2021

Torrey Peters, *Detransition, Baby*. One World: 2021.

Verónique Tadjo, *The Shadow of Imana: Travels in the Heart of Rwanda*, Waveland Press, 2015.

April 19, 2021

...preventing severe disease and hospital admission. S. Griffin 'Covid-19: AstraZeneca vaccine prevents 79% of symptomatic disease and 100% of severe disease, US study finds,' *BMJ* (2021); 372 :n793 doi:10.1136/bmj.n793

'gurneys in the gift shop.' Tim Arango, 'Southern California's Hospitals Are Overwhelmed, and It May Get Worse,' *New York Times* (December 31, 2020).

'...metal parts have begun to melt.' Alasdair Pai, 'Non-stop cremations cast doubt on India's counting of COVID dead,' *Reuters* (April 19, 2021).

...worse than they have ever been. Erin Cunningham and Siobhan O'Grady, 'New global coronavirus cases nearly double in two months,' *Washington Post* (April 16, 2021).

May 2, 2021

Arundhati Roy, 'We are Witnessing a Crime Against Humanity,' *The Guardian* (April 28, 2021).

Mohsin Hamid, *The Reluctant Fundamentalist*. Hamish Hamilton: 2007.

'Hope is a lapse in concentration.' Manu Joseph, *Serious Men*. HarperCollins: 2010.

'Hope for what? Not particularly, no.' Lucy Feldman, "My Wine Bills Have Gone Down.' How Joan Didion is Weathering the Pandemic,' *Time* (January 22, 2021).

May 8, 2021

aliens are real!... Gideon Lewis-Kraus, 'How the Pentagon Started Taking U.F.O.S Seriously,' New Yorker (April 30, 2021).

'...to underestimate the role of chance in events'... Daniel Kahneman, *Thinking, Fast and Slow*. Farrar, Straus, and Giroux, 2011.

Maggie Nelson, *On Freedom: Four Songs of Care and Constraint*. Graywolf, 2021.

May 15, 2021

The CDC's premature edict. 'CDC says fully vaccinated people can stop wearing masks indoors and outdoors', *NPR* (May 13, 2021). https://www.npr.org/2021/05/13/996582891/fully-vaccinated-people-can-stop-wearing-masks-indoors-and-outdoors-cdc-says

June 1, 2021

'I'm just not sure I want to...' Tim Kreider, 'I'm Not Scared to Reenter Society. I'm Just Not Sure I Want To', *The Atlantic* (May 30, 2021).

June 8, 2021

public schools need not require masks indoors in the fall...Jennifer Millman, 'NY to Eliminate Indoor Mask Rule for Schools, Camps, Monday; NYC to Keep Mask Requirement', NBC New York (June 4, 2021).

delusion that the pandemic is over...Melba Newsome, "Cave Syndrome' Keeps the Vaccinated in Social Isolation', *Scientific American* (May 3, 2021).

to believe those deaths will happen somewhere else...Jenni Fink, 'As CDC Eases Mask Restrictions, WHO Says 2nd Year of Pandemic Will Be 'Far More Deadly' Than First', *Newsweek* (May 14, 2021).

Cassandra syndrome... Kenneth Robertson, 'Adult Asperger's and The Cassandra Phenomenon' (June 19, 2019). Cf. 'Cassandra phenomenon: A systemic perspective.' https://www.connections-counselling.co.uk/blog/cassandra-phenomenon-a-systemic-perspective/

Second Summer: Forever

June 13, 2021

Yiyun Li, *Dear Friend, from My Life I Write to You in Your Life.* Random House, 2017; and *Where Reasons End.* Random House, 2019.

'Hygiene theater.' Derek Thompson, 'Hygiene Theater is a Huge Waste of Time,' *The Atlantic* (July 27, 2020). https://www.theatlantic.com/ideas/archive/2020/07/scourge-hygiene-theater/614599/

But the variants. James Gallagher, 'Covid: Is there a limit to how much worse variants can get?' *BBC* (June 12, 2021). https://www.bbc.com/news/health-57431420

...what Timothy Morton calls this 'hyper-object'. Morgan Meis, 'Timothy Morton's Hyper-Pandemic,' *New Yorker* (June 8, 2021). https://www.newyorker.com/culture/persons-of-interest/timothy-mortons-hyper-pandemic

June 25, 2021

'the most dangerous moment to be unvaccinated' Robert M. Wachter, 'This is the most dangerous moment to be unvaccinated', *Washington Post* (April 19, 2021). https://www.washingtonpost.com/opinions/2021/04/19/this-is-most-dangerous-moment-be-unvaccinated/

All prohibited. 'Ducey prohibits state universities from requiring masks, testing of unvaccinated students', *Tucson.com* (June 15, 2021). https://tucson.com/news/government-and-politics/ducey-prohibits-state-universities-from-requiring-masks-testing-of-unvaccinated-students/article_a2e64c4c-ce04-11eb-b189-a37a0d44748f.html#tracking-source=home-top-story-1

Solastalgia. Glenn Albrecht, Gina-Maree Sartore, Linda Connor, Nick Higginbotham, Sonia Freeman, Brian Kelly, Helen Stain, Anne Tonna, and Georgia Pollard, 'Solastalgia: the distress caused by environmental change,' *Australasian psychiatry* 15.sup1 (2007): S95-S98.

...bodies are continuing to wash up on the riverbeds. Om Gaur, 'The Ganges is Returning the Dead. It Does Not Lie,' *New York Times* (June 17, 2021). https://www.nytimes.com/2021/06/17/opinion/india-covid-ganges.html

...what I needed was to get hit by a truck. Hana Schank, 'I know the secret to the quiet mind. I wish I'd never learned it.' *The Atlantic* (June 7, 2021). https://www.theatlantic.com/health/archive/2021/06/car-accident-brain-injury/619227/

July 2, 2021

Plato's cave... Chiara Ricciardone [Chi Rainer Bornfree] 'Liberating Plato's Prisoners'. *The Philosopher,* Summer 2021. https://www.thephilosopher1923.org/post/liberating-platos-prisoners

July 9, 2021

...boiling to death in the Pacific Northwest. Sammy Westfall and Amanda Coletta, 'Crushing heat wave in Pacific Northwest and Canada cooked shellfish alive by the millions', *Washington Post* (July 8, 2021). https://www.washingtonpost.com/world/2021/07/08/canada-sea-creatures-boiling-to-death/

Lauren Berlant, *Cruel Optimism.* Duke University Press: 2011.

Hap. Thomas Hardy, 'Hap'. https://www.poetryfoundation.org/poems/46311/hap

July 16, 2021

Ben Quinn, 'England's Covid unlocking is threat to world, say 1200 scientists', *The Guardian* (July 16, 2021). https://www.theguardian.com/world/2021/jul/16/englands-covid-unlocking-a-threat-to-the-world-experts-say

July 23, 2021

'India's Pandemic Death Toll Estimated at About 4 Million: 10 Times the Official Count', *NPR* (July 20, 2021).

Teju Cole, *Every Day is for the Thief* (Random House, 2015), 112.

July 28, 2021

'The Delta Variant Upends the World's Pandemic Response', *Wall Street Journal* (July 25, 2021). https://www.wsj.com/articles/thedeltavariant-upends-the-worlds-pandemic-response-11627225200

August 11, 2021

Ben Okri. *The Freedom Artist.* Head of Zeus, 2019.

a new report out from the Global Sustainability Institute... King N, Jones A. An Analysis of the Potential for the Formation of 'Nodes of Persisting Complexity'. Sustainability. 2021; 13(15):8161. https://doi.org/10.3390/su13158161

Plato's myth of the flooding of Atlantis... Guy Middleton, 'Poseidon's Wrath', Aeon (Aug 2 2021). https://aeon.co/essays/how-a-vanished-ancient-greek-city-helps-us-think-about-disasters

August 19, 2021

'*...whose lives have been deemed irrelevant.*'... J. Daniel Elam, *World Literature for the Wretched of the Earth: Anticolonial Politics, Postcolonial Aesthetics.* Fordham University Press, 2020.

Second Fall: The Bottom Line

September 2, 2021

Make me as hard as a rock. Ishmael Reed, 'The Author Reflects on his 35th Birthday.' https://www.poetryfoundation.org/poems/42944/the-author-reflects-on-his-35th-birthday

September 16, 2021

...equal and opposite amount to the side of pain. 'In 'Dopamine Nation' Overabundance Keeps Us Craving More', Fresh Air with Terry Gross, *NPR* (August 25, 2021).

Catherine Rottenberg, *The Rise of Neoliberal Feminism* (Oxford University Press: 2018).

...more and more of the same. Dan Keating, Akilah Johnson, and Monica Ulmanu, 'The pandemic marks another grim milestone: 1 in 500 Americans have died of covid-19', *Washington Post* (September 15, 2021).

September 22, 2021

Plato, *Phaedo,* 60b-c.

Chiara Ricciardone [Chi Rainer Bornfree], 'What is the meaning of Socrates' last words? A multi-faceted approach.' Ancient Philosophy 39(2):267-293 (2019).

the only species which doesn't know how it is supposed to live... Martin Hagglund, 'The world to come: what should we value?' *The New Statesman* (August 26, 2020). https://www.newstatesman.com/world/2020/08/world-come-what-should-we-value

'never really at home in the interpreted world'... Rainer Maria Rilke, Duino Elegies, trans. A.S. Kline. https://www.poetryintranslation.com/PITBR/German/Rilke.php

September 30, 2021

adrienne marie brown, *Pleasure Activism: The Politics of Feeling Good.* AK Press: 2019.

Audre Lorde, 'The uses of the erotic: The erotic as power', *The lesbian and gay studies reader* (1993): 339-43.

Oswald de Andrade, 'The Cannibalist Manifesto', translated by Leslie Bary. *Latin American Literary Review* 19.38 (1991): 38-47.

Suketu Mehta, *Maximum City: Bombay Lost and Found*. (Vintage Book, 2004), 536,

October 8, 2021

Love the questions... Maria Popova, 'Live the Questions: Rilke on Embracing Uncertainty and Doubt as a Stabilizing Force', The Marginalia. https://www.themarginalian.org/2012/06/01/rilke-on-questions/

'Unforeseen and yet/only too well known'... W.S. Merwin, 'To Being Late', The Nation (July 29, 2005). https://www.thenation.com/article/archive/being-late/

'I wasn't I.'... Pessoa, Fernando. *The Book of Disquiet*. Translated by Richard Zenith, Penguin Books, 2003, p. 39-40.

'checklists specific to autism in women'... e.g. Samantha Craft, 'Females and Autism.' https://the-art-of-autism.com/females-and-aspergers-a-checklist

'in the cave ages in terms of understanding how viruses emerge'... German Lopez, 'Florida's mysterious Covid-19 surge', Vox (September 23, 2021). https://www.vox.com/22686423/covid-19-cases-rise-fall-florida-vaccines-weather

A carbon-backed coin called Klima... In Kim Stanley Robinson's *Ministry for the Future* (2020), a carbon-backed currency called carboni becomes a crucial driver of the messy social heave towards a livable future.

October 13, 2021

'Getting away with things is essential...' J. L. Austin, *How to Do Things with Words*, 30.

'...a desire to be and to know.' Natalia Ginzburg, *The Little Virtues*, translated by Dick Davis (Arcade, 1962, 1985), 97.

Arizona HEROES. https://azheroes.arizona.edu/join-az-heroes

October 19, 2021

'Sudden fits of rage'... 'Six most common causes of anger in relation to autism disorders,' https://www.pasadenavilla.com/resources/blog/common-causes-of-anger-autism/

'Compensatory mechanisms'... Tania Marshall, 'AspienGirl: Embracing the Strengths of Women with Autism', available from https://www.differentbrains.org/aspiengirl-embracing-strengths-women-aspergers-syndrome-tania-marshall-edb-51/

October 28, 2021.

But Covid still has me. Cf. Jim Moore, 'How to Come Out of Lockdown', on 'that long silence / which it is now time for me to admit I have loved / beyond any reason or defense.'

1 in 6 in Arizona. Arizona passed New York in terms of reported deaths per capita. See Annabelle Timsit, 'Arizona's pandemic outlook worries experts as mask and vaccine battles rage', *Washington Post* (October 25, 2021). https://www.washingtonpost.com/nation/2021/10/25/arizona-coronavirus-cases-surge-experts

40% of American children. Apoorva Mandavilli, 'Has the Virus Infected Huge Numbers of Younger Children?' *New York Times* (October 28, 2021). https://www.nytimes.com/2021/10/28/health/covid-vaccine-children.html

...his chronic pain may be significantly neuroplastic. Nathaniel Frank, 'Chronic Pain is surprisingly treatable—when patients focus on the brain,' *Washington Post* (October 15, 2021). https://www.washingtonpost.com/outlook/2021/10/15/chronic-pain-brain-plasticity/

Chicken and egg problems. Clarice Lispector, *The Foreign Legion: Stories and Chronicles,* translated by Giovanni Pontiero (New Directions, 1986).

November 5, 2021

Amitav Ghosh, *The Great Derangement*. University of Chicago Press, 2017.

November 12, 2021

Roy Scranton, *Learning to Die in the Anthropocene: Reflections on the End of a Civilization.* City Lights Books, 2015

Richard Powers, *The Overstory*. W.W. Norton & Company, 2018.

Covid is the leading cause of death.... Patty Machelor, 'Arizona the only state where COVID-19 the leading cause of death during pandemic,' *Tucson.com* (November 12, 2021). https://tucson.com/news/local/report-arizona-only-state-where-covid-19-the-leading-cause-of-death-during-pandemic/article_64571966-426c-11ec-9ce9-33204cf123ad.html

'the future of the virus has arrived.' David Leonhardt, 'How does this end? Thinking about covid and normalcy,' *New York Times* (November 12, 2021). https://www.nytimes.com/2021/11/12/briefing/when-will-covid-end.html. Cf. Joel Achenbach and Yasmeen Abutaleb, 'How does a pandemic start winding down? You are looking at it,' *Washington Post* (October 31, 2021). https://www.washingtonpost.com/health/2021/10/31/when-does-the-pandemic-end/

Dipesh Chakrabarty, 'Belatedness as possibility: Subaltern histories, once again', *The Indian Postcolonial* (Routledge, 2010), 181-194.

...learning to say more no's. Anna Holmes, 'How about never?' *The Atlantic* (November 5, 2021). https://www.theatlantic.com/ideas/archive/2021/11/liberating-power-no/620612/

November 18, 2021

Mohsin Hamid, *The Reluctant Fundamentalist*. Boston, Houghton Mifflin Harcourt, 2008.

John Williams, *Stoner*. Vintage Classics, 2012.

Claire Louise Bennet, 'Control Knobs', from *The Pond*, Riverhead Books, 2017.

'if I do, it might not be the same me'... As one reading of Heraclitus suggests: 'On those stepping into rivers staying the same other and other waters flow.' B12.

Rumi, 'Don't Go Back to Sleep', in Coleman Barks, Tr., *The Essential Rumi*. San Francisco: Harper Collins, 1995.

Second Winter: The End of the Beginning

December 25, 2021

'A child has been born unto us.' Hannah Arendt, *The Human Condition*, 2nd edition (University of Chicago Press: 1958), 247.

Arundhati Roy, *The God of Small Things* (Random House: 1997), 32, 156, 183.

Ling Ma, *Severance* (Farrar, Straus, and Giroux: 2018), 3.

Chang-rae Lee, *On Such a Full Sea* (Riverhead Books: 2014), 75.

C.D. Wright, *Steal Away: Selected and New Poems* (Copper Canyon Press: 2002), 179.

The failed and treacherous CDC. The People's CDC, 'The CDC is beholden to corporations and lost our trust. We need to start our own', *The Guardian* (April 3, 2022). https://www.theguardian.com/commentisfree/2022/apr/03/peoples-cdc-covid-guidelines

Patrick Blanchfield, 'Death Drive Nation,' *Late Light: A journal of Brooklyn Institute for Social Research* (December 17, 2021). https://late-light.com/issues/issue-1/death-drive-nation

Faith. Surrender. Renunciation. Lata Mani, *Interleaves: Ruminations on Illness and Spiritual Life* (Yoda Press: 2011)

Third Spring: Turn the Page

February 24, 2022

Thomas Kingsley, 'Iceland says it wants 'as many people as possible' to catch Covid after lifting all restrictions', *Independent* (February 23, 2022). https://www.independent.co.uk/news/world/europe/iceland-covid-lift-restrictions-b2021547.html

'5 minutes of freedom'... Masha Gessen, 'The Crushing Loss of Hope in Ukraine', *New Yorker* (February 23, 2022). https://www.newyorker.com/news/our-columnists/the-crushing-loss-of-hope-in-ukraine

Sheila Heti, *Pure Colour*. New York, Farrar, Straus and Giroux, 2022

BOOK THREE: THE WOODS

Third Summer: The Afterlife

June 28, 2022

20% chance it will, the CDC says... 'Nearly One in Five Americans Adults who have had Covid-19 Still Have 'Long Covid'', *CDC* and National Center for Health Statistics (June 22, 2022). https://www.cdc.gov/nchs/ pressroom/ nchs_press_releases/2022/20220622.htm.

July 6, 2022

Carlo Rovelli, *The Order of Time*, trans. Erica Segre and Simon Carnell. Riverhead Books, 2018

Rumi, 'The Sunrise Ruby', in Coleman Barks, Tr., *The Essential Rumi*. Harper Collins, 1995.

August 24, 2022

Anne Truitt, *Daybook: The Journal of an Artist*. Penguin Books, 1984.

September 20, 2022

'So are we really in the clear?' Ayana Archie, 'Joe Biden says the Covid-19 pandemic is over. This is what the data tells us', *Washington Post* (September 19, 2022). https://www.npr.org/2022/09/19/1123767437/joe-biden-covid-19-pandemic-over

'...will continue to be a threat beyond the rest of our lives.' Richard Martinello, quoted in Sabrina Malhi, 'Coronavirus Updates Newsletter,' *Washington Post* (September 19, 2022). https://www.washingtonpost.com/newsletters/ coronavirus-updates/. Cf. Nate Holdren, 'Pandemic Nihilism, Social Murder, and the Banality of Evil,' Bill of Health Blog (September 19, 2022). https://blog.petrieflom.law.harvard.edu/2022/09/19/pandemic-nihilism-social-murder-and-the-banality-of-evil/

Chaudhuri is considered to be 'literary'... Simon During, 'Calcutta's Via Negative,' *Public Books* (August 6, 2013). https://www.publicbooks.org/ calcuttas-via-negativa/.

'...The two happen simultaneously.' Amit Chaudhuri, *Friend of my Youth* (New York Review of Books, 2017), 143.

'It isn't absolutely certain when the writing ends.' Amit Chaudhuri, *The Origins of Dislike* (Oxford University Press, 2018), 293.

'Writing generates life.' Amit Chaudhuri, *Friend of my Youth* (New York Review of Books, 2017), 88.

Third Fall: The Strength

October 12, 2022

JTO, 'Why do they think that?' https://essaysyoudidntwanttoread.home.
blog/2022/10/09/why-do-they-think-that/

Nadia Bolz Weber, 'Not filling in the blank', *Substack* (October 10, 2022).
https://thecorners.substack.com/p/not-filling-in-the-blank?r=hckvp&utm_
campaign=post&utm_medium=email

Eleanor Gordon-Smith, 'I really don't want to get Covid, but the loneliness
gets greater every day.' *The Guardian* (October 6, 2022). https://www.
theguardian.com/lifeandstyle/2022/oct/07/i-really-dont-want-to-get-covid-
but-the-loneliness-gets-greater-every-day-how-do-i-keep-going

MC Barton, KV Bennett, JR Cook, GG Gallup, Jr, and SM Platek,
'Hypothesized behavioral host manipulation by SARS-CoV2/COVID-19
infection,' *Med Hypotheses.* 2020 Aug;141:109750. doi: 10.1016/j.
mehy.2020.109750. Epub 2020 Apr 22.

October 23, 2022

'the third space'... Homi Bhabha, *The Location of Culture* (Routledge, 1994).

a tripledemic of flu, RSV, and Covid... Apoorva Mandavilli, 'A 'Tripledemic'?
Flue, R.S.V. and Covid May Collide this Winter, Experts Say,' *New York
Times* (October 23, 2022). https://www.nytimes.com/2022/10/23/health/
flu-covid-risk.html

never—becoming strangers... Divya Victor, *Semblance: Two Essays* (Sputnik &
Fizzle, 2016), 29.

November 12, 2022

Elizabeth Strout, *Oh, William!* Random House, 2021.

Leo Tolstoy, 'The Three Questions.' https://www.plough.com/en/topics/culture/
short-stories/the-three-questions

*Hollywood is maintaining its strict Covid precautions...*Katie Kilkenny,
'Hollywood's Unions and Studios Extend COVID Protocols With Small
Modifications', in *Hollywood Reporter*, October 2022. https://www.
hollywoodreporter.com/business/business-news/hollywoods-covid-
protocols-extended-small-modifications-1235234314/

Long Covid does matter... see

B. Bowe, Xie, Y. & Al-Aly, Z. Acute and postacute sequelae associated with
SARS-CoV-2 reinfection. Nat Med 28, 2398–2405 (2022). https://doi.
org/10.1038/s41591-022-02051-3.

Brookings Institution. 'New data shows 'long COVID' is keeping as many as
4 million people out of work.' Brookings Institution (29 March 2021).
https://www.brookings.edu/research/new-data-shows-long-covid-is-
keeping-as-many-as-4-million-people-out-of-work/#:~:text=Using%20

COVID%2D19%20case%20counts,around%20%24200%20billion%20
per%20year
Yaneer Bar Yam, 'End Coronavirus.' www.EndCoronavirus.org

November 24, 2022

'immunity debt'...Haley Hernandez, 'Pediatric hospitals noticing number of critically ill patients increasing as common viruses surge,' *Click2Houston. com* (November 15, 2022). https://www.click2houston.com/news/local/2022/11/16/pediatric-hospitals-noticing-number-of-critically-ill-patients-increasing-as-common-viruses-surge/

*...about a gay couple's wedding...*Fenit Nirappil, 'My mom was finally ready to accept my gay wedding. Then she got Covid,' *Washington Post* (November 17, 2022). https://www.washingtonpost.com/lifestyle/2022/11/17/wedding-covid-pandemic/

December 10, 2022

Alexander Pope, 'An Essay on Criticism.' *The Norton Anthology of English Literature*, ed. Stephen Greenblatt, 9th ed., vol. 1, W.W. Norton, 2012, pp. 269-277.

Salman Rushdie, 'A Sackful of Seeds,' *New Yorker*, December 5, 2022. https://www.newyorker.com/magazine/2022/12/12/a-sackful-of-seeds

Forty-year-olds drop dead after a cold... Kevin Draper and Alan Blinder, 'Soccer Journalist Dies at World Cup After Collapsing at Argentina Game,' *New York Times* (December 9, 2022). https://www.nytimes.com/2022/12/09/ sports/soccer/grant-wahl-dead.html

Confusing cause and effect... Nietzsche's Four Great Errors, *Nietzsche, Friedrich. Twilight of the Idols. Edited by Duncan Large, Oxford University Press, 2008.*

Yasmin Tayag, 'It's Beginning to Look a Lot Like Another COVID Surge,' *The Atlantic* (December 9, 2022). https:// www.theatlantic.com/health/archive/2022/12/covid-us-new-cases-winter-surge/672415.

*Feminist Indigenous land education...*https://www.landeducationdreambook. com/introduction-to-land-education

December 20, 2022

*Chronic coughs all around seem like a big part of the post-Covid world and soundscape...*Sarah Mayberry Scott, 'Sonic Lessons of the Covid-19 Soundscape', *Sounding Out!* (August 2, 2021). https://soundstudiesblog. com/2021/08/02/sonic-lessons-of-the-covid-19-soundscape/

Third Winter: Fidelity

December 27, 2022

Julia Shapero, 'Nearly half of passengers from China to Milan have COVID:

Italian officials', *The Hill* (December 28, 2022). https://thehill.com/policy/healthcare/3790837-nearly-half-of-passengers-from-china-to-milan-have-covid-italian-officials/

'*The radical impacts of GPT-3*'...Josh Dzieza, 'How Kindle Novelists are Using Chat-GPT', *The Verge* (December 24, 2022). https://www.theverge.com/23520625/chatgpt-openai-amazon-kindle-novel

'*Far UV light...*'... 'New Type of Ultraviolet Light Makes Indoor Air as Safe as Outdoors', *Columbia University Irving Medical Center* (March 25, 2022). https://www.cuimc.columbia.edu/news/new-type-ultraviolet-light-makes-indoor-air-safe-outdoors/

most contagious variant yet takes off in NY...Eric Topol, 'A New Variant Alert: The XBB.1.5 variant is on a growth spurt in the US', *Substack* (December 23, 2022). https://erictopol.substack.com/p/a-new-variant-alert/

Terrifying pediatric health crisis... Madeline Halpert, 'Children's Tylenol in short supply–here's what parents can do', *BBC.com* (December 21, 2022). https://www.bbc.com/news/world-us-canada-64034568.

*Long-term illness crisis that is also economic...*Elliot Smith, 'A long-term illness crisis is threatening the UK economy', *CNBC* (December 28, 2022). https://www.cnbc.com/2022/12/28/a-long-term-illness-crisis-is-threatening-the-uk-economy.html/

January 8, 2023

'*It is only through the far distance that the object comes back to itself.*' Julie Beth Napolin, *The Fact of Resonance: Modernist Acoustics and Narrative Form* (Fordham University Press, 2020), 72.

'*I want to remove every trace of myself.*' Jhumpa Lahiri, *Whereabouts* (Knopf, 202), 142.

Bernadette Mayer, 'The Way to Keep Going in Antarctica', *A Bernadette Mayer Reader* (New Directions Publishing, 1968). https://www.poetryfoundation.org/poems/49723/the-way-to-keep-going-in-antarctica/

January 21, 2023

'*...you can get by with almost any how*'...Friedrich Nietzsche, 'Epigrams and Arrows', 12, in *Twilight of the Idols*.

'*That is how all distances, all measure, change*'... Rilke, *Letters to a Young Poet* (WW Norton,1929, revised 1993).

Carlo Rovelli, *Helgoland*, trans. Erica Segre and Simon Carnell (Penguin, 2021).

Chandra Prescott-Weinstein, *The Disordered Cosmos: A Journey into Dark Matter, Spacetime, and Dreams Deferred* (Bold Type Books, 2021).

January 31, 2023

'*...the idea of another order was still valid.*' Amit Chaudhuri, *Sojourn* (New York Review Books, 2022), 43

'*When freedom is the only reality, you're no longer free.*' Amit Chaudhuri, *Sojourn* (New York Review Books, 2022), 61

*The loss of China...*Helen Davidson, Verna Yu, and Chi Hui Lin, 'It was all for nothing: Chinese count cost of Xi's snap decision to let Covid rip,' *The Guardian* (January 29, 2023). https://www.theguardian.com/world/2023/jan/29/chinese-cost-covid-xi-lockdowns-china

The loss of Jacinda Ardern... Natasha Frost, 'Jacinda Ardern, New Zealand's Leader, Says She Will Step Down', *New York Times* (January 18, 2023). https://www.nytimes.com/2023/01/18/world/asia/jacinda-ardern-new-zealand.html

*unlearn [my] privilege as loss...*Donna Landry and Gerald MacLean, 'Introduction: Reading Spivak', *The Spivak Reader: Selected Works of Gayatri Chakravorty Spivak* (Routledge, 1996), 4-5.

Matthew Salesses, 'To Grieve is to Carry Another Time', *Longreads* (April 22, 2019). https://longreads.com/2019/04/22/to-grieve-is-to-carry-another-time/

Matthew Salesses, 'To Tell a Story is to Tell it Again, to Carry Another Time', *Catapult* (January 24, 2023). https://catapult.co/stories/matthew-salesses-grief-storytelling-another-time

February 9, 2023

Robert Frost, 'The Road Not Taken'. https://www.poetryfoundation.org/poems/44272/the-road-not-taken

Alain Badiou, *Metaethics*. See also, 'Happiness is a risk that we must be ready to take', *Verso* (June 10, 2015). https://www.versobooks.com/blogs/2032-alain-badiou-happiness-is-a-risk-that-we-must-be-ready-to-take

Daniel Kahneman, *Thinking Fast and Slow* (Farrar, Straus, and Giroux, 2011).

*Resilience...*Maria Konnikova, 'How People Learn to Become Resilient', *New Yorker* (February 11, 2016). https://www.newyorker.com/science/maria-konnikova/the-secret-formula-for-resilience

Georges Canguilhem, *The Normal and The Pathological* (Zone Books, 1991).

Ralph Waldo Emerson, 'The Transcendentalist', Virginia Commonwealth University, https://archive.vcu.edu/english/engweb/transcendentalism/authors/emerson/essays/transcendentalist.html

'*Upsurge in organizing Covid-Zero intentional communities*'... See 'Cult of Last Resort' (Vermont), https://docs.google.com/document/d/1M8DxeJj2uddylRm6LHq1sDx26UR_1I9oW5hoOqN6VGk/mobilebasic?fbclid=IwAR06ZBHdBJd-INXaqw8QJseks5FftJuAOqFpfDfSGayI90kHWn6hb6rxwBY&urp=gmail_link; 'Still-Coviding' (Mid-Atlantic); https://www.facebook.com/groups/497272482564321/>;

March 4, 2023

'*organized abandonment*'...Ruth Wilson Gilmore, *Abolition Geography: Essays Toward Liberation*. Verso, 2022.

Nate Holdren, 'Broken Sociality', *Peste* (February 21, 2023). https://www.pestemag.com/lost-to-follow-up/broken-sociality/

Fourth Spring: Two Roads

March 22, 2023

John Snow Project, 'We Need to Talk about Covid-19'. https://johnsnowproject.org/

Kwam Um School of Zen, 'Bad luck or good luck?' (September 24, 2018). https://kwanumzen.org/teaching-blog/2018/9/24/bad-luck-or-good-luck/

Sebastien Bubeck, et al, 'Sparks of Artificial General Intelligence: Early Experiments with GPT-4', Arxiv (Rev. April 13, 2013). https://arxiv.org/abs/2303.12712/

*...help you plan a death camp or impersonate a lover...*Julian Togelius, 'The Banality of AI', *Twitter* (March 20, 2023). https://twitter.com/togelius/status/1638938289074741253?s=20

...plan a meal... Robert Leib, *Exoanthropology: Dialogues with AI* (punctum books, 2023); 'ChefGPT'. https://www.chefgpt.xyz/

...fantasy of Trump being arrested... Debate Society of Berkeley, 'AI is getting out of hand', *Twitter* (March 21, 2023). https://twitter.com/BerkeleyDebates/status/1638219431087095808?s=20.

...plan a trip... Candice Cai, 'This Can't be Real': Singaporean Woman Uses AI to plan Vietnam Travel Itinerary', *AsiaOne* (March 22, 2023). https://www.asiaone.com/lifestyle/cant-be-real-singaporean-woman-uses-ai-plan-vietnam-travel-itinerary-netizens-disbelief/

Khan Academy, 'Khanmigo [*AI tutor*]'. https://www.khanacademy.org/khan-labs/

March 29, 2023

'*... it establishes a hierarchy utterly corrosive*'... Garth Greenwell, 'A Moral Education', *The Yale Review* (March 20, 2023). https://yalereview.org/article/garth-greenwell-philip-roth/

John Patrick Shanley, *Doubt: A Parable* (Dramatists' Play Service, 2005).

*...three pieces of Covid news...*Wilson Andrews and Lisa Waananen Jones, 'The Times Switches to CDC Covid Data, Ending Daily Collection', *New York Times* (March 22, 2023). https://www.nytimes.com/2023/03/22/us/covid-data-cdc.html

Dan Diamond and Tyler Pager, 'White House disbanding its Covid-19 team in May', *Washington Post* (March 22, 2023). https://www.washingtonpost.com/politics/2023/03/22/biden-disband-covid-team/

Mary Ellen McIntire and Niels Lesniewski, 'Senate votes to overturn Covid-19 national emergency order', Roll Call (March 29, 2023). https://rollcall.com/2023/03/29/senate-votes-to-overturn-covid-19-national-emergency-order/

'sociological production of the end of the pandemic'...Artie Vierkant and Beatrice Adler-Bolton, 'The Year the Pandemic 'Ended' (Part 1): A Timeline of Covid Normalization in the US in 2022,' *The New Inquiry* (December 21, 2022). https://thenewinquiry.com/the-year-the-pandemic-ended-part-1/

Victory for 'normal people'...Gabrielle Bauer, 'Normal People Say 'No Mask,' *Wall Street Journal* (March 13, 2023). https://www.wsj.com/articles/normal-people-say-no-mask-covid-pandemic-return-to-normalcy-conferences-fitness-travel-handshake-76c20281

Devi Sridhar, 'Covid struck and Britain locked down. Here's what we learned from that–and what we must do next time.' *The Guardian* (March 23, 2023). https://www.theguardian.com/commentisfree/2023/mar/23/covid-britain-locked-down-three-years-trauma

Epilogue: Fifth Spring

May 2024 | Rearranging the World

Anne Lamott, *Bird by Bird* (Anchor Books, 1994).

May 2024 | Looking directly at the Sun

'breach with the status quo'...Robyn Maynard and Leanne Betsamasoke Simpson, *Rehearsals for Living* (Haymarket Books, 2022), 253.

'what it means to be human'...Rustom Bharucha, *The Second Wave: Reflections on the Pandemic through Photography, Performance and Public Culture* (Seagull Books, 2022), xviii.

BBC Channel Four, 'Letters in Lockdown', https://www.channel4.com/programmes/letters-in-lockdown

Jiang Jiehong, ed. *The Otherness of the Everyday: Twelve Conversations from the Chinese Art World During the Covid-19 Pandemi* (Intellect, 2021)

Hoyt Long, Richard Jean So, and Kaitlyn Todd, '#COVID, Crisis, and the Search for Story in the Platform Age', *Critical Inquiry* 49.4 (2023), 532.

'Together Apart,' *Orion Magazine,* https://orionmagazine.org/2020/04/together-apart-a-new-web-series/.

'think together about what it means [to] build livable lives'...Maynard and Simpson, 10.

books of letters... Pam Houston and Amy Irvine, *Air Mail* (Torrey House Press, 2020); Jack Miles and Mark C. Taylor, *A Friendship in Twilight: Lockdown Conversations on Death and Life* (Columbia University Press, 2022); Maynard and Simpson, *Rehearsals for Living* (2022); Alice Kaplan and Laura Marris, *States of Plague: Reading Albert Camus in a Pandemic* (The University of Chicago Press, 2022); The Black | Indigenous 100s Collective, *Say, Listen: Writing as Care* (np:, 2024).

'reevaluation of our priorities'...Irvine and Houston, 6.

Judith Butler, *What World is This?* (Columbia University Press, 2022).

'collective feeling'... Kate Zambreno, *The Light Room: On Art and Care*

(Riverhead, 2023), 34.

the possibility, at least, of such large-scale transformation'... Maynard and Simpson, 124.

a time tailor-made for utopian thinking'... Grant Farred, *Only a Black Athlete Can Save Us Now* (University of Minnesota Press, 2022), xv.

'We *truly are "all in this together"*'... Michelle Fishburne, *The Way We Are Now: Stories of What Americans Lost & Found during the Covid-19 Pandemic* (University of North Carolina Press, 2023), 296.

'[E]*verything is possible beyond our wildest dreams....*'...Irvine and Houston, 35-37.

Arundhati Roy, 'The Pandemic is a Portal,' *Financial Times* (April 3, 2020).

mask wearing as an obligation of public life'...Butler, 28.

Zadie Smith, *Intimations: Six Essays* (Penguin, 2020), 7, 22, 16.

sociological production of the end of the pandemic'... Artie Vierkant and Beatrice Adler Bolton, 'The Year the Pandemic 'Ended", *The New Inquiry* (December 21, 2022).

V. S. Naipaul, *The Enigma of Arrival* (Viking, 1987).

the longer we are home'... Houston and Irvine, 113.

At the very least...'...Farred, xxiii.

Mohsin Hamid, *How to Get Filthy Rich in Rising Asia* (Riverhead, 2014), 221.

Amitava Kumar, 'Against Nostalgia', *Bombay-London-New York* (Routledge, 2002), 32-36.

things can change in a day'...Arundhati Roy, *The God of Small Things* (Random House, 1997), 183.